STORM OVER
CAROLINA

STORM OVER CAROLINA

THE CONFEDERATE NAVY'S STRUGGLE FOR EASTERN NORTH CAROLINA

R. THOMAS CAMPBELL

CUMBERLAND HOUSE

NASHVILLE, TENNESSEE

STORM OVER CAROLINA
PUBLISHED BY CUMBERLAND HOUSE PUBLISHING, INC.
431 Harding Industrial Drive
Nashville, Tennessee 37211

Cover design by Gore Studio, Inc., Nashville, Tennessee

Library of Congress Cataloging-in-Publication Data

Campbell, R. Thomas, 1938–
    Storm over Carolina : the Confederate Navy's struggle for eastern North Carolina /
R. Thomas Campbell.
        p.   cm.
    Includes bibliographical references and index.
    ISBN-13: 978-1-58182-486-5 (pbk. : alk. paper)
    ISBN-10: 1-58182-486-6 (pbk. : alk. paper)
    1. North Carolina—History—Civil War, 1861–1865—Naval operations.
2. Confederate States of America. Navy—History. 3. United States—History—Civil
War, 1861–1865—Naval operations, Confederate. 4. Atlantic Coast (N.C.)—
History, Naval—19th century. I. Title.
    E596.C367 2005
    973.7'57—dc22   2005026002

Printed in the United States of America

1 2 3 4 5 6 7 8 9 10—10 09 08 07 06 05

CONTENTS

Acknowledgments

S*TORM OVER CAROLINA HAS* been, off and on, eight years in the making. During this time there have been many people and organizations that have provided information and offered encouragement. To all of these, I am extremely grateful.

Several individuals and institutions deserve special thanks. In no particular order they include: Bob Holcombe of the Civil War Naval Museum in Columbus, Georgia; Henry Harris of Chapel Hill, North Carolina; Chris Fonvielle, author of *Fort Anderson* and *The Wilmington Campaign;* Bob Elliott, author of *Ironclad of the Roanoke;* William J. Clark of Norfolk, Virginia; the Cape Fear Museum and Research Library; the Virginia Historical Society; the Chester County Library; the CSS *Neuse* State Historic Site; and many, many others that I am sure I have forgotten to mention.

In addition, my wife, Carole, garners an honorable mention as my editor and critic and for her enduring patience as I spent many evenings at the computer.

INTRODUCTION

THE STRUGGLE FOR CONTROL of the eastern waters of North Carolina during the War Between the States was a bitter, painful, and sometimes humiliating one for the Confederate States Navy. No better example exists of the classic axiom "too little too late." Burdened by the lack of adequate warships, construction facilities, and even ammunition itself, the South's naval arm nevertheless fought bravely and recklessly to halt the Federal invasion of North Carolina from the sea.

For most of the war the navigable portions of the Roanoke, Tar, Neuse, Chowan, and Pasquotank rivers were occupied by Union forces. The Albemarle and Pamlico sounds, as well as most of the coastal towns and counties, were also under Federal control. From about the middle of the war onward, however, the presence of Confederate naval forces in the form of ironclads, gunboats, and underwater torpedoes—or mines as they are known today—helped prevent the continued advancement of Union forces into the interior of the state. More fighting (most of it naval) occurred in these inland waters of North Carolina than in all other sections of the state combined. There were excellent reasons for this. Enticing strategic objectives in this area could possibly lead to a quick Federal victory and the end of the war . . . if only they could be taken. A simple glance at a map reveals why.

The Wilmington and Weldon Railroad snaked through the low-lying hills and marshes of the eastern piedmont. This line, stretching from the blockade-running port of Wilmington to the south and the Virginia border to the north, became the main supply route for Robert E. Lee's Army of Northern Virginia. Other rail lines passed through North Carolina to be sure; however, these brought supplies from the Deep South, and as this portion of the Confederacy was overrun, more and more dependence was placed upon the vital Wilmington and Weldon. Any severance of this line by the enemy could prove disastrous for the Virginia front—and for the nation itself.

The eastern counties of North Carolina were some of the most successful in the state in terms of food production, and much of this was shipped north to Virginia. Prior to the commencement of hostilities between North and South, the inland waterways, consisting of the Albemarle and Pamlico sounds and the many rivers flowing into them, constituted an important means of shipping these products to northern markets. These intracoastal waterways connected with the ocean to the east via a series of inlets and with Virginia by way of the Dismal Swamp Canal and the Albemarle and Chesapeake Canal. Domination of these waters would give an enemy control of fully one-third of the state of North Carolina.

What made this area so attractive, both from a commerce as well as from a military point of view, was the protection afforded by those long windswept stretches of sand dunes known as the Outer Banks. Protruding far out into the gray Atlantic, this thin line of barrier islands served as a sanctuary from the howling ocean gales in addition to providing protection against an invading enemy. There were only seven inlets through these islands, and not all of them were navigable to large warships. Those inlets that were accessible were dangerous because of rough seas and shifting sandbars. Whoever controlled the inlets controlled the Outer Banks, and whoever controlled the Outer Banks would control the sounds and rivers and a good portion of the state.

Confederate military planners recognized early in the conflict the importance of holding the islands and waters of eastern North Carolina. Unfortunately, their pleas and those of state officials for men, ships, and guns fell mostly on deaf ears in Richmond. Not that the Confederate government failed to appreciate the danger, but with Federal armies within striking distance of the capital itself, there was little that it could do to help. It became evident to the local army and navy commanders, therefore, that they would have to make do with what they had. The Confederate navy, in particular, received little or no assistance from the central government, and other than a few cannon salvaged from the Gosport Navy Yard at Portsmouth, Virginia, it was left to convert existing river steamers and tugboats into makeshift ships of war. Nevertheless, with these frail and poorly armed steamers, Southern sailors gamely fought the imposing and vastly superior Union navy in a hopeless and desperate effort to halt the invasion. Not until the loss of the sounds, including the inland towns and counties, was the enemy finally stopped. But stopped they were, and while Northern commanders also had problems convincing their government to commit the necessary forces to seize the state, a good deal of credit for the Federal failure to complete the subjugation of North Carolina must be given to the Confederate navy.

The Southern navy's struggle for the eastern waters of North Carolina is a saga of crushing defeats interspersed with moments of brilliant victories. It is also the story of dogged determination and incredible perseverance in the face of overwhelming odds. With the building of the river ironclads, the Confederate navy at last could strike a telling blow against the invaders, but it was slowly and surely being overtaken by events elsewhere. With the war grinding to a close, the last Confederate vessel in North Carolina waters was destroyed, William T. Sherman approached from the south, Wilmington was lost, and the Confederacy reeled from a mortal blow. For the Confederate navy, and especially for the besieged citizens of eastern North Carolina, these were indeed stormy days. The narrative that follows is the story of their ordeal.

STORM OVER CAROLINA

1

THE COMING STORM

THE SUN HAD BEEN up for only two hours, and already it looked like it was going to be another sweltering July day on the inland waters of eastern North Carolina. The early morning ocean breeze, blocked by the rolling sand dunes of the narrow strip of beach known as Brodie Island, failed to reach the crew of the North Carolina gunboat anchored in Pamlico Sound. Even now perspiration was dripping from the brows of the men as they went about their morning tasks on deck. It was even hotter belowdecks in the engine room where steam pressure was slowly rising in the boilers. The coolest spot on the ship seemed to be forward where the thirteen men of the gun crew were laboring to learn the intricacies of loading and firing a large naval cannon.

North Carolina was at war.

There was talk that the few ragtag vessels of the North Carolina navy and their volunteer crews were soon to be transferred to the Confederate navy; however, the men of the NCS *Beaufort* so far had seen no evidence of this. For now, the red-and-white banner of the Old North State flew proudly from the masthead.

The little gunboat had been constructed as the *Caledonia* at Wilmington, Delaware, in 1854, and was an eighty-five-foot screw tugboat. She had been purchased by the state of North Carolina and refitted early in the war at the Gosport Navy Yard at Portsmouth, Virginia. There a heavy gun, a long 32-pounder, was mounted on a forward pivot. On July 9, 1861, she was commissioned as the NCS *Beaufort* and Lt. R. C. Duval of the newly formed North Carolina navy took command. Sailing the same day, she passed through the Dismal Swamp Canal and into the waters of Pamlico Sound in eastern North Carolina.[1]

The *Beaufort's* primary task was to guard the narrow channel of Oregon Inlet that provided entrance from the turbulent surf of the Atlantic Ocean to the placid waters of the sound. For several days Federal warships had been cruising slowly past the hastily erected sand fortifications adjacent to the inlet, and nine days earlier, July 12, 1861, two of them had opened fire on the works, completely stampeding the green North Carolina troops. It was, therefore, with pulse-quickening excitement that the crew of the *Beaufort* noticed the signal flags flying from the Brodie Island lighthouse at 8:20 on the morning of July 21. Lieutenant Duvall lifted his marine glass to study the flags. There could be no mistake. The signal read: "Man-of-war steamer in sight to the northward!"[2]

The steamer sighted by the lookouts was the USS *Albatross,* a three-masted screw steamer carrying five guns. Her captain was Cmdr. George A. Prentiss. His orders were to cruise off Oregon Inlet and intercept any Southern privateers that might attempt a passage through the channel. Early in the war the Confederate government had issued letters of marque and reprisal to private shipowners who were willing to pursue and capture enemy merchant vessels. The inland sounds of North Carolina offered a secure sanctuary for these craft, most of which were civilian operated. The most successful of the lot, however, was another vessel of the North Carolina navy—the NCS *Winslow* commanded by Lt. Thomas M. Crossan. Operating out of Hatteras Inlet, the *Winslow* had captured sixteen prizes in just six weeks. Northern shippers were up in arms and clamored for Washington to do something about the "pirates" that infested North Carolina waters. Although still some distance away, Prentiss had spotted one of the "pirates" on the other side of Brodie Island, and he was determined to destroy her.[3]

Knowing that his lone gun would be no match for the Federal warship, Duvall quickly dispatched a scribbled note to Col. Elwood Morris, commanding the troops huddled in the sand fortification. The paper informed Morris of the approaching warship and "alluded to the two guns which he had mounted and the good effect it would certainly produce if he would have them served." Upon receipt of the note, Morris hurried to the beach where he informed Duvall that the guns, contrary to reports, were not yet properly mounted and that he had no crew to serve them. Unfortunately, he could offer no help. The *Beaufort* would have to face the Federal warship on her own.

Duvall cleared his ship for action. The *Albatross* rounded to just off the ocean side of Brodie. The *Beaufort's* gun crew had already loaded the 32-pounder and was now swinging it around. They had barely finished aiming the piece when a bluish puff of smoke erupted from the forward pivot rifle of the Union ship. Within seconds the shell screamed across the *Beaufort* and splashed in the sound some distance behind her, where it exploded. The report of the exploding shell had barely died away when the order "Fire!" was shouted by the *Beaufort's* gun captain.

With a jerk of the firing lanyard, the long 32-pounder roared to life. The little gunboat trembled as smoke and flame spewed from the gun's muzzle while a solid shot, barely skimming the intervening sand hill, arched gracefully toward the enemy vessel. Duvall was not sure, but he thought the shot struck the Federal vessel between her main and mizzen masts. Only later would he learn from observers on the island that his shots, while true in line, all fell approximately two hundred yards short. Duvall suspected as much, but he could get no more elevation out of the gun.

The *Beaufort's* captain described the action that followed in his official report:

> The firing then became general, the enemy during the engagement
> throwing rifle-cannon shot and shell, and from the distance the 32-
> pound shot and shell carried, the gun must have been of the 62-

hundredweight class. We answered every shot as long as we could get our gun elevated to graze the sand hill, throwing the shot beautifully in line. I either sighted or adjusted the sight in person, though this action has given me entire confidence in the coolness and judgment of the captain of the gun crew, who is also my chief boatswain's mate. The enemy finally, not fancying our shot, cowardly moved around and dropped farther to the southward behind a higher sand bank, which completely prevented us from firing a shot, the line of our greatest elevation striking near the base of the hill behind which our soldiers on shore were placed for protection. The enemy's vessel being higher out of the water enabled his guns to rake us over the hill, while we could not fire a single gun. The frigate's first shot from this position passed near our smokestack and struck the water about 30 yards from us, the second passed between the captain of the gun and the man next to him and struck the water about 20 feet from our port bow. You may imagine my feelings at this stage of the action.[4]

Duvall saw no point in presenting his little steamer as a target for the heavier Union warship if he could not return the fire, so in company with the steamer *Currituck,* which had arrived from Roanoke Island towing a schooner laden with one hundred troops, he moved out of range. It was not much of a battle as naval battles go. The *Beaufort* fired eight shots, all of which fell short, while the *Albatross* had fired approximately a dozen rounds.

The report from Commander Prentiss of the *Albatross* makes no mention of his moving behind a higher sandbank; however, it would have been a wise move if he had: "I opened fire upon her, which she returned from a heavy gun upon her spar deck. After exchanging some twenty shots with her, she hauled off, with the other steamer apparently in a crippled condition."[5]

Neither vessel was struck and each claimed a victory. In a few days the *Beaufort* and her crew was transferred to the Confederate navy, where she served until the end of the war. The little gunboat's single gun would be heard from again—at such places as Roanoke Island, Elizabeth City, Hampton Roads, and the James River. But perhaps her most notable achievement was that the soon-to-be CSS

Beaufort had the dubious distinction of firing the first shot in the Confederate navy's defense of eastern North Carolina.

☆   ☆   ☆

On November 5, 1860, the telegraph wires carried the disquieting news to North Carolina that Abraham Lincoln had been elected president of the United States. While many in the state were dismayed and concerned, their anxiety paled in comparison to their fellow Southerners in the Deep South. The election of the "Black Republican," as Lincoln was called by many, instituted a chain of events that resulted in the secession of seven states in the lower South. The general sentiment among most citizens of North Carolina, however, was one of watchfulness and waiting. While some radicals clamored for the governor to call a special convention of the General Assembly, most North Carolinians felt that Lincoln should be given a reasonable amount of time to reveal his intentions.

On November 19, 1860, the General Assembly met at the state capitol in Raleigh. Governor John W. Ellis addressed the convention, his remarks finding particular favor among the Secessionists or radicals who favored immediate action by the state. While not specifically calling for a secession convention, the governor urged that North Carolina call a conference with "those states identified with us in interest and in the wrongs we have suffered; and especially those lying immediately adjacent to us." Ellis also suggested that following this conference a convention of the people of the state be convened and that the militia be strengthened.[6]

Those in favor of secession were pleased and welcomed the speech; however, the governor's words were severely condemned by conservatives. For the next month the legislative halls of the state capitol resounded with the rhetoric of those favoring and those opposed to secession. Throughout the state public debate reached a fever pitch, with those urging secession seemingly gaining in prominence. And then, on December 20, came the sensational news of the secession of South Carolina.

Nowhere did this news create more excitement than in the state's largest city, Wilmington. One hundred guns fired a salute to South

Carolina, and groups of citizens gathered in the streets to discuss the latest news arriving hourly by telegraph. Only thirty-eight miles above the South Carolina state line, Wilmington felt a close kinship with the citizens of the Palmetto State. Throughout the remainder of North Carolina, however, the action of South Carolina was generally viewed with alarm. Many felt that it now would be even more difficult for other Southern states to receive fair treatment from the Federal government.

North Carolina Governor John W. Ellis

    In the midst of all this excitement came word on January 8, 1861, that a group of Wilmington citizens had seized Forts Caswell and Johnston at the mouth of the Cape Fear River. Even though the state was still firmly a part of the Union, the first naval action undertaken to defend the coast of North Carolina had taken place. Militia Col. John L. Cantwell later described this episode:

Early in January, 1861, alarmed by the condition of affairs in Charleston Harbor, they [the Secessionists] determined to risk delay no longer. A meeting of the citizens of Wilmington was held in the courthouse, at which Robert G. Rankin, Esq., presided, who afterwards gave his life for the cause on the battlefield of Bentonville. A Committee of Safety was formed, and a call made for volunteers to be enrolled for instant service under the name of "Cape Fear Minute Men." The organization was speedily effected, John J. Hedrick being chosen commander.

    On 10 January, Major Hedrick and his men embarked on a small schooner with provisions for one week, the Committee of Safety guaranteeing continued support and supplies, each man carrying such private weapons as he possessed. Arriving at Smithville [now Southport] at 3 p.m., they took possession of the United States barracks known as Fort Johnson, and such stores as were there in

Cols. John J. Hedrick (*left*) and John L. Cantwell (*right*)

charge of United States Ordnance Sergeant James Reilly, later Captain
of Reilly's Battery. The same afternoon Major Hedrick took twenty
men of his command, reinforced by Captain S. D. Thurston, commander of the "Smithville Guards," and a number of his men and
citizens of Smithville, but all acting as individuals only, and proceeded to Fort Caswell, three miles across the bay, where they demanded, and obtained, surrender of the fort from the United States
Sergeant in charge.[7]

While Governor Ellis fully understood the patriotic motives behind the seizures, he could not in good conscience sanction such action as long as North Carolina remained an integral part of the
United States. Acting quickly, the governor dispatched Colonel
Cantwell to Wilmington with instructions for the militia to return
the forts to the U.S. caretakers. Four days after the seizures, the Stars
and Stripes once more floated over Forts Johnston and Caswell.[8]

As one after another of the states in the Deep South withdrew
from the Union, North Carolina, for the most part, remained committed to a "wait and see attitude"—but little by little the Secessionists were gaining in strength. The General Assembly was pressured to
call a special convention that could consider secession, and on January 29, 1861, as a consequence of dwindling conservative opposition,

the governing body adopted a measure directing the citizens of North Carolina to vote on the question. With instructions to elect 120 delegates, the election was set for February 28. Radicals and conservatives campaigned hard across the state in the short period of time prior to the vote, while newspaper headlines screamed the cause of the Unionists or Secessionists, depending upon their editor's political leanings. The whole state seemed to be caught up in the debate, but on the day of the vote the question of calling a convention went down to a resounding defeat. For now, North Carolina would remain in the Union.[9]

Despite the results of the vote, no one in North Carolina considered the issue as settled. With the secession of South Carolina, Mississippi, Florida, Alabama, Georgia, Louisiana, and Texas an accomplished fact, both sides of the controversy realized that North Carolina must soon decide whether to side with her sister states of the South or to remain firmly entrenched in the Union. Then on April 13, 1861, came the electrifying news from South Carolina of the bombardment and surrender of Fort Sumter in Charleston Harbor.

Two days later President Lincoln issued a call upon the states for seventy-five thousand troops to suppress the Southern "insurrection." The War Department wired Governor Ellis that North Carolina's quota was two regiments of militia for immediate service. The time for decision was now.

Almost overnight the mood in the state changed from one of division to one of unanimity. To wage war upon the Southern states was abhorrent to Governor Ellis, and he immediately telegraphed Secretary of War Simon Cameron on April 15, 1861:

> Your dispatch is received, and if genuine, which its extraordinary character leads me to doubt, I have to say in reply that I regard the levy of troops made by the administration for the purpose of subjugating the States of the South as in violation of the Constitution and a gross usurpation of power. I can be no party to this wicked violation of the laws of the country, and to this war upon the liberties of a free people. You can get no troops from North Carolina. I will reply more in detail when your call is received by mail.[10]

On the same day, Governor Ellis ordered Colonel Cantwell to seize Forts Caswell and Johnston at the mouth of the Cape Fear River below Wilmington, while Militia Capt. M. D. Croton and his Goldsboro Rifles were ordered to occupy Fort Macon on Bogue Banks at Beaufort Inlet. Unknown to the governor, a group of volunteers had already taken possession of Fort Macon the previous day. The unoccupied masonry fortification was quietly turned over to the group by its lone caretaker, Ordnance Sgt. William Alexander. Fort Macon had been completed in 1832 but had since fallen into a sad state of disrepair. Capt. Josiah Pender commanded the North Carolina militiamen now manning the bastion, and he reported on its sad condition:

> This work was taken possession of by the troops of the State of North Carolina about the middle of April. It was at that time in bad repair; the woodwork of the quarters and barracks and of one of the drawbridges required renewing and painting; the iron-work and door and window fastenings were much rusted; the shingled interior slope was very much rotted, and the masonry in many places required repointing. The embankment of the causeway needed repairing, and the bridge across the canal to be rebuilt. A few guns (four, I believe) were mounted on the southeast or sea front, but the carriages were decayed and weak.[11]

Meanwhile, Colonel Cantwell was moving to carry out his orders to occupy Forts Caswell and Johnston. On the morning of April 16, Governor Ellis had telegraphed him to "take possession of the same in the name of the State of North Carolina. This measure being one of precaution merely, you will observe strictly a peaceful policy, and act only on the defensive."[12]

The previous day, April 15, Cantwell ordered all of Wilmington's militia companies to assemble "fully armed and equipped, ready for duty." Early the next morning a signal gun was fired, and men from the Wilmington Light Infantry, the Cape Fear Light Artillery, the German Volunteers, and the Wilmington Rifle Guards assembled at the corner of Market and Front streets. From there they were marched amidst an enthusiastic crowd to the end of Front Street where they embarked on the steamer *W. W. Harlee* and the schooner *Dolphen*. With a crowd of well-wishers cheering them on, and with the schooner in tow, the *Harlee* cast off her lines and headed down-river toward Smithville.[13]

By 4:00 p.m. the *Harlee* was at Smithville, and Ordnance Sergeant Reilly again had the dubious distinction of surrendering Fort Johnston to the forces of North Carolina. Colonel Cantwell placed Lt. James M. Stevenson and his company of artillery in charge, and he proceeded to Fort Caswell with the rest of his command. Here Sergeant Walker handed over the facility but was soon placed in close confinement in his quarters "in consequence of the discovery of repeated attempts to communicate with his government."[14]

Much like Fort Macon, Cantwell found Fort Caswell in a deplorable condition. Two thousand sandbags for reinforcing the walls arrived from Wilmington the next day, but Cantwell felt so exposed he rushed an urgent message to the governor: "Unless I am adequately reinforced or am prohibited by orders from you, I shall cause the lights at the mouth on the river to be extinguished tomorrow night, the present garrison being totally inadequate to the defense of this post."[15]

On April 20 and 22 the branch mint at Charlotte and the Fayetteville arsenal respectively were seized. Union sentiment throughout the state all but disappeared, and Governor Ellis issued a proclamation calling the General Assembly into special session for May 1,

The U.S. Arsenal at Fayetteville was seized by state troops on April 21, 1861.

1861. With secession now only a matter of time, Ellis began preparing North Carolina for war. Additional militia troops were dispatched to Forts Macon, Caswell, and Johnston, and numerous instructional camps were set up throughout the state. With high hopes and almost fanatic enthusiasm, the sons of North Carolina flocked to the colors.

When the General Assembly met in Raleigh, Governor Ellis recommended a convention to the legislators as the only means by which secession could be legally accomplished. A convention bill was quickly passed, and the election was set for May 13, after which the elected delegates were to assemble within seven days.

On the prescribed day, May 20, 1861, the convention gathered in Raleigh. With little debate, an ordinance of secession was passed, and within an hour another ordinance was passed ratifying the Provisional Constitution of the Confederate States. A few hours later the 120 members of the convention gathered in the chambers of the House of Representatives for the formal signing ceremony. Many years later, a former militia officer, Capt. Hamilton C. Graham, recalled this momentous moment:

> As a youthful soldier and eye-witness of the scene, it made an impression on me that time has never effaced. The convention then in session in Raleigh was composed of men famous in the history of the commonwealth. The city was filled with distinguished visitors from every part of the State and South. The first camp of instruction, located near by, under command of that noble old hero, D. H. Hill, was crowded with the flower of the old military organizations of the State, and sounds of martial music at all hours of the day were wafted into the city. When the day for the final passage of the ordinance of secession arrived, the gallant and lamented [Stephen Dodson] Ramseur, then a major of artillery, was ordered to the Capitol grounds with his superb battery to fire a salute in honor of the event. The battery was drawn up to the left of the Capitol, surrounded by an immense throng of citizens. The convention in the hall of the House of Representatives was going through the last formalities of signing the ordinance. The moment the last signature was fixed to the important document, the artillery thundered forth, every bell in the city rang a peal, the military band rendered a patriotic air, and with one mighty

shout from her patriotic citizens, North Carolina proclaimed to the world that she had resumed her sovereignty.[16]

As the jubilant citizens celebrated in Raleigh, it was with the knowledge that all coastal fortifications were now securely in North Carolina's hands. On their own, however, in spite of the overwhelming patriotic enthusiasm throughout the state, the three lonely sentinels guarding the windswept beaches along the Atlantic coast would do little to stem the Federal storm that was about to break over the shores of the Old North State.

2

PREPARATION

IN 1877 J. THOMAS SCHARF published his outstanding history of the Confederate navy. Scharf, who had been a midshipman in the Southern navy, devoted a chapter to the war in North Carolina waters. The beginning of his chapter 15 describes the problems facing the Tar Heel State as she went to war with the most powerful nation on earth:

The most cursory examination of the map of the Southern states will show to the reader that the sounds of North Carolina were no less important to the defense of that State than Hampton Roads was to that of Virginia, and that if the blockade of the Southern coast was to be effective indeed, then these sounds, as coaling stations and harbor[s] of refuge, were of prime importance to the United States. The long, low sandy islets that separated the waters of the ocean from those of the sounds, were indented with inlets, which often changing positions, and always treacherous, were yet, at one or two points always navigable for vessels that could ride with safety in the shoal waters of the sounds.

From Cape Charles to Cape Lookout that island chain extended but inclosed no inland water of importance until Albemarle Sound was reached; there Roanoke Island separated that sound from the

larger and deeper water of Pamlico Sound, upon the eastern border of
which Cape Hatteras jutted farthest out into the ocean, and Hatteras
Inlet and Ocracoke Inlet offered the only safe and reliable entrances
from the ocean. Oregon Inlet, near Roanoke Island, had been at all
times unsafe for any but the smallest of crafts. The command of the
broad waters of these sounds, with their navigable rivers extending
far into the interior, would control more than one third of the State
and threaten the main line of railroad between Richmond and the
sea-coast portion of the Confederate States. Roanoke Island, between
Albemarle and Pamlico Sounds, was the commanding position in
those waters. These sounds were connected with the waters of Hampton Roads by the Albemarle and Chesapeake Canal, capable of passing vessels of light draft from Norfolk to Elizabeth City. From
Albemarle Sound, the Pasquotank River afforded navigation to Elizabeth City; the Perquimans River to Hertford; the Chowan River to
Winton; and the Roanoke River to Plymouth.

From Albemarle Sound, the Pamlico River extended to Washington,
from whence the Tar River was navigable to Tarboro; the Neuse River
opened wide and deep communication with Newberne, and further up
to Kingston and Beaufort, and Morehead City, below Cape Lookout,
were accessible also from Pamlico Sound. A large portion of the popu-
lation of this large and fertile area was, if not actually hostile to the
Confederate cause, so indifferent to its success, as to avail themselves
of the first and every opportunity to evade the duty of defense and to
secure the protection of the enemy for their persons and property.[1]

No one was more cognizant of the vulnerable condition of the
coast and the great potential that the sounds offered than Governor
John W. Ellis. Even before the state had formally drafted its ordinance of secession, the governor wrote a confidential letter to Confederate President Jefferson Davis in Montgomery, Alabama:

The State is to all intents and purposes practically out of the old Union,
and we are deciding on the speediest mode of giving legal sanction to
this state of facts. All lights have been extinguished on the coast. Vessels have been sunk in the Ocrachoche [sic] Inlet and a fleet of armed
vessels (small) is now being fitted out to protect our grain crops lying

on the inland waters of the [northeastern] part of the State. A good ship canal connects those waters with the Chesapeake at Norfolk.

Beaufort harbor, protected by Fort Macon is a most eligible point for privateering etc. We have on these waters some bold and skillful seamen who are ready to go out as privateers at once. The forms required in procuring letters of Marque present a great obstacle. Had you an authorized agent here who could deliver letters and receive the bonds etc., the work would be greatly facilitated. The enemy's commerce between N. York and all the West Indies and South American ports could be cut off by privateers on the coast of North Carolina.[2]

In spite of the dearth of heavy guns to fortify the coast, the governor ordered that vessels be purchased and armed to patrol the sounds and that batteries be erected at Hatteras, Oregon, and Ocracoke inlets. To accomplish this the legislature created the Military and Naval Board to oversee the state's military affairs, including coastal defense. The coast was divided into two sections: that from the Virginia border to the New River in Onslow County was in charge of Brig. Gen. Walter Gwynn; the area from New River to the South Carolina line was under the command of Brig. Gen. Theophilus H. Holmes.

While Governor Ellis was eager to begin privateering from the sounds, he recognized that the first priority was to strengthen the

Brig. Gens. Theophilus H. Holmes (*left*) and Walter Gwynn (*right*)

BOTH: NORTH CAROLINA REGIMENTS

three existing fortifications: Forts Macon, Caswell, and Johnston. In addition, other areas were totally unprotected and would require that new fortifications be constructed. With this in mind, work on Fort Fisher south of Wilmington was begun and batteries were planned for each of the navigable and unguarded inlets along the Outer Banks.

The task of building defenses on the Outer Banks was a formidable one. With few inhabitants, the area to the north was little more than a barren windswept strip of sand infested with mosquitoes in the summer and buffeted by fierce cold winds in the winter. Thanks to the abandonment by the Federals of the Gosport Navy Yard in Virginia, some heavy guns were available, but they had to be transported by barge via the Dismal Swamp Canal from Norfolk. Water and all supplies had to be transported by boat, the nearest source being New Bern, almost ninety miles away. The citizens of the surrounding counties were urged "to send laborers, slaves or free Negroes" at once, for both Gwynn and Holmes knew it was only a matter of time before the enemy would strike.[3]

While the two generals struggled to have batteries erected on the Outer Banks, the naval board was negotiating the purchase of steamers to serve as gunboats on the sounds. The first of these was the *J. E. Coffee,* a 207-ton side-wheel steamer that had plied the waters between Norfolk and the eastern shore of Virginia. At Portsmouth,

Lt. Thomas M. Crossan (*left*) and Capt. Thomas J. Lockwood (*right*)

NORTH CAROLINA REGIMENTS

NAVAL HISTORICAL CENTER

across the Elizabeth River from Norfolk, the *Coffee* was fitted out at the Gosport Navy Yard. A single 32-pounder was mounted forward on a pivot and a small brass 6-pounder rifle was mounted aft. Commissioned as the NCS *Winslow,* and commanded by Lt. Thomas M. Crossan, formerly of the U.S. Navy but now commissioned in state service, the gunboat left Norfolk bound for the sounds of North Carolina in late June or early July 1861. (Crossan's name does not appear on any register of Confederate naval officers; he may have remained in the North Carolina navy even after the state's men and ships were transferred to the national flag.)

The next vessel commissioned and converted at Gosport was the NCS *Beaufort,* a screw tug of 85 tons, mounting one gun and commanded by Lt. R. C. Duvall. It was during her passage south from Norfolk that she engaged the USS *Albatross* at Oregon Inlet. Next came the NCS *Raleigh,* an iron-hulled, propeller-driven towboat of 65 tons, armed with one pivot gun and commanded by Lt. Joseph W. Alexander. Last, the NCS *Ellis,* armed with a 32-pounder and a small brass howitzer, was captained by Cmdr. William T. Muse. By the end of July 1861 these four vessels constituted the North Carolina navy and were on station in Pamlico Sound just south of Roanoke Island.[4]

By this time Northern shippers were clamoring for the Washington government to put a stop to the constant privateering forays of Southern vessels such as the *Winslow, Beaufort,* and others. Operating from the protected waters of the sounds, Crossan and the *Winslow* had been very active in dashing out through the inlets and capturing unsuspecting U.S. merchant vessels. While the *Winslow,* owned by the state, was not, strictly speaking, a privateer, that distinction made little difference to the merchants who were losing their ships and cargoes.

One of the most successful raiders at the time was a true privateer, a speedy side-wheel steamer from Charleston, South Carolina, the C.S. privateer *Gordon.* The *Gordon* had been a packet boat before the war, serving between the ports of Charleston and Fernandina, Florida. She was 519 tons and carried a crew of fifty. Armed with three heavy guns, her letter of marque and reprisal had been received only ten days before her arrival from Charleston. She was commanded by the venerable Thomas J. Lockwood, a sea captain who was destined to become a household word throughout the South for his many daring and successful exploits as a blockade-runner. The accounts of her escapades define in a large measure why so much alarm was generated in the North.

Shortly after sunrise on July 25, 1861, the *Gordon* was approximately forty miles off Cape Hatteras when the cry "Sail ho!" rang from the masthead. The vessel to which the lookout was excitedly pointing was the brig *William McGilvery* of Bangor, Maine, carrying a cargo of molasses to Boston. The statement of the brig's master, Hiram Carlisle, taken at an inquiry in New York sometime after the event, described the the capture:

> On 25th July, about 40 miles E. by S. from Hatteras, was fired at by the privateer steamer, *Gordon* of Charleston, S. C. The first shot fell short, the second went between the head stays and foresail. We then hove to, when the steamer came up alongside and ordered us to launch our boat and the captain and 4 men to go on board the steamer. This I refused to do, when they threatened to sink us. After being so threatened, ordered out the boat and took four men and went on board. At the same time they sent a boat with six men on board the brig, armed with cutlasses, pistols, and bowie knives. (They) wore the brig around with her head to the westward, took her in tow, and towed her into Hatteras Inlet. Upon anchoring they sent us ashore to the fort, and after about three hours they sent us off to the steamer, where we were put in irons for the night. Next morning the irons were removed and we were sent out to the brig under a guard of four armed men, where we remained four days, when they gave us a pass by [the] steamer *Albemarle* to New Bern, N. C. Remained there eight days; was at liberty all the time; was provided [for] by the quartermaster. Left there August 10 on schooner *Priscilla,* of Baltimore, which vessel had been seized as a prize, but afterwards released. The C. S. Government paid our passage to Baltimore.[5]

The *Priscilla* had been seized by one of the North Carolina steamers, but she was released when her Maryland nationality was discovered. Carlisle was very observant while he was a prisoner and made a careful mental note of all the privateer activity: "At Hatteras Inlet there is 14 feet of water. The privateer force consists of four steamers, sometimes as many as 6, besides several small sailing vessels, sent as pilot boats, etc. When leaving there they had sixteen prizes in all."[6]

Steaming out through Hatteras Inlet, the *Gordon* was soon prowling for additional victims. On July 28 she apprehended the schooner *Protector* from Philadelphia, which was loaded with tropical fruit from the Cuban port of Mantazas. Lockwood exercised his gun crew again and sent a shot whistling across the *Protector*'s bow. The *Gordon* passed a line, and the little schooner was towed quickly into Pamlico Sound. Two days later, while searching the rough seas off Hatteras, the *Gordon* was spotted by an American warship, which gave chase. Lockwood pointed the privateer's stern toward the enemy and, with the throttles held wide open, ran for Beaufort, North Carolina.

On Saturday, August 4, 1861, despite numerous rain showers, visibility was fair to good from the Hatteras lighthouse. As daylight broke over the gray eastern horizon, the lookout on this lofty tower signaled to the numerous privateers in the sound that several sails were in sight. Soon steam hissed in the *Gordon*'s engine room, pressure built rapidly in the boilers, and within minutes Lockwood had the steamer pounding through the swells outside the entrance to the inlet. Perched high on the main mast above the deck, the lookout scanned the patches of ocean among the scattered squalls of rain. It was not long before the cry, "Sail ho!" was shouted. Rapidly approaching a small schooner, the morning air was awakened by a roar from one of the *Gordon*'s guns. The *Henry Nutt* from Key West, bound for Philadelphia, quickly rounded into the wind. She carried a rich cargo of logwood and mahogany, which would bring a high price on the auction block at New Bern. Placing a small prize crew on board, Lockwood ordered the *Gordon* off toward another sail. Once again the boom of the privateer's gun brought a Northern schooner rounding into the wind. She was the *Sea Witch*, which was returning to New York from Baracoa, Cuba, after picking up a load of tropical fruit. Passing a line to the *Henry Nutt*, Lockwood towed both prizes into the sound.[7]

Forays by the *Gordon, Mariner, Raleigh, Teaser, Winslow, York*, and many others were becoming an embarrassment to the Union navy. As a consequence, preparations were soon under way to put an end to the Hatteras privateers. The alarm now spread, and Northern merchantmen gave the Outer Banks a wide berth. As a consequence, even though Lockwood kept the *Gordon* at sea for the next several weeks, not one sail was spotted. Then, on August 27, while steaming out through the inlet, ten vessels were sighted on the distant northern horizon. Seven of them appeared to be man-of-war steamers, and three were sail-driven transports. Lockwood quickly determined that the little *Gordon* was no match for this armada and so turned the vessel southward. That night he put in to Wilmington, where the privateer remained for two days. Early on the morning of August 30 the *Gordon* steamed down the Cape Fear River and set a course for home. Later that same day she arrived in Charleston. The armada that had necessitated Lockwood's hasty departure would soon spell disaster for the Confederate land and naval forces defending Hatteras Inlet.[8]

While the vessels of the North Carolina navy, which by the end of July had been transferred to the Confederate navy, and the privately owned vessels were preying on Northern commerce, work was progressing on the two forts designed to protect the channel at Hatteras Inlet. The most strategically important was Fort Hatteras, situated about one-eighth of a mile from the inlet, and another, Fort Clark, a smaller fortification east of Fort Hatteras and closer to the ocean. The two together could provide a crossfire over the inlet and hopefully prevent all enemy vessels from entering the sounds.

Daniel A. Campbell, master of the brig *Lydia Francis,* was detained at Fort Hatteras after his vessel was wrecked at Hatteras Cove. Upon his release on July 19 he submitted a detailed report to the Navy Department describing the facilities around Hatteras Inlet:

> Hatteras Inlet. There is no light here. The iron can buoys which marked the channel have been sunk. The channel is over 200 yards in width, and vessels drawing 15 to 16 feet can pass through it and for a distance of about 1 mile into Pamlico Sound, where they meet a swash upon which at high water there is a depth of about 8 to 9 feet, and over which large vessels have to lighten their cargoes.
>
> Saw vessels of 100 to 150 tons beat out through the inlet. Large vessels could only work in and out with a free wind, unless towed by a steam tug. While there saw as many as 50 vessels pass in through the

inlet (9 of them prizes) and as many go out, some bound to Liverpool and Halifax [Nova Scotia], and the larger number reported bound to the West Indies, loaded with naval stores, rice, lumber, etc.

There are 4 armed vessels stationed there which go out to make prizes of vessels passing along the coast:

1. The steamer *Warren Winslow,* of Norfolk, commanded by Lieutenant Crossan, who is said to have belonged formerly to the U. S. Navy. This vessel came from Norfolk through the canal into Pamlico Sound. Armament, 1 32-pounder and 1 smaller rifled gun.

2. The steamer *Gordon* (believed to be), of Charleston; 3 guns.

3. The steamer *Marion* (*Mariner?*); 8-pounder.

4. The pilot-boat *York;* 1 rifled gun, 8-pounder.

Fortifications at Hatteras Inlet:

1. On the right-hand side entering the inlet, and near the western point of the strip of land or beach, is an octagon-shaped fort [Fort Hatteras], which completely commands the channel. The wall or embankment is built of sand, covered with turf. It is about 5 feet high, about 25 feet wide on the top, and sloping on the outer side at an angle of about 45 degrees. On the inner side the wall or embankment is perpendicular, and is formed of pieces of turf about 2 feet square and 8 inches thick, piled upon each other. This turf was brought from a place in the center of the beach about 2 miles distant. On the 19th of July they had 8 guns mounted, viz, 2 64-pounders and 6 32-pounders. Two were on pivots, 6 on ordinary ship gun carriages.

Chart showing the locations of Forts Hatteras and Clark

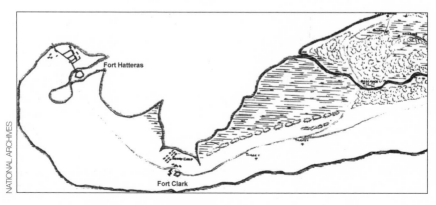

They intended to mount 12 more, making 20 in all. In the center of the fort there is a bombproof tent about 100 yards long, and the covered way is about 12 feet wide and 6 feet high, built of timber and plank. The sides are covered with sand about 10 feet in thickness, Sloping out at an angle of 45 degrees, and the top with sand about 5 feet in depth, the whole being covered with turf.

2. Shortly before the 19th of July they commenced building a second fort [Fort Clark], situated about 1 mile to the eastward of the other, on the seaward side of the beach. In form it is like the other, constructed in the same manner, but only about half as large; at that time they had 4 guns mounted, and intended to mount 8 more, making 12 in all. Both forts were constructed, or constructing, under the supervision of Colonel [William B.] Thompson, said to have been formerly in the U.S. Army. The laborers employed were about 180 Negroes, said to be free, and brought from different parts of the State. The troops stationed there at the time consisted of three companies, under command of a Major [William S. G.] Andrews. The supply of ammunition was very short. They had only about 100 kegs of powder. The soldiers on guard or picket duty were not allowed to carry their muskets loaded, but carried their cartridges in their pockets, not being provided with cartridge boxes. Water is obtained by sinking wells in the sand to the depth of 5 or 6 feet. Water can be had in this way in many places on the beach. It is not very good, but answers. They brought some water from the mainland. In calm, smooth weather they extend their pickets nearly 10 miles up the beach; in rough weather, about a mile.

The object is to discover or prevent a landing. The bark *Linwood,* drawing 15 feet water, stranded about 400 feet distant from the beach. With the wind offshore, troops could be landed anywhere along the beach without the use of surf-boats or difficulty, if not opposed by a force on the land.

The beach to the northeast of the forts along the water's edge for a width of about 300 feet is flat and hard, but would be to some distance, it is thought, commanded by the guns of the smaller fort. The center of the beach is higher, its surface more uneven, composed of loose sand, and troops advancing over it in daylight would hardly find shelter within the range of the guns of the forts. Vessels drawing over 20 feet can approach to within about 1 mile of the forts.[9]

By the beginning of August, General Gwynn had been able to mount approximately a dozen 32-pound smoothbores at Fort Hatteras and an additional five 32-pounders and two smaller guns at Fort Clark. These guns, firing solid round balls with a maximum range of only about 3,000 yards, were effective coastal pieces against wooden sailing vessels during the War of 1812; however, they would prove woefully inadequate against the powerful rifled shell guns of the U.S. Navy. In addition, only token amounts of powder had been sent with the guns from Norfolk.

Even more distressing to Gwynn was the lack of trained troops. In spite of almost continuous pleas to Richmond (where the Confederate government had been relocated) for the return of one or two North Carolina regiments stationed in Virginia, Gwynn was only able to muster 350 men from the Seventh North Carolina Infantry and a few detachments of the Tenth North Carolina Artillery at Fort Hatteras. Several smaller units guarded the beaches, and a few men were at Oregon and Ocracoke inlets, but the total number of troops, all unseasoned and a few without arms, totaled no more than 580.[10]

While Gwynn endeavored to mount his guns on the barren windswept beaches of the outer banks, and the crews of the diminutive vessel of the North Carolina navy struggled to learn the intricacies of firing naval guns, the first of many setbacks struck the Old North State. Governor Ellis's health steadily declined until he died from tuberculosis on July 7. He had been a steady hand in the early days prior to and during the secession of the state from the Union, and now his reasonableness and intelligence would be sorely missed. He was replaced by Henry T. Clark, speaker of the state senate, and while an energetic and devoted leader of the Southern effort, Clark was nearly overwhelmed by the magnitude of his duties and lacked the influence with Richmond that Ellis had enjoyed.

As early as June 1861, Union Gen. Benjamin F. Butler had proposed a plan to the War Department in Washington for taking the Outer Banks along the North Carolina coast. At first not much heed was paid to his suggestions; however, there were now two reasons to reconsider his proposals. First, the destructive marine losses to privateers and to what had become known as the "Mosquito Fleet" of the Confederate navy had become unbearable. The second reason

for securing stretches of the North
Carolina coast was to provide repair and refueling stations for the
blockading squadrons stationed
offshore. Without these depots it
would be next to impossible to
keep steamers on station long
enough to make the blockade effective.

Finally, on August 9, 1861,
Commo. Silas Stringham received
confidential orders at Fort Monroe
stating that "the obstruction on
the North Carolina coast" should
be "thoroughly attended to." He

Commo. Silas H. Stringham

was instructed to level the two forts guarding the entrance at Hatteras Inlet and to sink stone-laden ships in the channel as obstructions. Butler requested a force of 25,000 men, but with the Federal
government reeling from the ignoble defeat at Manassas, Virginia, he
was only assigned 880.

Stringham assembled a force consisting of seven warships—
*Cumberland, Harriet Lane, Minnesota, Monticello, Pawnee, Susque-
hanna, Wabash*—mounting a total of 143 heavy guns. Two transports
were chartered to carry the troops, and each vessel towed an old
hulk loaded with stone. On Monday, August 26, Stringham's fleet
weighed anchor and sailed for the North Carolina coast. The storm
was about to break.[11]

3

DISASTER ON THE OUTER BANKS

AUGUST 27, 1861, WAS a hot and muggy day. If it hadn't been for the light breezes blowing in off the Atlantic, that Tuesday would have seemed almost unbearable in the blazing summer sun. While the green North Carolina troops sought out what shade they could find and swatted sand fleas and mosquitoes, gangs of black workers, seemingly unmindful of the heat, labored on the still unfinished parapets and traverses of both Forts Clark and Hatteras. One young army officer, however, seemed oblivious to the oppressive heat. It was around 4:00 p.m. when Col. William F. Martin, commander of the meager forces manning the two fortifications, stood on the sloping rampart of Fort Clark, the work nearest the ocean, a pair of field glasses pressed to his eyes. He did not like what the glasses revealed.

Far out to sea, and barely discernible on the northeastern horizon, was the ominous and unmistakable silhouette of a fleet of ships. Within only an hour the images became remarkably more distinct. With an aide at his side scribbling notes on a wrinkled piece of paper, Martin began to count: "Seven large war steamers, two transports apparently crowded with men, and two or three small tug steamers."[1]

Knowing that his small force of approximately 350 men could not successfully resist such a force, Martin hurried a dispatch to Lt. Col. George W. Johnston at Portsmouth, North Carolina, urging him to bring to Hatteras as many remaining companies of the Seventh North Carolina Infantry as he could muster. No steamer was available, and the message had to be dispatched utilizing a small sail-driven pilot boat. Portsmouth, a small village farther south on the island chain, was more than twenty-five miles distant. By the time Johnston received Martin's note, loaded his men on the *Winslow* and a small schooner that the gunboat had in tow, and then set out, it would be early evening of the following day before he could arrive. Even after dispatching the message, Martin suspected that if the enemy fleet attacked the next day—which they most probably would—he would have to make do with what he had.

It must have been a restless, sleepless night for the men huddled behind the sand embrasures of Fort Clark. Anchored just a few miles offshore was the largest congregation of enemy vessels that any of them had ever seen. The morrow would most certainly bring a storm of shot and shell upon them. All they could do was try to sleep and await the coming of the dawn.

The storm, in all its violent fury, did break the following morning. Colonel Martin, in his official report filed while he was a prisoner of war, described the fateful day of August 28, 1861:

> On the morning of the 28th, between 8 and 9 o'clock, a heavy fire was opened from the steamers *Minnesota, Susquehanna, Wabash,* and other war vessels upon Fort Clark and upon almost all parts of the island, particularly at the point where they intended landing troops. The fire was continuous upon Fort Clark, and upon all the skirts or woods where troops might possibly be concealed, for several hours. Being a fire of shells only, it might well be spoken of as a flood of shells. The fire of the enemy was promptly returned by Captain J. C. Lamb, Company D, Seventh Regiment North Carolina Volunteers, who was in charge of Fort Clark, and was regularly kept up by him until every charge of powder and every primer was exhausted. . . . Captain Lamb and his lieutenants, all of whom were present, and the men under their command, displayed great coolness and bravery.

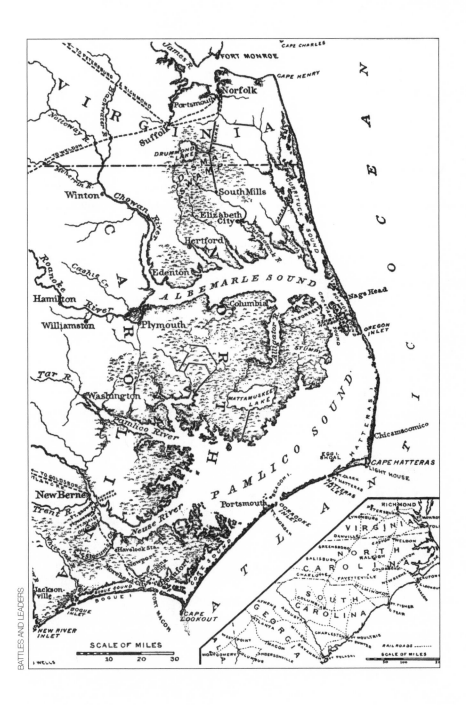

Their fire was well directed, guns well managed, and whilst most of their shot fell short, yet some reached the enemy, doing, however, but little damage, as they were all round shot that were fired.

Our ammunition being entirely exhausted at Fort Clark, and the enemy having landed some forces, I called the officers together who were at Fort Clark, and it was unanimously agreed that it was advisable to render useless the guns and fall back upon Fort Hatteras. This being agreed to, I sent orders to the various bodies of men whom I had stationed in the skirts of wood to resist the advance of the enemy upon Fort Clark, that Fort Clark could not be held, and they must fall back upon Fort Hatteras. The guns at Fort Clark were as effectually spiked as it was possible to do with nails, having no proper spikes; everything taken off that we could carry, and we fell back, under a most terrible fire of shell, upon Fort Hatteras. We reached there about 1 o'clock.

I regret to state that while some of the men were passing from Camp Gwynn, which was on the sound shore and about 2 miles from Fort Hatteras, one man and possibly two were killed by shells of the enemy. I have not been able to learn their names.

Having collected all the troops at Fort Hatteras, I determined to make as good a resistance as possible. Consulting with Captain [John Thomas P. D.] Cohoon, of

Fort Hatteras (*above*) and Fort Clark (*right*) were the primary defenses of the Outer Banks.

Company B, Seventh Regiment North Carolina Volunteers, who had charge of Fort Hatteras with his company, we agreed that it was useless to expend our shot on the enemy, as we were beyond reach, so we must endure until they came nearer. Fort Hatteras submitted to the fire for some hours without returning a shot. At about 4 o'clock p.m., one of the enemy's steamers undertook to go through the inlet, when we opened fire upon her and drove her back, putting several round shot into her, but doing her, I suppose, no material damage.

The firing between Fort Hatteras and the enemy continued until nightfall, or rather the fire of the enemy upon the fort continued, for they kept so well beyond the reach of our guns that we only wasted our ammunition in firing at them.[2]

The steamer that attempted to enter the inlet was the USS *Monticello* captained by Cmdr. John P. Gillis. The fire from Fort Hatteras was surprisingly accurate as attested to by the *Monticello*'s skipper:

As we turned the point on Spithead, finding so little water that we would be compelled to turn and work the vessel out again if possible, the large fort opened a brisk fire upon us, which we promptly returned with our pivot gun and port battery (two 32-pounders abaft); ship striking often as we backed and filled to turn her head seaward. By keeping the engine in motion we succeeded, with the aid of the swell, in getting out of the inlet, firing 5-second shell rapidly and with precision at the battery. We were about fifty minutes in this tight place, during which time we fired thirty shells. The fort fired slow as we came out and did not return our last three shot, owing, no doubt, to the promptness with which the flag-officer and the other vessels opened upon them for our relief. We were struck by 8-inch shot and shell, once amidships on port side, shot lodged in knee; another amidships on port side, which carried away boat davit and drove the fragments of shell and davit through the armory, pantry, and galley; another shot carried away a part of the foretopsail yard and sail on the port yardarm; another on the starboard bow. This shot lodged in the knee at forward end of shell locker. Another shot amidships on the starboard side passed through across berth deck, through locker and bulkhead, across fire room, and lodged in

Federal bombardment of Fort Hatteras

FRANK LESLIE'S THE AMERICAN SOLDIER IN THE CIVIL WAR

the port coal bunker, ripping up the deck in the gangway over it. Whaleboat's bottom shot away and gig injured.[3]

All of the shots that struck the *Monticello* were round solid shot, and, as Martin surmised, did her little material damage. In the fading light the men of Fort Hatteras could discern the Stars and Stripes floating jubilantly over Fort Clark three-quarters of a mile away. Because of the rough surf and strong southeast winds, however, the Federals had been able to land only 318 men and 2 small howitzers. But unknown to Martin, these men were extremely vulnerable to a counterattack. Most of their ammunition had been ruined by seawater, they had no drinking water except what was in their canteens, which had long since been consumed, and they were bone tired from their day of exertion. Demoralized though they might be, they constituted the first enemy foothold on North Carolina soil.

Amid all of the smoke and confusion experienced by the *Monticello*, Commander Gillis had noticed a steamer with another vessel in tow approaching from the west. It was the CSS *Winslow* with approximately 250 of the Portsmouth garrison. Also on board the Confederate gunboat was Capt. Samuel Barron Sr., newly appointed commander of the naval defenses of Virginia and North Carolina. As soon as the *Winslow* had been secured to the rickety wooden dock that jutted into the sound behind Fort Hatteras, Barron hurried off to confer with Colonel Martin. The army colonel was "utterly pros-trated" from the day's fighting, and after conferring with some of his equally exhausted officers, requested that Barron take command. With some misgivings, Barron accepted.

> I was requested by him and Major [William S. G.] Andrews, com-manding the post, to assume command of the fort, to which I as-sented, Colonel Bradford volunteering to assist me in the duty of defense. In assuming this grave responsibility I was not unaware that we could be shelled out of the fort, but expecting from New Berne the arrival of a regiment of North Carolina volunteers at or before midnight (the fleet having put to sea, and appearances indi-cating bad weather), we designed an assault on Fort Clark, three-fourths mile distant from Fort Hatteras, which had been taken possession of by a party landed from the shipping, but unfortunately the regiment did not arrive until the following day after the bom-bardment had commenced.[4]

Samuel R. Barron Sr. had entered the U.S. Navy as a boy on Janu-ary 1, 1812. Appointed a midshipman, he was serving his appren-ticeship on the USS *Brandywine* when that warship conveyed the Marquis de Lafayette to France in 1825. Two years later he was ad-vanced to lieutenant and then to commander on July 15, 1847. In 1855 he had obtained the rank of captain, and at the outbreak of the

SANTORIOUS, PICTORIAL WAR RECORD 1882

The interior of Fort Hatteras after the surrender

war, he was in charge of the Office of Bureau of Details in the U.S. Navy Department. Barron, who was from Virginia and had spent more than forty-nine years in the service of the United States, resigned his commission on April 22, 1861, and on June 10 was commissioned a captain in the Confederate navy. Ironically enough, just six months prior to his setting foot on Hatteras Island, he had been in command of the USS *Wabash,* one of the vessels now poised to shell the island's last remaining fortification.[5]

Maj. W. S. G. Andrews, an artillery officer who had arrived with Captain Barron on the *Winslow,* was ordered to organize the men and work through the night in an effort to strengthen Fort Hatteras. His initial inspection was not encouraging. Only two guns were mounted on the side facing Fort Clark, both old 32-pounders. Two additional guns faced the channel where they could fire on the enemy fleet, and working throughout the night he was able to bring one more gun to bear in this same direction. One of the guns mounted on a navy carriage was placed under the command of navy Lt. William H. Murdaugh and assisted by Midshipman James M. Stafford from the CSS *Ellis,* which now had arrived on the scene. Eight sailors from the *Winslow* volunteered to work the gun.[6]

For some it was backbreaking work all night; for others, it was a night filled with apprehension and dread for what the morrow

Gov. Henry T. Clark (*left*) and Capt. Samuel R. Barron Sr. (*right*)

would bring. Gun crews attempted to find some much-needed rest by their guns, while other men wrote last-minute letters to loved ones. On the eastern horizon the first streaks of morning light revealed a clear and cloudless sky broken only by plumes of black smoke emanating from the stacks of numerous enemy warships. Confederate soldiers and sailors peering over the ramparts of Fort Hatteras could see plainly that the Federal vessels were already on the move. The sea was glassy smooth with hardly a swell to disturb its surface. The enemy's fire, they knew, would be deadly accurate.

In his report, Captain Barron graphically described this tragic day on the Outer Banks:

On the next morning [August 29, 1861] at 7:40 a.m. the fleet, consisting of the *Minnesota, Wabash, Susquehanna, Cumberland, Pawnee,* and *Harriet Lane* (other steamers being in company), took their position and opened fire. In addition to the batteries of the ships the enemy had during the night erected a battery of rifled field guns near to Fort Clark, which also opened on us.

During the first hour the shells of the ships fell short, we only firing occasionally to ascertain whether our shot would reach them, and wishing to reserve our very limited supply of ammunition till the vessels might find it necessary to come nearer in. But they, after some practice, got the exact range of the IX, X, and XI-inch guns, and did not find it necessary to alter their positions, whilst not a shot from our battery reached them with the greatest elevation we could get.

This state of things, shells bursting over and in the fort every few seconds, having continued for about three hours, the men were directed to take shelter under the parapet and traverses. I called a council of officers, at which it was unanimously agreed that holding out longer could only result in a greater loss of life, without the ability to damage our adversaries; and just at this time the magazine being reported on fire, a shell having fallen through the ventilator of the bombproof into the room adjoining the principal magazine, I ordered a white flag to be shown. When the firing ceased, the surrender was made upon the conditions of the accompanying articles of capitulation.[7]

In a remarkable display of interservice admiration, which would seldom be the case in coming months, Major Andrews singled out special praise for the navy men:

> I desire especially to speak of the conduct of the officers and men at the naval gun, who fired frequently to try the range. Lieutenant Murdaugh was badly wounded; Lieutenant Sharp was knocked down by a shot which passed through the parapet near his head and brought the blood from his ear and cheek in considerable quantity, killing a man at his side, at the same time knocking down and covering Colonel J. A. J. Bradford with sod and earth. Midshipman Stafford cheered on the men, behaving in a most gallant manner. After the fall of Lieutenant Murdaugh, his men bore him to the commodore's boat [*Winslow*] and he escaped.[8]

Both the *Winslow* and the *Ellis* escaped with most of the navy men, but Captain Barron and Lieutenant Sharp were taken prisoner along with approximately seven hundred men, mostly from the Seventh North Carolina Infantry. They were all herded aboard the Federal warships and were soon on their way to New York. Confederate casualty figures vary, listing anywhere from four to fourteen soldiers killed and wounded. The Federals did not lose a single man. Recognizing the great potential that a Federal presence could offer if they controlled the entrance to Pamlico Sound, General Butler, in a rare display of sound military logic, decided to disobey his Washington instructions and garrison the captured Confederate positions at Hatteras Inlet.

News of the victory was met with wild jubilation in the North, coming on the heels of the embarrassing defeat the previous month at Manassas, Virginia. In the South, however, it was a different story. Secretary Stephen R. Mallory was shocked when he heard the account, although it should not have come as a complete surprise to him. For weeks it had been rumored that the Federals were planning the attack, and Governor Clark had pleaded with the secretary and the War Department almost daily to send more men and munitions to the Outer Banks. Even the engineers who designed and supervised the construction of Forts Clark and Hatteras were censured,

R. THOMAS CAMPBELL

Present-day location of Fort Hatteras as seen from inside the sound

and the Ordnance Department was blamed for not supplying better guns, shells, and adequate powder. Allegations of drunkenness, inefficiency, and even cowardice surfaced, and Captain Barron was berated for not being more aggressive. On September 11 the *Raleigh Register* lamented: "Why did not our force of seven or eight hundred men kill, drive into the sea, or capture the enemy's force of 300 or 400 men who spent the night 600 yards of our troops?"[9]

To add insult to injury, the fledgling Confederate navy had been unable to even annoy the enemy, much less defend the inlet. While Lieutenant Murdaugh's crew fought bravely, even though their gun could not reach the Union warships, the *Winslow* and *Ellis* with their single 32-pounders were powerless to prevent the disaster. Fortunately, with the exception of Captain Barron and Lieutenant Sharp, the navy men escaped to fight another day.

One of those navy men, an officer on the *Ellis*, felt certain he knew the cause for the loss of Fort Hatteras. In an anonymous letter to the *Washington (NC) Dispatch* he explained:

Nearly all night we were employed in making the fort impregnable, as we then thought. Much of the disaster which occurred on Thursday may be attributed to the fact that we did not possess ourselves of Fort Clark by the bayonet that night, but wiser and older heads than mine thought otherwise. Certain it is, in my opinion, it was one of the causes, second only to the shameful neglect of the authorities in not properly fortifying the coast, that caused our defeat. From these two causes we have the following result: the possession of Hatteras, the key of the Sound; the road open to invasion at any moment; Capt. Barron, Lieut. Sharp, and about 700 or 800 gallant men prisoners, taken by the Abolition Kangaroos, besides prolonging, in my opinion, the war for half a year.[10]

While the defeat was bemoaned throughout the Confederacy, the loss was most keenly felt among the citizens, soldiers, and sailors from North Carolina. One North Carolina soldier, writing from his regiment in Virginia, expressed the sense of embarrassment felt by many of his fellow Tar Heels: "Must history record in after years that in our struggle for freedom, the first repulse our cause received was on the soil of the Old North State?" Some even felt that the surrender had so shaken the confidence of the people that the ultimate success of the Southern effort was now in jeopardy.[11]

With the fortifications at Hatteras Inlet now occupied by Union troops, and the inlet itself open to the Federal navy, the stout and well-built forts at Oregon Inlet to the north and Ocracoke Inlet to the south were incredulously abandoned without a fight. On August 31 the steamer *Governor Morehead,* with a schooner in tow, arrived at Fort Ocracoke, where, after spiking the guns and setting fire to their platforms, the garrison was evacuated and carried to Washington, North Carolina. After the evacuation several Confederate steamers, including the side-wheeler *Albemarle,* visited Fort Ocracoke on Beacon Island and the nearby small town of Portsmouth with the intent of recovering some of the guns. Few if any were carried off, and on September 16 a Federal landing party of soldiers and marines destroyed eighteen guns in the abandoned fortification and four more that were found lying on the beach at Portsmouth.[12]

At Fort Oregon a council of war was called, and it was decided to evacuate the fortification and transport as many of the guns as possible to Roanoke Island. The designer and builder of the fort, Col. Elwood Morris, protested vehemently against the plan stating, "The evacuation of a strong fortress just finished, just mounted with its armament, and not even threatened by the enemy, was not justified by any military necessity."

The remaining officers, however, disagreed, arguing that with Hatteras and Ocracoke now open to the enemy, and with Federal warships in the sound, it would be only a question of time until they too would be forced to surrender. With the decision made, the garrison was loaded onto four schooners and the steamer CSS *Raleigh*. An attempt was made to remove the guns, but nine of them had to be spiked and left behind. Only three cannons were transferred to the schooners, but in a combination of tragic errors, an accident dumped these overboard. Some men did manage to set fire to the rudimentary wooden barracks before they left.

Although it was not fully appreciated at the time, the loss of the inlets to the sounds of North Carolina was a serious blow to the entire Confederacy. Not only did it shut down the sounds as a haven for blockade-runners, government commerce raiders, and privateers, but it provided a base of operations from which the enemy could launch further operations. These operations would soon threaten the interior of North Carolina, Norfolk, and southern portions of Virginia. Writing from the Federal prospective after the war, Union Adm. David D. Porter summarized it best:

> This was our first naval victory, indeed our first victory of any kind, and [one that] should not be forgotten. The Union cause was then in a depressed condition, owing to the reverses it had experienced. The moral effect of this affair was very great, as it gave us a foothold on Southern soil and possession of the sounds of North Carolina if we chose to occupy them. It was a deathblow to blockade running in that vicinity and ultimately proved one of the most important events of the war.[13]

For the men and officers of the Confederate navy, whose small makeshift gunboats were already being referred to derisively as the Mosquito Fleet, the storm was about to intensify.

4

THE CHICAMACOMICO RACES

REPARATIONS HAD BEGUN EARLIER that morning with three small steamers that now sat tied to the boat landing at Fort Huger on Roanoke Island, North Carolina. Wisps of wood smoke curled upward from their stacks as steam hissed through their pipes and valves. It was a beautiful autumn day, October 1, 1861, and the calm waters of Croatan Sound shimmered in the early morning sun. Waiting in line to board the vessels over rickety gangplanks were three companies of the Third Georgia Infantry with the imposing names of Dawson Grays, Governor's Guards, and the Athens' Guards. Excited over their upcoming "cruise," the Georgia troops laughed and sang like schoolboys on a Sunday-school picnic. Except for their trip through the Dismal Swamp Canal from Norfolk aboard an old leaky barge, most of the tall, lanky Georgians had never set foot on a steamboat.

While the men from the red clay state may have stared in wonder at the waterborne monsters with their roaring furnaces and hissing engines, experienced navy men on board were not very impressed. In fact, their vessels were so small and weak, so pathetically armed, that they had begun even before the fall of Fort Hatteras referring derisively to themselves as the Mosquito Fleet. But for the Confederate navy, guarding the inland waters of North Carolina on this sunny Tuesday morning, they were all that was available.

Although the Mosquito Fleet would eventually number seven or eight vessels, only three were being loaded this morning with the men from Georgia. Capt. William F. Lynch, who had replaced the captured Samuel Barron as commander of Confederate naval forces in the coastal waters

BENDANN BROTHERS, BALTIMORE

Capt. William F. Lynch

of North Carolina, had chosen these three for the expedition because they were the most reliable. Lynch's objective was to determine what the Federals were up to in Pamlico Sound since their easy conquests of Forts Hatteras and Clark on August 29. Word had reached him and Col. A. R. Wright, senior army commander on Roanoke Island, that Union forces had established a camp at the desolate village of Chicamacomico, approximately twenty-six miles north of the Hatteras light on the Outer Banks. It was rumored that this camp was to become a jumping-off point for an attack on Roanoke itself, and Lynch was determined to investigate it.

Lynch was a naval officer of the old school, having entered U.S. service in 1819 at the age of eighteen. Born and reared in Virginia, Lynch had served his country for his entire adult life, rising to the rank of captain before he resigned on April 21, 1861, to offer his sword to his native state. He had served in the Virginia navy until that state's forces were transferred to the Confederacy, and then he had been in charge of the naval batteries along the Aquia Creek until tapped by Secretary Mallory for the defense of North Carolina. With the Richmond government's eyes focused on the Virginia front, Lynch's task was destined to be a frustrating one, for there was never enough men, ships, or guns—as had already been proven at Hatteras Inlet—to adequately defend the Carolina coastal region.[1]

Cmdr. Thomas T. Hunter (*left*) and Lt. Joseph W. Alexander (*right*)

Captain Lynch flew his flag from the CSS *Curlew,* the largest of the three steamers that were now about to cast off from Roanoke Island. Commanding the *Curlew* was another Virginian, Thomas T. Hunter, who, having achieved the grade of commander in U.S. service, resigned and was appointed a commander in the Confederate navy on June 10, 1861. The *Curlew* had been constructed as a tug at Wilmington, Delaware, in 1856 and had been purchased at Norfolk in 1861 by the Confederate government. She was a 260-ton side-wheel steamer, 150 feet long, and could make about 12 knots. Her draft of 4.6 feet meant that she was well suited for the shallow waters of Pamlico Sound. A 32-pounder that had been rifled and banded at the Gosport Navy Yard was removed from Fort Bartow and installed on a makeshift pivot in her bow. An old 12-pounder smoothbore was mounted on a field carriage and positioned on her stern.[2]

The *Raleigh,* under the command of Lt. Joseph W. Alexander, was a small propeller-driven steamer that had seen service with the North Carolina navy until transferred to Confederate service in July 1861. The 65-ton steamer had operated as a towboat on the Albemarle and Chesapeake Canal. She had been armed with one 32-pounder on her bow when she was taken over by the state of North Carolina in May 1861. Alexander, the son of distinguished Judge Julius Alexander of Charlotte, North Carolina, had been graduated from the Naval Academy at Annapolis in 1861 and had commanded the *Raleigh* since the early days of her commissioning in the North Carolina navy.[3]

The third vessel of Lynch's expedition was another small screw-propeller that had operated on the inland waters and canals of North Carolina before the commencement of the war. The 79-ton *Junaluska* had been built in Philadelphia in 1860, and like the *Raleigh,* had been purchased by the Confederates while she was at Norfolk. Two 6-pounder howitzers were mounted on her narrow deck, and she was under the direction of Midshipman William H. Vernon, assisted by Midshipman James M. Gardner.[4]

Now that the frolicking troops were on board, and the inexperienced gun crews, comprised of army details from the Third Georgia, were at their stations, Captain Lynch gave the order to cast off. With the men cheering and the captains blasting their steam whistles, the Mosquito Fleet chugged into Pamlico Sound and headed south. Just over forty miles in that direction, another steamer, the USS *Fanny,* flying the Stars and Stripes, was on its way north.

Several days before, Col. Rush C. Hawkins, Federal commander at Fort Hatteras, had dispatched Col. W. L. Brown's six-hundred-man Twentieth Indiana Infantry to the northern end of Hatteras Island near Loggerhead Inlet. There, on the windswept dunes near the village of Chicamacomico, they established an outpost to guard against possible Southern attacks from Pea Island to the north. Early on the morning of October 1, while the Georgia boys were clambering aboard the Mosquito Fleet to the north, Hawkins dispatched the army tug *Fanny,* loaded with supplies for the regiment, to Loggerhead Inlet.[5]

The *Fanny,* armed with a rifled 32-pounder, an 8-pounder rifle, and under the command of J. H. Morrison, arrived opposite Chicamacomico at around 1:00 p.m. and dropped anchor in eight feet of water. There the *Fanny's* gun crew and twenty-five members of the Twentieth Indiana who were on board as reinforcements, lounged on deck while waiting for Colonel Brown to send a lighter to unload the supplies. It was two and one-half hours before the first boat pulled alongside. Once loaded, the small craft started for shore, then suddenly someone shouted that there was a vessel rapidly approaching from the west.

Captain Lynch had spotted the anchored Federal steamer and had turned his flotilla of three ships directly toward her. Bells rang in the Confederate steamers' engine rooms as engineers opened the valves and threw the levers for full speed. The *Curlew* was in the lead, and her army gun crew scrambled to load and train their cannon on the distant target. The soldiers had spent two days practicing with the 32-pounder before it was mounted on the *Curlew,* but because of the shortage of powder, they had yet to fire the weapon. At a range of a mile and one-half, the firing lanyard was pulled, and the Confederate gun responded with a thunderous blast. The startled Georgia troops had never seen anything like it. Smoke, which initially shrouded the bow of the boat, quickly blew to the rear as an explosive shell streaked low over the sound and splashed near the *Fanny.*

The *Raleigh* and the *Junaluska* now joined in, their excited gunners sending shells splashing near and far but not hitting the Federal steamer. The Union gunners were not idle. Swinging their two pieces around, they opened a brisk and accurate fire on the approaching Mosquito Fleet. Morrison later claimed that one shell exploded on the bow of the lead vessel, but there is no mention of a hit in any Confederate report. Steadily the Confederate flotilla advanced, their enthusiastic gunners firing wildly. Geysers of water, thrown up by near misses from the return fire, cascaded upon the little steamers, drenching everyone on board. The range had diminished by now, and presently a shell from the *Curlew* was seen to explode on the *Fanny*'s deck. A few moments later a white shirt knotted to the halyards was run up, and Lynch shouted for his gunners to cease firing. The *Fanny* had surrendered, and within a few minutes Colonel Wright's men were tumbling aboard the Union steamer. When the Stars and Bars were run up, the ecstatic Georgians shouted until they were hoarse. Compared with what was to come later in this long and brutal war, it was not a very impressive victory. However, after the disasters at Hatteras Inlet and the loss of Forts Hatteras and Clark, it was a sweet victory, indeed, for those Southerners who were there, and the first victory of the war for the Confederate navy.[6]

In addition to the forty-nine prisoners, the *Fanny* yielded a large cache of ammunition, a thousand overcoats (which were distributed to the Third Georgia), a thousand dress coats and pants, and a thousand pairs of shoes. The Third Georgia might look like a regiment of Yankees during the coming winter, but at least they would be warm. Putting a crew on board, Lynch's men hoisted the captured steamer's anchor and triumphantly steamed the now CSS *Fanny* back to Roanoke Island in company with the Mosquito Fleet. Along the way, illustrating yet another example of the many shortages with which Lynch was faced, the Confederate vessels stopped along the shore to allow the crews to gather firewood for fuel, there being no coal available.

Among the few surviving Confederate reports of the capture of the *Fanny* is one by Col. A. R. Wright of the Third Georgia:

> I have just returned from an expedition against the Yankees. We received information yesterday morning that the Yankees were about landing men near Chicamacomico, and immediately left this post, taking 150 men on board the steamers *Curlew, Raleigh,* and *Junaluska,* Commodore Lynch being in command of these vessels. At 5 o'clock p.m. we came in sight of a steamer (Federal), which proved to be the *Fanny,* having on board a quantity of quartermaster and commissary stores for the Twentieth Indiana Regiment, in command of Captain Hart. After an engagement of thirty-five minutes the *Fanny* surrendered, and we made prisoners of the entire force—47 men, 2 officers, and 1 Negro. The *Fanny* mounted two rifled cannon and made a gallant resistance, but the superior weight of our guns gave us the advantage. The gun of the *Curlew* was manned by a crew from Captain

The USS *Fanny* under fire from the *Curlew,* the *Raleigh,* and the *Junaluska*

McWhorter's company of this regiment, and worked their gun beautifully. All behaved well. We had to return for want of fuel, and I am
now engaged with all my men cutting wood, and as soon as I can get
a supply we will return and endeavor to capture the Federals who are
encamped at Chicamacomico. We cannot send the prisoners up
today for want of fuel. Indeed, we are almost helpless here on this account. We will demolish the light at Hatteras if we do no more. The
captured Federals report a large force at Hatteras, but I think we can
manage them.[7]

The Union outpost at Chicamacomico posed a serious threat to
the entrenched Confederates on Roanoke Island. Lt. Col. Claiborne
Snead of the Third Georgia explained:

The situation of the Confederates was alarming. It was evident that
the new position taken by the enemy was intended as a base of operations from which to assail Roanoke Island and capture the small garrison thereon. The Third Georgia Regiment and Col. Shaw's North
Carolina regiment (8th North Carolina), with Commodore Lynch's
"Mosquito Fleet," comprised our entire defense, while reinforcements could not be obtained nearer than Norfolk by a long and difficult route through Albemarle Sound, Dismal Swamp Canal, and the
Elizabeth River. On the other hand, the Federal forces, daily accumu-
lating at Fort Hatteras, had behind them on the open sea, a powerful
navy, efficient both in attack and in the transportation of troops.[8]

The capture of the *Fanny* and the intelligence concerning the
Federal outpost at Chicamacomico, set into motion one of the most
confusing and bizarre campaigns of the war. Wright and Lynch for-
mulated a plan whereby all available Confederate troops would be
transported by the Mosquito Fleet to a point just north of the Union
camp. There the Third Georgia would splash ashore and attack the
enemy, driving him down the island to the south. Meanwhile, Col.
H. M. Shaw's Eighth North Carolina would proceed down the sound
and effect a landing near the Hatteras lighthouse, thus acting as a
blocking force. Once the Indiana regiment was disposed of, the Confederate troops would destroy the Hatteras light, and in conjunction

with the Mosquito Fleet, attack and attempt to retake Forts Hatteras and Clark. It was an ambitious plan.[9]

By October 4 Lynch had his fleet ready. A visitor to the island described the scene where he found the Mosquito Fleet:

> All very busy in making preparations and embarking troops. . . . I remained with them until just before they left. The scene was very animating. The evening was calm and the Sound smooth as glass. Steamers and barges crowded with troops were anchored off from the shore. Cheers of welcome arose from the troops on board, as new companies marched down to embark. I went on board a schooner to return to N. H. [Nags Head] and remained near the steamer and barges until about 10 o'clock at night. Everything was animate with excitement. From my position and the favorable state of the atmosphere you could hear every word that was said. From one steamer the lively notes of Dixie filled the air; from another the notes of the violin floated on the air and from others the solemn service of praise and prayer to God, rendered more solemn by the circumstances, went up from the mingled voices of a large and apparently devout congregation of worshippers.[10]

In addition to the *Fanny,* now under the command of Midshipman James L. Tayloe, Lynch had rounded up two more of his steamers, making six in all for the mission. They included the 120-ton side-wheeler *Empire,* armed with two guns, and the 85-ton *Cotton Plant,* another side-wheel steamer that may have been unarmed. The *Empire,* whose name was later changed to *Appomattox,* was under the command of 1st Lt. Charles C. Simms, while the name of the *Cotton Plant's* captain is unknown. At approximately 1:00 a.m., amid the flickering glare of pine torches and the blasting of steam whistles, the Mosquito Fleet got under way.[11]

Colonel Snead described their arrival at Loggerhead Inlet:

> Passing through Croatan Sound into and down Pamlico Sound, the little fleet arrived off Chicamacomico, and about three miles therefrom, just after sunrise. All the vessels were of too deep a draft to get nearer this point of the island, except the *Cotton Plant,* which was

enabled to advance a mile further on. Upon her, Colonel Wright, with
three companies of the third Georgia, and two six-pound boat howitzers, . . . proceeded toward the shore, the officers and men wading
in the water up to their middies for three fourths of a mile, and opening a rapid fire upon the enemy, who stood in line of battle on the
beach, twelve hundred strong according to their muster rolls. [Only
six hundred men from the Twentieth Indiana were present.] Soon
after the firing commenced they began a retreat, moving hastily and
in great disorder toward Fort Hatteras.[12]

Thus ensued what would be fittingly referred to later as the
"Chicamacomico Races."

While the remainder of the Third Georgia waded ashore, Lynch
pulled out his Mosquito Fleet and headed south with the Eighth
North Carolina. The Confederate fleet would attempt to land them
near the Hatteras light, and if successful, they would trap the Twentieth Indiana. While Lynch's steamers raced south to set up the
blocking force, the chase went on. Neither side was accustomed to
forced marches, let alone a hectic pace in loose sand. Colonel Snead
remembered, "The attacking party scarcely numbered seven hundred men, some of whom, with their own hands, drew the two
howitzers through the deep sand, (and) pursued the retreating foe
flying pell-mell for twenty-six miles, killing eight and capturing
forty-two men."[13]

Man after man, Confederate and Union, fell from the ranks, but
the majority kept going. It was a hot day for October, and the sun
beat down unmercifully upon the heads of friend and foe alike. It
was maddening—the roaring surf only a few feet away and yet not a
drop of water to drink. The chase continued all day, while farther
down the sound, the Eighth North Carolina was not faring very well.
By late afternoon the Mosquito Fleet was in position, but because of
the shallowness of the sound at this location, none of the vessels
could approach the landing nearer than two miles. Determined to
give it a try, the Tarheels jumped overboard and began splashing toward shore. After wading about a mile, the bottom of the sound
dropped off so sharply that they could not keep their heads above
water, and reluctantly, the North Carolinians returned to their boats.

Finally, near midnight, the weary Twentieth Indiana reached the lighthouse, and using it as a rough-and-ready fortification, the Hoosiers dropped down in the sand to get some rest. The fatigued Third Georgia, unaware of Colonel Shaw's failure to land the Eighth North Carolina, fell exhausted onto the sand just south of the village of Kinnakeet. But the Chicamacomico Races were not yet over. The next morning, when it was learned that there was no blocking force to cut off the fleeing Federal troops, Colonel Wright gave the order for his Third Georgia to return to Chicamacomico.

Col. Ambrose R. Wright

The disgusted and bone-tired Georgians, many with blistered feet, had just begun their countermarch when the Ninth New York, having hurried up from Fort Hatteras during the night, suddenly appeared in their rear. Now it was the Confederates who were being chased. Back they went pell-mell over the loose sand dunes and rough scrub that characterized the bleak island. Soon, as an officer of the Georgia regiment recalled, they had another problem: "After marching only a few miles upon our return, a Federal steamer anchored off the coast and opened fire upon us with shell, shot, and grape shot. They fired the first gun at 5 minutes after 1 o'clock, and continued the fire till dark, throwing by Commander Lynch's count 441 shot. It was a miracle that numbers of us were not killed."[14]

It was the USS *Monticello* that was lobbing the shells at the harried Confederates, and to avoid her fire as much as possible, the men marched on the west side of the island. This necessitated their wading across the numerous little inlets that dot the western shore, but even here, because of the narrowness of the island, the *Monticello* and her thundering guns were at times only five hundred yards away. At last the panting Southern troops arrived at their starting point and hurriedly began reboarding the steamers that had returned from their abortive part of the mission. Shooting over the island, Lynch opened fire on the *Monticello* with several of his rifled guns, but the distance was too great and the shells fell short. The Chicama-comico Races were over, and with each side contending that it had won a great victory, the Confederates returned to Roanoke Island and the Federals to Fort Hatteras.[15]

Confederate Brig. Gen. Benjamin Huger, army commander of the region, gave a cryptic account of the affair to Adj. Gen. Samuel Cooper: "I hear that Colonel Wright, with his command, attacked and drove the Lincolnites on the 4th. They ran. He captured some 40 prisoners and a large amount of provisions, &c. Colonel Wright has returned to Roanoke Island, and none of the men have come up. No official report yet."[16]

Federal authorities in Washington were now keenly aware that the seizure of Hatteras Inlet was a barren victory unless they could control all the inland waters of eastern North Carolina. Preparations were soon under way in the Federal capital to secure once and for all this important inroad into the heart of the state. Rear Adm. Louis M. Goldsborough and Brig. Gen. Ambrose E. Burnside were busy planning what would be styled in February the Burnside Expedition.

With the recent setbacks in the area, Confederate officials were very worried about the North Carolina sounds, but with Union forces pushing into Virginia and Tennessee, there seemed little the Richmond government could do. Governor Clark continually stressed to Richmond the importance of the North Carolina sounds and the absolute inability of the state to defend them. One immense

Exhausted troops of the Third Georgia Infantry return to their boats.

BATTLES AND LEADERS

OFFICIAL RECORDS NAVY

The USS *Monticello* fired more than four hundred rounds into the ranks of the retreating Confederates.

problem was the shortage of arms. Clark reminded the War Department that in addition to arming all of the North Carolina troops, which were now in Virginia, the state had also "loaned" to the Confederacy thirteen thousand stand of arms for the equipping of troops from other Southern states. Because of this generosity, the harried governor was now attempting to purchase arms from private citizens. On October 25, 1861, in a letter to the War Department, Clark reiterated his case:

> We feel very defenseless here without arms, and I will not again report to you that this has been affected by our generosity to others. . . . We see just over our lines in Virginia, near Suffolk, two or three North Carolina regiments, well-armed, and well-drilled, who are not allowed to come to the defense of their homes—and two of them posted remote from any point of attack. . . .
>
> Our forts might resist their attack and landing, but out of reach of the forts we cannot concentrate a force of any magnitude. We have now collected in camps about three regiments without arms, and our only reliance is the slow collection of shotguns and hunting rifles, and it is difficult to buy [these] because the people are now hugging their arms to their own bosoms for their defense.[17]

Captain Lynch too could expect little in the way of reinforcements for his Mosquito Fleet. Although a plan for the construction of one hundred gunboats to serve on Pamlico Sound was approved, few boats were actually completed, and none before the attack on Roanoke Island. The resources of the state were sadly lacking, and the few vessels that were constructed later were built mostly at makeshift shipyards, sometimes no more than cornfields along a river bank. Lynch was also not satisfied with the preparations made by the army, and in correspondence with the Navy Department, suggested ways of strengthening the Roanoke defenses. On September 17, prior to the Chicamacomico Races, Lynch wrote a letter to theater commander Brig. Gen. Benjamin Huger:

> So great is the breadth of Croatan Sound [between the island and the mainland] with a channel of 6 feet near the mainland, 3 miles distant, that I am reluctantly forced to the conclusion that but little dependence can be placed upon the batteries for its defense. After a careful reconnaissance, I am persuaded that the defense of this sound must be made at the marshes, 7 miles below, with floating batteries and gunboats, there being no soil wherewith to construct redoubts.[18]

5

THE BATTLE FOR ROANOKE ISLAND

ROANOKE ISLAND, WHICH DIVIDES the waters of Pamlico Sound from those of Albemarle Sound, was the key to the defense of North Carolina. If it fell to the enemy, the whole eastern third of the Tarheel State would be open to the invader. Of major concern was the Weldon Railroad that linked the upper Confederacy and the war front in Virginia with the supplies from the Deep South. If the sounds and rivers were captured, Union troops would be only a day's march from this very important lifeline. The ever popular Brig. Gen. D. H. Hill, who had been placed in charge of the defenses of Pamlico and Albemarle sounds, completed an inspection tour of his district in early October 1861, and in a letter to Secretary Stephen R. Mallory, he described the deplorable condition of the state's defenses. After describing the lack of guns and the shortage of powder at such places as Fort Macon, New Bern, and Washington, North Carolina, Hill got to the crux of the problem:

> Roanoke Island is the key to one-third of North Carolina, and its possession by the enemy would enable him to seize the great railway

connection between north and south of the Confederacy. This all important island is in want of men and guns. It should have at least 6 more rifled cannon. Feeling that everything depended upon holding it, I came up last night (to Portsmouth, Virginia) to apply to the Navy Department for ordnance and ordnance stores. I found Commodore Forrest, Captain Fairfax, and General Huger fully as much concerned about the island as I was, but they could do nothing for me without your order. Under these circumstances I most earnestly appeal to you for 6 additional rifled cannon—4 for Fort Macon and 2 for Roanoke Island. There ought to be, however, 4 at least for the latter place. I am confident that Manassas itself is not more important than it.[1]

By the end of the year, with the constant demand for men in other theaters siphoning off what few good troops the state could muster, there were, exclusive of the garrisons in the three forts, only 1,473 Confederate soldiers on Roanoke Island. These included 475 men of the Thirty-first North Carolina, 568 men of the Eighth North Carolina, and 450 soldiers of Wise's Legion, a Virginia unit that had been formed by Brig. Gen. Henry A. Wise, now immediate army commander on the island. This was a pitifully small force that was expected to defend and hold the island against the storm that was about to break.

Lynch's Mosquito Fleet was no better off, for only eight light steamers would be all that were available for the coming battle. The *Seabird,* commanded by 1st Lt. Patrick McCarrick, was a wooden side-wheel steamer that mounted just two guns. The only other side-wheeler was the iron-hulled *Curlew,* still under the command of Lieutenant Hunter, while all the rest were small screw steamers. They included the *Ellis,* captained by Lt. James W. Cooke; the *Beaufort,* 1st Lt. William H.

Brig. Gen. Henry A. Wise

CONFEDERATE MILITARY HISTORY

Parker; the *Raleigh*, still commanded by Alexander; the *Forrest*, Acting Master James L. Hoole; the *Fanny*, Midshipman Tayloe; and the *Appomattox*, under Simms. All the small-propeller steamers each carried one gun. (The venerable *Winslow* had struck a sunken hulk near Ocracoke Inlet on November 7 and was lost.) Lynch also had available an excellent schooner, the *Black Warrior*, armed with two 32-pounders and under the command of Master Frank M. Harris. In addition to the weakness of his vessels, Lynch had another problem. On January 22, 1862, in a letter to Navy Secretary Mallory, he explained:

> But my greatest difficulty is in the want of men. So great has been the exposure of our crew that a number of them have necessarily been invalided; consequently the complements are very much reduced, some of them one-half. I have sent to Washington, Plymouth, Edenton, and Elizabeth City for recruits without success, and an earnest appeal to Commodore Forrest brought me only four. To meet the enemy I have not more than sufficient number of men to fight half the guns.[2]

Burnside's forces rendezvoused at Annapolis in early January, and on the night of January 11, Goldsborough led his fleet to sea. By February 4, 1862, all of the Federal warships and transports, after

First Lt. Patrick McCarrick (*left*) and son, Acting Master's Mate J. W. McCarrick (*right*)

much difficulty fighting gale-force winds and heavy seas, managed to cross the bar at Hatteras Inlet and anchor in the sound. The Burnside Expedition consisted of twenty warships of Goldsborough's fleet mounting 62 guns, with 15 of these being the new and deadly 9-inch rifles. Burnside, in addition to the numerous army transports carrying his soldiers, had assembled his own fleet of gunboats, which added an additional 108 pieces that could be brought to bear. Early on the morning of February 5, this grand armada of 170 guns and 13,000 troops headed north up Pamlico Sound. The largest amphibious landing in American history, up to that time, was about to take place.[3]

Roanoke Island is approximately twelve miles long and about three miles across at its widest point. Badly situated on the western shoreline guarding Croatan Sound, and running from north to south, were three turfed sand forts—Bartow, Blanchard, and Huger. These fortifications mounted a total of twenty-five guns, few being rifled. Ammunition was in short supply, and the demoralized and untrained troops who manned them had never seen a large gun until a few days before. Fort Bartow, situated midway down the western shore, would be the only bastion to offer resistance, the others being out of range. Across the sound on the mainland was Fort Forrest. Constructed on two old barges that had been hauled up in the mud, Fort Forrest contained seven 32-pounders. The east side of the island was defended by a two-gun battery positioned on Ballast Point, and an eighty-foot redoubt in the middle of the island commanded the only road that ran the length of Roanoke. This three-gun emplacement was flanked on both sides by breastworks and deep cypress swamps that were thought to be impassable. Just to the north of Fort Bartow, a double row of derelict ships and barges, stretching between the island and the mainland, had been sunk to provide obstructions to any invading flotilla. Behind the sunken vessels a row of pylons was in the process of being put down, and behind these protective obstructions, Captain Lynch positioned his tough little Mosquito Fleet.[4]

At 6:00 p.m. the Burnside Expedition anchored ten miles south of Roanoke Island. The next morning, Thursday, February 6, dawned cold and rainy with poor visibility. At 7:45 a.m. the armada got under way, and a little after 10:00 a.m. it entered Croatan Sound.

By noon, however, a thick fog shrouded the invasion fleet. Goldsborough ordered the advance stopped, and further operations for the
day were canceled. Confederate officers on Roanoke Island had been
well informed concerning the Burnside Expedition, and now the
Federal armada's final objective was clear. At 1:00 p.m. Navy Lt. Benjamin P. Loyall, commander of Fort Bartow, scratched an urgent message to Colonel Shaw: "The fog has cleared away from below, and I
can distinctly see that the enemy is about 8 miles from us, in full
force. I can make out more than fifty vessels, either at anchor or underway, in tow of steamers. I believe that they are at anchor. I am of
opinion that they have stopped to consider, but it requires a bright
lookout to keep the run of them."[5]

Lieutenant Parker of the *Beaufort* remembered well this calm before the storm. He and Lynch were warm friends, and he poignantly
recalled their evening together before the battle:

> At sunset, as we saw no disposition on the part of the enemy to move,
> we anchored and all hands went to supper. . . . After getting something
> to eat I went on board the *Seabird* (the flagship) to see Commodore
> Lynch. I found him in his dressing gown sitting quietly in his cabin
> reading *Ivanhoe*. He expressed great pleasure at seeing me and said he
> had thought of signaling me to come aboard, but knew I must be very
> tired and he did not wish to disturb
> me. . . . We talked for a long time of
> what the next day would probably
> bring forth, and our plans for de-
> fense, etc. Neither of us believed
> that we would be successful, nor
> was there a naval officer in the
> squadron who thought we would.
> The force opposed to us, both naval
> and military, was too overwhelm-
> ing. Ten thousand men to our two
> thousand on land, and nineteen
> vessels and 54 guns to our eight
> vessels with 9 guns on the water.
> After talking some time on the

First Lt. William H. Parker

subject, we insensibly got upon literature. Lynch was a cultivated
man and a most agreeable talker. . . . We commenced on Scott's nov-
els, naturally, as he held one of the volumes in his hand; incident
after incident was recalled and laughed over, and I never spent a
more delightful evening. We were recalled to our senses by the ship's
bell striking 8 (midnight). I jumped up exclaiming that I did not
know it was so late and that I had not intended keeping my gig's crew
up so long. The Commodore's last words to me at the gangway were:
"Ah! if we could only hope for success, but," said he, "come again
when you can."[6]

In the still air of the following morning, tiny plumes of smoke
spiraled skyward from the Mosquito Fleet as the galley fires were lit
and the crews piped to breakfast. Looking south across the line of
obstructions, the anxious Confederate sailors could clearly see a for-
est of masts and spars, which comprised the enemy fleet. It was
impossible not to comprehend the tremendous odds arrayed against
them. With grim determination, however, the Southern crews were
soon busy preparing their boats for action. The overwhelming
Union force was also visible from Fort Bartow. After a sparse morning meal, Lt. Benjamin P. Loyall marched his men to their guns at
10:00 a.m., their usual hour for instruction. Within thirty minutes of
reaching their positions, the horizon to the south went black with
smoke. The Federal assault was coming.

The men hurried to load their 32-pounders, knowing that this
time it was no drill. A sudden boom out on Croatan Sound announced the opening shot from one of the Federal steamer's rifled
guns. The green Confederate gunners watched as the shell, with its
sputtering fuse, streaked low over the sound and impacted on the
sand parapet, exploding into a thousand fragments. Someone
shouted, "Fire!" and the 32-pounders thundered in response, their
shells screaming toward the Federal armada only to splash short of
their targets. The firing now became general with approximately
twenty-two of Goldsborough's fleet opening up on Fort Bartow. Only
three guns in the fort could be brought to bear, and Lieutenant Loyall instructed his gunners to fire conservatively and aim precisely, for
powder was in very short supply.

Meanwhile, Lynch and his Mosquito Fleet had moved into line of battle behind the barricades. The *Appomattox* was dispatched to Edenton in search of powder, and the *Black Warrior* was anchored near Fort Forrest and out of range. This reduced the Mosquito Fleet to seven vessels and only eight guns that could be brought to bear on the enemy. Lt. William H. Parker well remembered this opening of the battle:

> At 11:30 the fight commenced at long range. The enemy's fire was aimed at Fort Bartow and our vessels, and we soon became warmly engaged. The commodore at first directed his vessels to fall back in the hope of drawing the enemy under the fire of Forts Huger and Forrest, but as they did not attempt to advance, and evidently had no intention of passing the obstructions, we took up our first position and kept it during the day. At 2 p.m. the firing was hot and heavy and continued so until sunset.[7]

Whenever the vessels of the Mosquito Fleet drew near, the Federal gunners would switch their fire from Fort Bartow to concentrate on the Confederate boats. When this happened, the Southern steamers would be almost smothered with screaming shot and shell. In spite of the firestorm tearing into their boats and splashing around them, Lynch's inexperienced crews kept their guns hammering away at the enemy. It was not without a price, however. A Federal shell exploded on the *Forrest,* the spinning fragments striking Master Hoole in the head, blinding him in one eye and leaving what was thought at the time a mortal wound. But Hoole recovered. Another shell slammed into the *Ellis,* taking off the right arm of Midshipman Robert A. Camm at the shoulder and injuring several others.

Thick gray smoke spread over the sound as the air shook from the concussion of the guns and the bursting of shells. The *Forrest* was disabled and had to be towed out of action, and then the flagship, the *Curlew,* took a mortal hit. Parker recalled:

> Towards 4 o'clock in the afternoon a shot or shell struck the hurricane-deck of the *Curlew* in its descent, and went through her decks and bottom as though they had been made of paper. Her captain

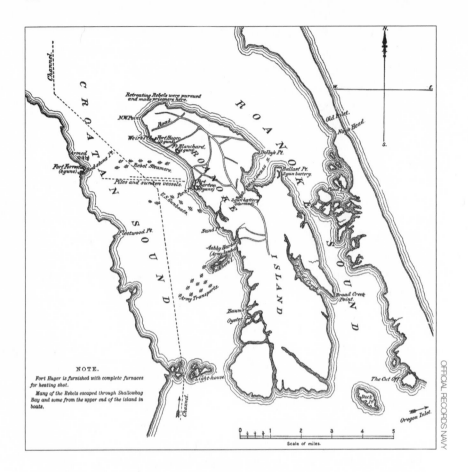

[Hunter], finding she was sinking, started for the shore and as he passed me, hailed; but I could not make out what he said, and he being a very excitable fellow [the North Carolinians called him "Tornado Hunter"] I said to Johnson that I thought there was nothing the matter with him. "Oh yes there is," said J., "look at his guards." And sure enough he was fast going down. I put after him in the *Beaufort*, but he got her ashore in time.[8]

Unfortunately Hunter beached the sinking *Curlew* right in front of Fort Forrest, completely masking its guns. The crew of the sunken gunboat scrambled to safety in the marshes, but the vessel could not be fired for fear of burning the battery on the canal barges that comprised the fort. Hunter was indeed an excitable fellow, and

Parker remembered: "He told me afterward that during the fight this
day that he found to his surprise that he had no trousers on. He said
he could never understand it, as he had certainly put on a pair in the
morning. I told him I had heard of a fellow being frightened out of
his boots, but never out of his trousers!"[9]

Ammunition was running low and Lynch sent an urgent message to Fort Huger requesting more, but they could spare only ten
charges. The entire Federal force now concentrated its fire on Fort
Bartow, and the sand fort was smothered in bursting shells. Adding
to the carnage, the fort's barracks caught fire, and thick black smoke
rolled skyward mixing with the blue-gray gun smoke that drifted in
from offshore. Around 4:00 p.m. Lieutenant Loyall spotted what he
feared most. Union troops were splashing ashore south of him at
Ashby's Landing and were pushing inland against no resistance. If
they succeeded in passing the redoubt guarding the center of the island, Loyall's position would be turned.[10]

As the afternoon sun mercifully began to disappear over the
horizon, one by one the roaring guns of the Mosquito Fleet fell
silent. They were out of ammunition. Fortunately for them, the Federals ceased firing also. Parker noted: "A little after sunset the firing
ceased on both sides, and as we felt sure the enemy would not attempt to pass the obstructions by night as he had declined them by
day, we ran in and anchored under Fort Forrest. We lit our galley

The interior of Fort Bartow during the Federal bombardment

BATTLES AND LEADERS

fires, and as we had been fighting all day, were glad enough to get something to eat. Upon the whole I was rather surprised to find myself alive, and congratulated myself upon having one more night before me. I directed my steward to serve out the cabin stores to the men and let them have a good supper."[11]

Parker was very pleased with the behavior of the *Beaufort's* crew. He was exceptionally proud of gun captain Jack Robinson and gunner's mate John Downard. Both men had trained on the British gunnery ship HMS *Excellent* and both wore the Crimean Medal, which they had earned during that conflict. Some men needed a little extra persuasion, however, and Parker related an amusing incident that occurred during the battle:

> During the afternoon, when the battle was at its height, I ordered the engineer to send me all the men he could spare from the fire-room to work at the gun. One of the men sent up was my green coal-passer, who evidently did not like the appearance of things on deck. However, he went to the side tackles of the gun as ordered. After awhile, [with] a shell bursting overhead, I called to the men to lie down, and when it was over I ordered them to jump up and go at it again. All promptly obeyed but the coal-passer, who still lay flat on his stomach. "Get up," I called to him from the hurricane deck just above him. He turned his head like a turtle and fixed his eye on me, but otherwise did not move. "Get up," I said, "or I will kill you!" at the same time drawing a pistol from my belt and cocking it. He hesitated a moment, and then sprang to the gun and behaved well during the rest of the engagement.
>
> As I went aft to my cabin after the battle, my steward being busy forward, I called to the engineer to send a man to make a fire in my stove. I had just seated myself before it when who should come in but my friend the coal-passer. He kneeled down in front of me and commenced blowing up a fire. Knowing that the man had not the slightest idea of the discipline of a man-of-war, and wishing to encourage him, I remarked, "Well, my man, I am glad you did your duty so well at the gun after I spoke to you." He blew awhile, and then looking back he said, "I tell you what, captain, I was mighty skeered; but," he said after another blow, "I saw you were going to kill me, so I thought I might as well take my chances with the enemy." After a few minutes more blow-

ing, he said, "I warn't much skeered after that; it's all in getting used to it, Cap." Well, I thought, you have the philosophy of it after all![12]

With no ammunition for his guns and no additional ordnance supplies available, Lynch was in a dilemma. It would be useless to expose his vessels and their crews to enemy fire in the morning if they had no way of defending themselves, and yet to leave would appear as though they were abandoning the army. Later that evening Lynch called his commanders to the flagship and explained his decision. After the conference, one by one, the Confederate vessels pulled out with no lights showing and headed north.

Lynch reported: "I felt sure that Pork Point battery [Fort Bartow] could hold out, and earnestly hoped that, profiting by the mistake at Hatteras, the enemy, who had landed on a point of the marshes, would be attacked and defeated during the night. With this conviction and in this hope, with the *Forrest* in tow, I proceeded with my little squadron to Elizabeth City, 35 miles distant, for ammunition, but finding only a small quantity there, dispatched Commander Hunter express to Norfolk for it."[13]

Back on Roanoke Island, Union troops continued to wade ashore at Ashby's Landing, and by midnight there were nearly ten thousand of them huddled around their blazing campfires trying to stay warm. Confederate authorities would sorely regret not contesting this landing when they had had the opportunity, for at daylight these troops pushed inland, and soon Colonel H. M. Shaw and his North Carolinians were hotly engaged. During the morning the weary gunners in Fort Bartow waited for the Federal fleet to resume the attack, all the while listening to the sound of heavy musketry fire growing closer in their rear. Around noon the redoubt covering the island road was flanked, and the demoralized Tarheel troops pulled out and retreated toward the north end of the island. With the defeat of this line, Roanoke Island was lost, and Shaw sent messengers to the forts advising their abandonment.[14]

Loyall's gunners were incensed. They still had ammunition and were ready to continue the fight with the Federal fleet, but with Union troops surging up the center of the island, it was time to retreat. Angrily throwing their remaining sacks of powder into the

Present-day location of Fort Huger on Roanoke Island

watery sand, they destroyed what equipment they could, spiked the guns, and headed north. With haste they marched along the sandy paths until they came to the camp of the Eighth North Carolina. When they arrived, a white flag was flying from Colonel Shaw's tent pole. It was all over. A battalion of men from Wise's Legion, who had landed on the northern end of the island as a relief force, arrived just in time to be included in the approximately twenty-five hundred Confederate soldiers who laid down their arms.[15]

Meanwhile, at Elizabeth City an exasperated Captain Lynch, unaware of the catastrophe that was happening on Roanoke Island, was still searching for cartridges to supply his vessels. Finding little at Elizabeth City, he had dispatched Cmdr. Thomas T. Hunter overland to Norfolk, and now sent Lt. Joseph W. Alexander and the *Raleigh* up the Dismal Swamp Canal to the same place, where it was hoped he could acquire an adequate amount of powder. Not wanting to lose any more time, however, Lynch decided to take two boats and return to the scene of the battle:

Having procured fuel and ammunition sufficient for two steamers, I left Elizabeth City in the *Seabird,* with the *Appomattox* in company, on

The Dismal Swamp Canal is still in use today as part of the Intracoastal Waterway.

the 9th instant for Roanoke Island with the purpose of rendering what assistance we could. At the mouth of the river we met a boat, from which we learned that our forces on the island had capitulated. We then continued on in the hope of rescuing the men stationed at the Croatan floating battery [Fort Forrest], but were forced to retire upon the appearance of a division of the enemy's fleet, steering toward the river.[16]

The Union flotilla that chased the *Seabird* and the *Appomattox* upriver consisted of thirteen warships of Goldsborough's fleet commanded by Stephen Rowan. The Federal captain's instructions were to find Lynch's Mosquito Fleet, attack, and destroy it. Arriving back at Elizabeth City after dark, Lynch noted with relief that the enemy had anchored for the night about ten miles below the town. The Confederate commander was well aware that he had only the remaining hours of this cold February night to prepare for their arrival.

Elizabeth City is on the western shore of the Pasquotank River, approximately twelve miles from its mouth. Between two and three miles below the city, at Cobb's Point, was a battery consisting of four 32-pounder smoothbores. These guns were under the charge of an army engineer and several North Carolina militiamen. Lynch arranged his vessels—*Appomattox, Beaufort, Ellis, Fanny,* and *Seabird*—in line abreast stretching across the river opposite the battery. The schooner *Black Warrior* was positioned across the river and slightly below the fort. During the night the men worked feverishly to distribute the small amount of ammunition available among all the vessels. Well after midnight, preparations were as complete as could be expected. Lynch believed that the enemy flotilla, as they had done at Roanoke Island, would halt and attempt to subdue the guns on Cobb's Point before advancing on the Mosquito Fleet. Events, however, proved he was sadly mistaken.[17]

Lynch roused his exhausted crews long before daylight on Monday, February 10, 1862. Quietly, each crew shuffled off to breakfast. As the eastern sky began to lighten, the galley fires were extinguished, shot lockers opened, and preparations made to man the guns. Down below, coal-heavers swung chunks of green wood into the furnaces (coal being unavailable), while in the engine rooms, steam hissed and banged through the pipes and valves. Engineers watched their gauges with a practiced eye as the pressure in the boilers began to rise. Other sailors squeezed by their engine rooms to take up stations in the cramped passageways where they could pass the few remaining shells and bags of powder up to the gundeck.

As daylight broke over the river, the Confederate gunners could see that the Federal vessels were under way and headed toward them. Parker described the sight:

The enemy was coming up at full speed, and our vessels were underweigh ready to abide the shock, when a boat came off from the shore with a bearer of a dispatch for me; it read: "Captain Parker with the crew of the *Beaufort* will at once take charge of the fort—Lynch"

"Where the devil," I asked, "are the men who were in the fort?"

"All run away," said the messenger. And so it was. The enemy vessels were by this time nearly in range, and we were ready to open fire. I did not fancy this taking charge at the last minute, but there was no help for it, so I put the men in the boats with their arms and left the *Beaufort* with the pilot, engineer and two men on board. [Parker also took all of the *Beaufort*'s ammunition.] I directed the pilot to slip the chain and escape through the canal to Norfolk if passable, otherwise to blow the steamer up rather than be captured. He "cut out," as Davy Crockett says, accordingly.[18]

When Parker and the men from the *Beaufort* reached the battery, they found only the army engineer standing by the guns. Parker's men quickly rammed the charges down the smoothbores. Within minutes the 32-pounders, one by one, roared to life. With no time to organize themselves, and finding the pieces difficult to train, the resultant shots were wild and missed their targets. By now the guns of the Mosquito Fleet had also opened fire, and the Federals, who were still plowing upriver at full speed, returned the fire. Four Union vessels in line abreast led the charge, the river being too narrow for the others who followed behind. Confederate fire from the gunboats, while it lasted, was thick and sometimes deadly. Several hits caused numerous Federal causalities. The report of the thundering guns reverberated in the still morning air, while smoke and flames covered the river and made visibility difficult. Shells whizzed through the air, crisscrossing one another as they sped toward their intended targets. Lynch's gig was cut in half by a shell, and he was stranded at the guns with Parker. The Confederate commander stood on the parapet of the Cobb's Point battery and watched with dismay as the Federal warships sped past, paying no attention to Parker's hammering fire. Lynch watched helplessly as the Union boats headed straight for his Mosquito Fleet.[19]

The Union vessels never slackened their pace, and with engines belching fire and smoke, they steered directly for the Confederate squadron. Southern gunners fired their last remaining charges and began abandoning their boats in the face of such overwhelming force. Harris set fire to the *Black Warrior* and ordered his crew to escape to shore. Amid a scattering of musket and pistol fire, a Federal vessel slammed hard into the side of the *Seabird*. Union sailors tumbled aboard, and forty-two Confederates were made to surrender as the *Seabird* began to founder. The *Ellis* was boarded, and with most of the crew escaping over the side, Lieutenant Cooke stood bravely with cutlass and pistol in hand and refused to surrender. He was finally knocked down and subdued after being severely wounded.

Midshipman William C. Jackson leaped overboard and was swimming toward shore when a pistol ball caught him in the back. Taken on board a Federal steamer, he was well cared for, but the seventeen-year-old officer died at 10:00 p.m. that evening.

Suddenly a tremendous explosion rocked the area. Having been set ablaze, the *Fanny* ran ashore and her magazine exploded. The *Forrest,* drawn up on the ways to repair her damaged propeller shaft, was set afire and abandoned. His ammunition gone, Simms turned the *Appomattox* upstream and ran for the Dismal Swamp Canal. A Federal gunboat gave chase, and Simms banged away at him with a little howitzer on his stern, finally leaving the Union boat behind. Arriving at the lock to the canal, the men of the *Appomattox* stared in disbelief—the boat was two inches too wide! Simms torched her, and the disheartened men trudged along the canal on a painful trek toward Norfolk.

Parker, not being able to train his guns on the Union vessels now milling about above his battery, and seeing that all was lost, ordered

The *Seabird* sinks as the Mosquito Fleet is destroyed at Elizabeth City.

NAVAL HISTORICAL CENTER

the guns spiked, the flag hauled down, and the men to retreat to the woods to their rear. From there it was hoped that they could elude the victorious Federals by slipping around Elizabeth City to the west and continuing on toward Norfolk. The Union gunners now turned their attention to the exposed side of Parker's battery, and grape and canister began to whistle around the men. Quickly they raced for the wood line. Parker turned to leave and saw that Captain Lynch was standing quietly, gazing upon his shattered Mosquito Fleet that had just been destroyed in front of him. Parker sadly remembered:

> I knew pretty well what his feelings were. Turning to him I said, "Commodore, I have ordered the fort evacuated."
>
> "Why so, sir?" he demanded. I pointed out the condition of affairs, . . . and he acquiesced. Arm in arm, we followed the retreating men.[20]

6

MORE DISASTERS

THE DESTRUCTION OF THE Mosquito Fleet for all intents and purposes eliminated the Confederate navy as a viable force in the sounds of North Carolina. With no waterborne resistance to oppose them, Federal warships were free to push up the numerous rivers and estuaries leading to the interior of the state. The first to experience the panic of the approaching Union forces was, of course, Elizabeth City. Richard B. Creecy was a young planter living in lower Pasquotank County at the time the Federals arrived. He described that fateful day:

> Returning from town one day, we heard when in town that the Yankees were getting their gunboats ready to come to town. The rumor had greatly excited the town, and the people were much disturbed what to do when they came. We got home late, communicated the startling news to our disturbed household, and retired. About midnight a messenger from Elizabeth City roused us from sleep and delivered a message from Rev. E. M. Forbes, Rector of Christ Church, saying that a statement had reached town that the Yankee gunboats were preparing to leave Roanoke Island for Elizabeth City, and re-

quested that we would send up wagons to remove his books and valuables to our home in the country for safety. We hurried Isaac off immediately with a farm wagon, a three-mule cart with driver, and little Peter with a single box wagon. We rose early next morning, in fact, we didn't go to sleep any more that night. While at breakfast, a servant ran into the room from upstairs saying with great alarm that the river was full of steamboats going up towards town, like a wedge, that there was mor'n forty of 'em. We ran upstairs, looked out of an upper window, and there they were, moving like a phalanx, to disturb our peace and happiness. When we went down, Isaac had returned with the debris of Mr. Forbes' goods, wares, and chattels. Great drops of bead sweat were rolling down his ebony cheeks, and his emotions overcame his utterance.

"Well, Isaac, where's Mr. Forbes' things?"

"Lord o' massy, Master Richard, I tell you how dat is. Dey's scattered all along the road from here to' Lizabeth."

Finishing our hasty breakfast, we mounted our horse and set out for town, and our eyes opened on a sight we hope never to see again. All the people of the town were on the road, most of them were afoot, shoe-tops deep in mud and slush, muddy, bedraggled, unhappy, wretched. They were looking for an asylum of safety among country friends. We met scores of our town friends, forlorn and miserable. We asked for others, and they told us the town was on fire and was deserted, and that a naval engagement was raging in the harbor; that two Confederates were killed and three Yankees. We soon met General [Charles Frederick] Hen[n]ingsen on the road, flying before an unseen enemy. We met some ladies afoot, unhappy, looking for an asylum. We met Piemonts in "Little Billy's" three-mule cart, looking for our house. They told us of the distress. That it was a dead town. That it was dead as a graveyard, that all had left, some never to return. We asked after our friends. They said that some had set fire to their houses and made tracks for Currituck, that others had done the same and that the whole town was then on fire, to spite the Yankees; that the Elliotts had started on foot for Oxford, that the Martins were in a buggy, flying for Oxford, that Rev. E. M. Forbes was staying in town to meet the Yankees when they landed on the wharf, surrender them the town and ask protection; that Mr. Forbes, when they left, was putting on his ecclesiastical vestments, in order that they might respect his sacred office. It was a grand, gloomy and peculiar time, such as the town had never seen before, has never seen since, and we trust may never see again.[1]

On February 11, Federal forces arrived in Edenton, a small town at the western end of Albemarle Sound, and within days other Union forces obstructed the Albemarle and Chesapeake Canal. The citizens of North Carolina were now thoroughly alarmed. In the space of one week, the Burnside Expedition had captured Roanoke Island, two small towns, obstructed a major canal, and annihilated the Confederate navy in the area. The headlines of the *North Carolina Standard* screamed, "TO ARMS! TO ARMS!"

The response was immediate. On February 17 Governor Henry T. Clark was able to report that the invasion of the state had "infused quite a spirit of volunteering for the war. Within the last two days seven companies have tended themselves, and I hear of many more recruiting successfully."[2]

The rush to the colors by the sons of the Tarheel State could not hide the reality—in fact, it confirmed it—that a great calamity had overtaken North Carolina and indeed the whole Confederacy. The *Richmond Examiner* termed the loss of an entire army at Roanoke Island and the destruction of the Mosquito Fleet as the "most painful event of the war." "The Roanoke affair," the editor continued, was "perfectly incomprehensible. The newspapers are filled with extravagant laudations of our valor; the annals of Greece and Rome offer no parallel. Whole regiments were defeated by companies, and we yield only to death. [Yet] our men finally surrendered with no blood on their bayonets."[3]

In Raleigh the Secession Convention, meeting in secret heated session, discussed the Roanoke loss and the "total incapacity of . . . Governor Clark."[4] In Richmond the Confederate Congress established an investigating committee to look into the affair. Meanwhile, in spite of the increase in volunteers for the army, most of whom were shipped to the Virginia front, other towns along the sounds prepared for the worst. One of these was Winton, a small community of three hundred souls up the Chowan River. Federal excesses against this small town were remembered with intense bitterness for generations to come.

Winton was of interest to Burnside for two reasons: first, it offered the possibility of a forward base of operations with the key rail junction of the Weldon and Norfolk Railroad within easy striking distance, and second, there were reports of five hundred Union sympathizers in Winton who had supposedly taken over the town. While the rumor concerning the Unionists proved to be false, the strategic importance of the town was not lost on Confederate authorities. With unusual promptness several militia companies— comprised of Lt. Col. William T. Williams's First Battalion of North Carolina Volunteers and a four-gun Virginia battery commanded by Capt. J. N. Nichols—rushed to the town. The Confederate force totaled approximately four hundred men.[5]

Early on February 18 a Federal flotilla led by Commander Rowan began the ascent of the Chowan River. His forces consisted of eight gunboats carrying approximately one thousand men of the Ninth New York Zouaves and several elements of the Fourth Rhode Island Infantry, all under the command of Col. Rush C. Hawkins. There was, of course, with the destruction of the Mosquito Fleet, no Confederate naval force to oppose them. At 4:00 p.m. on the afternoon of February 19, an excited North Carolina militiaman reported a Federal steamboat rounding the bend in the river about a mile below town.

The village of Winton was situated on a high bluff and hidden from the river by oak trees and dense underbrush. Colonel Williams dispersed his men among this cover and arranged for Martha Keen, a young black woman and the wife of a local brick mason, to stand on the wharf and signal the approaching Federals that it was safe to land. Because of the height of his position, Williams reasoned that the Union vessels would not be able to elevate their heavy guns enough to return his fire. The inexperienced North Carolinians buried themselves in the undergrowth and watched with pounding hearts as the first Federal gunboat drew near. Below them, Keen stood on the wharf and waved her handkerchief.

The Federal vessel approaching was the USS *Delaware*, Commander Rowan's flagship and the lead gunboat of the flotilla. Colonel Hawkins, evidently suspicious that the report of Union sympathizers in the town might be false, was in the cross-trees of the *Delaware* scanning the bluff through his binoculars. Approximately 350 yards from the wharf where Keen was waving her handkerchief, he caught the glint of something high on the bluff. Realizing at once that it was the sun reflecting off of Confederate rifle barrels, Hawkins shouted to the pilot, "Ring on, sheer off, Rebels on shore!" The pilot obeyed, but the momentum of the *Delaware* carried her within ten feet of the wharf. At that moment, Williams's North Carolinians opened fire.

The tangled undergrowth and oak tress exploded in a sheet of flame and smoke—Enfield rifle slugs slammed into the *Delaware* sending wooden splinters flying in all directions. Hawkins quickly abandoned his perch, so quickly in fact that the Confederates later reported a lookout in the rigging fell to the deck "presumed dead." Williams's artillery also opened fire, but the gunners miscalculated the effects of firing downhill, and their shells screamed over the *Delaware* and splashed in the river beyond.

The gunboat's paddle wheels thrashed as she attempted to turn around in the narrow river. The Confederates continued to pour musket fire into the struggling Federal when suddenly, from down the river, the USS *Commodore Perry* opened fire. Canister tore through the undergrowth, and shells began to explode among the North Carolinians. With little stomach for the fire of heavy guns, the Confederates pulled out. The *Delaware* and the remaining vessels of Rowan's command retreated downriver and anchored approximately seven miles below Winton. The *Delaware* had been "pierced like a sieve." Union sailors later counted 125 bullet holes in the vessel's deck and superstructure.[6]

A conference of Rowan's officers, including Hawkins, was held that night aboard the flagship. An ominous sentence in Hawkins's official report bares stark testimony to the fate that would befall not only Winton but countless North Carolina towns and homes as the war continued: "A consultation was held, and it was agreed to return the next morning and burn the town if found to be occupied by the rebels."[7]

Infuriated by being lured into an ambush, Rowan led his flotilla upstream next morning at full throttle. There would be no debacle this time.

After a night of celebration, the Confederate troops and citizens of Winton were startled when someone shouted that the Union warships were once more steaming up the river. But instead of meeting the enemy on the commanding heights of the bluff, Colonel Williams had his men withdraw to a set of breastworks at Mount Tabor Church several miles away. As frightened civilians streamed along after him, shells began bursting among the stately oak trees lining the bluff. Chunks of reddish clay, splintered stones, tree limbs, and hot shrapnel flew in all directions. Rowan was taking no chances. Once satisfied that there was no return fire, the Union commander ordered the landing party ashore: six companies of the Ninth New York, led by Colonel Hawkins and supported by three boat howitzers. The Zouaves charged up the bluff and burst into the town, finding only a few slaves and a small number of infirm townspeople.[8]

One who had stayed behind in the town recounted later for the *Wilmington Journal* what he observed:

About 10 o'clock, a.m. on Thursday, 20th inst. they came up as far as Barfield's [two miles below Winton] and commenced bombarding the town; landing 1,500 men at Barfields who marched off to intercept our retreat. . . . [Then] the gunboats came up to Winton, and placed 300 men on the wharf. The entire force entered the village, rolled a barrel of tar into the courthouse, burst it in and set it on fire. The stately building which cost the county $30,000 in 1833, is now in ruins. With the exception of a few books saved by the County Court clerk, our records are all destroyed. The entire town, from Captain Hiram Freeman's embracing Col. Jordan's Hotel and buildings, the beautiful residence of the late Jno. A. Anderson, and all buildings down to the bank of the Chowan, are all destroyed. The jail is uninjured. . . . In the retreat, the Confederates left some $3,000.00 or $4,000.00 worth of commissary stores. . . .

While at Winton the federal soldiers committed divers depredations on private property; poultry of all kinds and pigs were rapidly driven off. All the houses, which the federals burned, were first rifled of such valuable contents as could be taken on board the gun-boats, the rest destroyed.[9]

Hawkins simply allowed his Zouaves to run wild. In a frenzy of looting and burning, the Union troops dragged beds and stuffed chairs into the streets, ripped them open with their bayonets and set them on fire. Pictures, books, velvet drapes, carpets—anything that would burn—were heaved into the fires. Pianos were carried outside and smashed to pieces with rifle butts. Every pig, cow, and chicken that could be found was bayoneted or shot. The Northerners staggered under the load of pots and pans, silverware, mounds of clothing and other possessions as they returned to their ships. Anything not consumed by fire was carried off. Winton was totally destroyed.

Through it all Williams and his troops sat safely in their breastworks only a few miles away. His men outnumbered the rampaging Federals and could have easily ambushed and defeated them. Williams did nothing, however, and was soundly criticized for his inaction. He resigned from the army in disgrace in 1863.[10]

Fortunately for North Carolina and the Confederacy, Commander Rowan felt that with no Union sympathizers in the area the two railroad junctions were out of reach, and he retired his flotilla back down the Chowan. While his ultimate objective had not been realized, the expedition displayed just how much misery could be inflicted on the people of North Carolina because of the absence of a viable naval force to contest the coastal rivers. With the inlets,

The ruins of Winton

Roanoke Island, and Albemarle Sound in his possession, Burnside was able to turn his attention to the next stage of his campaign—New Bern.

While a detailed account of the land battles in eastern North Carolina is beyond the scope of this work, the battle for and loss of New Bern is important in order to gain a perspective of the grim disasters now facing the state and, in particular, the Confederate navy. As had been the case at Winton, there was no Southern naval force to prevent the landing of Federal troops for an advance on New Bern.

Burnside's army sailed from Roanoke Island under a bright sunny sky on March 11, 1862. His force consisted of approximately eleven thousand troops embarked on Rowan's ships. Meanwhile, Goldsborough was ordered to Hampton Roads, Virginia, to help relieve the disaster to the Federal navy caused by the CSS *Virginia*. Command of the Union navy on the North Carolina sounds was passed to the aggressive Rowan. By March 13 Union troops splashed ashore twelve miles below New Bern at Slocum's Creek under an umbrella of naval gunfire from Rowan's gunboats. The naval fire was unnecessary, however, for there were no Confederates in the area.[11]

Upriver at New Bern, Brig. Gen. Lawrence O'Bryan Branch had less than four thousand untested North Carolina troops—a woefully inadequate number to man the elaborate defenses below the city.

Brig. Gen. Lawrence O'Bryan Branch

NORTH CAROLINA REGIMENTS

These earthworks had been constructed before Branch's arrival in November of the previous year, and he immediately had set about strengthening them. He was hampered, however, by a lack of implements and laborers, much of which was attributed to the area's lukewarm support for the Confederacy. After circulating handbills all over the state and running ads in local newspapers, Branch was only able to muster a few free blacks and one slave. He finally was forced to detail five hundred soldiers a day to

A view of New Bern from across the Neuse River

work on the breastworks. Repeated requests to Raleigh and Richmond for more troops to man the defenses went unanswered.[12]

The line along which the battle was to be fought began on the Neuse River with Fort Thompson, a thirteen-gun earthen fortification approximately six miles below New Bern. But only three of the fort's guns could bear on the land approaches to the city. Stretching westward for approximately one mile was a series of breastworks leading to the Atlantic and North Carolina Railroad. To take advantage of terrain features, Branch dropped the line back 150 yards at the railroad and then continued westward in a series of redans ending at Brice's Creek, which was bordered by an impassable swamp. This arrangement left an unprotected 150-yard gap in the line at the railroad where a large brick kiln was situated. Into this gap, the weakest point of the line, Branch positioned a battalion of North Carolina militia under the command of Col. H. J. B. Clark.[13]

The Federals attacked on the foggy morning of March 14 in three columns. Rowan's gunboats, aiming over trees at the smoke and noise of battle, began dropping shells on friend and foe alike, adding to the noise and confusion. Although the left and right Federal columns met strong resistance from the regular North Carolina regiments, the center column advancing up the railroad struck the militia at the brick kiln. The militiamen fired one volley from their hunting rifles and shotguns and then fled in terror. The Union troops then assailed the next nearest Confederate unit in the flank, and they too gave way. Although the Thirty-third North Carolina plugged the hole for a short while, it was soon overwhelmed and began to pull back. Even with the Twenty-sixth North Carolina standing firm on the right side of the railroad, Branch knew his line was broken and ordered a general retreat. By the end of the day, New Bern was in Federal hands. For the next two days former slaves and Union soldiers and sailors ransacked and pillaged the city. Burnside was finally forced to bring in a strong guard of troops to restore order.[14]

Before the Northern general could launch any further penetrations into the interior of the state, he had to secure his rear. With that in mind, and with New Bern now firmly in Union hands, Burnside turned his attention to Fort Macon, the last remaining Confederate position on the coast north of Wilmington. Fort Macon was situated on the eastern tip of Bogue Banks and guarded the entrance to Beaufort and Morehead City. In addition, Beaufort, being an excellent deep-water port, was much prized by the Federal navy as a coaling

Federal ships firing on Fort Thompson

BATTLES AND LEADERS

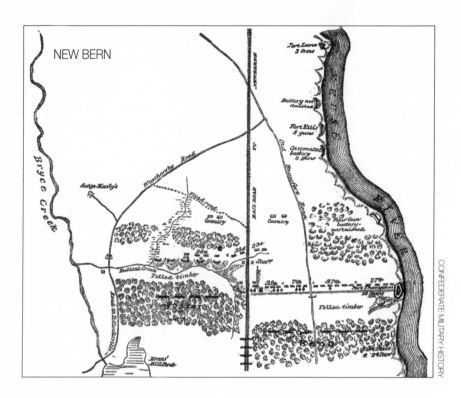

and refitting facility. Another desirable feature was that, once in Federal hands, the port would provide a safe haven for Union blockaders from the fierce Atlantic storms.

Fort Macon had been completed in 1834 and was garrisoned by five companies of North Carolina artillerymen. On paper the force totaled approximately 479 men, but only about 300 were fit for duty. The fort was commanded by Col. Moses J. White, and at the time of Burnside's investment of the bastion, he could count on 54 guns of various calibers. Although the garrison had labored day and night to construct firing platforms facing the land side on Bogue Bank, the majority of the fort's guns still bore on the ocean. Another frustrating deficiency, as events would soon show, was the lack of small mortars that could have dropped their shells among the Union work parties who labored in relative safety behind the sand dunes. In spite of these deficiencies, White was determined not to surrender Fort Macon without a fight.[15]

Unlike Winton and New Bern, there was a Confederate naval

"presence" at Fort Macon, but it could add nothing to the defense of the area. Back on February 28, there was considerable excitement among the garrison when the CSS *Nashville* eluded the fire of a blockader's guns and steamed triumphantly into Beaufort Harbor. Commissioned as a cruiser by the Confederate government, the paddle-wheel steamer had been the first warship to carry the new country's flag to England. Her commander was Lt. Robert P. Pegram, and in his official report to Secretary of the Navy Stephen R. Mallory, he explained why Beaufort was his choice for a return:

> Upon leaving England I had determined to make direct course for one of our Southern ports, but finding that the *Nashville* could not weather in safety continued northerly gales, and that far more coal had been consumed than was anticipated, I shaped our course for Bermuda, anchoring in the harbor of St. George on the 20th of February. Whilst

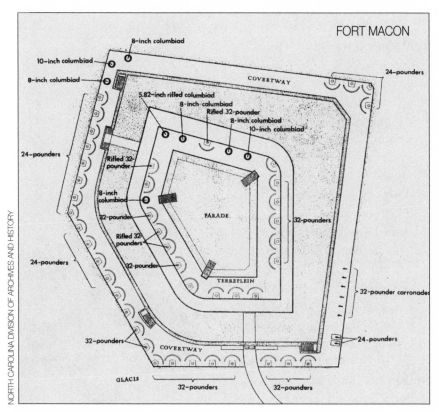

receiving on board a supply of coal, I learned that the owner and master of the Confederate schooner *Pearl,* which had run the blockade from Beaufort, N. C., and had run aground on the northern part of the Island of Bermuda, was then at Hamilton, and I determined on seeking an interview with the person in charge. Before, however, I could carry out this resolution, Captain J. Pender, the owner of the *Pearl,* came on board the *Nashville,* and in the most patriotic and praiseworthy manner volunteered his services, and those of his master, Mr. J. Beveridge, a practiced pilot, to pilot the *Nashville* into Beaufort, N. C., speaking with the utmost confidence of our ability to run into that port.[16]

Four days after touching at Bermuda, the *Nashville* steamed out of St. George, bound for Beaufort. With pilot Beveridge on board for the run to the Southern coast, Pegram was confident that they would have no trouble reaching the Carolina port. A sharp lookout was kept, for they were now entering the waters patrolled by the Federal blockaders, and despite heavy seas, the *Nashville* continued on her course. Pegram described his arrival to Mallory:

At daylight on the morning of the 28th of February we found ourselves near the harbor of Beaufort, N. C., and the first thing seen was the enemy's ship blockading the port. I stood directly toward her, hoisting the American flag and the ship's private number. This was replied to by the enemy. As soon, however, as I had passed her, I ordered the United States flag to be hauled down and hoisted the Confederate flag at the foremast head and at the peak, while my pennant was run up the main. When the United States flag was hauled down on board the *Nashville,* the Federal vessel's captain endeavored to bring her broadside to bear, but before the ship could be swung we were out of range of his guns.

Col. Moses J. White

This Federal vessel was the USS *State of Georgia,* commanded by James F. Armstrong. He had been deceived by the *Nashville's* close resemblance to the USS *Keystone State* and allowed the Confederate cruiser to pass, believing she was delivering the mail. Pegram added: "In spite of this the enemy fired twenty-one shots, but without the slightest effect. I answered the enemy's salute by firing one gun, finding it useless to waste more powder. At shortly after 7 a.m. we had passed the lines of Fort Macon and were safely moored alongside of the railroad wharf at Morehead City."[17]

The arrival of the *Nashville* in Southern waters signaled the end of her career as a Confederate naval warship. When Pegram arrived in Richmond, he was informed that the vessel had been sold to Fraser, Trenholm and Company, the Charleston and Liverpool–based banking firm, which intended on operating the speedy steamer as a blockade-runner. Returning to Morehead City, Pegram ordered all government property removed and the vessel prepared for movement to Charleston where the new owners would take delivery. After braving the guns of the Federal blockaders and the winter storms of the North Atlantic, however, the *Nashville* was now threatened with destruction from another quarter. Lt. William C. Whittle, executive officer on the trip to England who had been placed temporarily in command, described this new danger:

> General Burnside's movement upon Newbern, N. C., was then being executed, and Captain Pegram, with the officers and crew of the *Nashville,* went through on one of the last trains that could escape, after which all communication inland was completely cut off. Burnside's expedition was moving upon Morehead City, and the capture of the *Nashville* seemed inevitable. The blockading fleet had been increased to two steamers and one sailing vessel, and the Federal troops were on the march to seize the vessel as she lay tied up at the wharf.[18]

While Federal infantry inched closer and closer, siege batteries were constructed on the mainland to batter the masonry fort into submission, and Union navy guns shelled the fort from offshore. With Federal warships off the bar, and heavy guns in their rear, the plight of the now unarmed *Nashville* was dark indeed.[19]

Whittle's narrative explained:

> Without a crew or means of defense, without even a chart or chronometer, short of coal and provisions, the idea of saving the ship was simply vain. There seemed a single chance, however, and I determined to take the chance. The fall of Fort Macon was only a question of time, and a very short time at that; the blockade must therefore, be broken. Quietly and secretly we set to work, and being assured by my chief engineer [James Hood] that with his small force and assistance of the deck hands he could keep the vessel under steam, we made ready to run through the blockading fleet. I was fortunate in securing the services of Captain Gooding, an excellent coast pilot, who was then in command of a sailing ship blockaded in the harbor. He brought with him a chart, chronometer and sextant, and such instruments as were deemed absolutely necessary for navigation, with the promise that if his efforts were successful the ultimate command of the ship would be given him by the purchasers.

Whittle and his men worked feverishly to get the *Nashville* ready. The young lieutenant was determined that the Confederate steamer

The CSS *Nashville*

HARPER'S WEEKLY

The shelling of Fort Macon

would not fall into the hands of the enemy, and accordingly made preparations to destroy her if it became necessary. When all was ready, Whittle dropped down under the guns of Fort Macon, and there planned the final steps of his escape. Colonel White came aboard and apprised Whittle of the Federal schemes to capture the *Nashville*. Whittle informed the colonel that he had no intention of allowing the enemy to lay hands on the cruiser, and divulging his plans for running out, asked that White make sure that his men did not fire on them as they passed in the dark. White assured him that he would forward the message and wished him God speed.[20]

On the evening of March 17, 1862, between sunset and moonrise, the moon being nearly full, I tipped my anchor and ran out. As soon as I was under way a rocket was sent up from the lower side of Brogue Island, below Fort Macon, by an enemy's boat, sent ashore from the blockaders for the purpose of watching us, giving me the assurance that our movement had been detected.

Steaming toward the entrance at the bar, I found the three vessels congregated close together under way and covering the narrow channel. . . . We were going at full speed, say fourteen knots per hour. I was in the pilot house with Gooding, and two others were at the wheel. The blockaders, under way and broadside to me, were across my path. I ran for the one furtherest to the northward and eastward,

The interior of Fort Macon today

with the determination to go through or sink both ships. As I approached rapidly I was given the right of way and passed through and out under a heavy fire from the three vessels. They had commenced firing as soon as I got within range and continued until I passed out, firing in all, as well as we could determine, about twenty guns. The moon rose clear and full a short time afterward and found us well out to sea, no attempt being made to pursue us that we could discover.[21]

At dawn on April 25, the Federal batteries that had been emplaced behind the sand dunes on Bogue Banks opened fire on Fort Macon. Ten minutes later the Confederate guns replied. Soon guns of the Federal warships began sending their shells into the masonry fort. For a time the firing was wild and inaccurate on both sides. Many of the shells from the Federal batteries screamed low over the fort and splashed in the bay beyond while Confederate gunners watched in disgust as their shots skipped from the top of one sand dune to another. Without mortars Colonel White had little hope of damaging the enemy.

Gradually, however, the Federal land batteries, aided by a lookout with signal flags on the mainland, zeroed in on the fort. All morning and into the afternoon the Union guns continued their rapid fire with increasingly telling effect. By late afternoon nineteen Southern guns had been dismounted and several soldiers killed, and Confederate fire, plagued by a shortage of ammunition and disabled guns, had slackened considerably. The only bright spot for Colonel White was on the ocean side, which was designed for this type of encounter, where accurate Confederate gunners drove the Federal warships out of range. By late afternoon, however, White concluded that to resist further would only cause needless causalities and so ordered a white flag raised. Fort Macon, and a fine deep-water port, were now in the hands of the enemy.[22]

By the end of May 1862, the ports of Plymouth and Washington were also under Union control. Only Wilmington remained firmly in Confederate hands. To the frightened citizens of eastern North Carolina it was painfully evident that their towns and homes had become a hateful no-man's-land. Pillaged by the enemy, abandoned by their government, their pain would endure for three long years. With the siphoning off of Confederate troops for distant battlefields, and the total absence of the Confederate navy, Federal forces were free to overrun the eastern part of the state.

Something had to be done, or Lee's army, struggling to hold the enemy at bay in Virginia, would be threatened from behind. The seriousness of the naval situation was not lost on Secretary of the Navy Mallory. Somehow, the navy must reestablish itself and take back the sounds, bays, and rivers of eastern North Carolina, or at the very least, halt any further advances into the interior of the state.

7

THE WHITE HALL GUNBOAT

THE NAVAL DISASTERS THAT besieged the Confederacy during 1861 and 1862 had prompted Stephen R. Mallory to change his thinking concerning Southern shipbuilding. The naval secretary had always felt that armored vessels were the only viable means to successfully counter the naval strength of the United States. Initially he and others at the Navy Department had emphasized large ironclad gunboats, such as the *Arkansas, Louisiana,* and *Virginia,* operating in conjunction with smaller wooden gunboats. Mallory had envisioned that these behemoths, in addition to defending the major seaports, would take to the sea and wreak havoc among the Union blockade. European-built cruisers, meanwhile, were to make war upon Northern merchant shipping. With their deep draft, low freeboard, and heavy weight of armor, however, these large ironclads had not proven seaworthy. Now, with their loss, coupled with the alarming disasters in North Carolina, some in the department were urging Mallory to pursue a different course.

Heeding advisers such as constructor John L. Porter and Cmdr. John M. Brooke, Mallory determined to abandon the construction of wooden gunboats, except for those well under way or nearing

completion, and concentrate instead on smaller, light-draft, iron-
plated gunboats. Hopefully, the
armored warships that were cur-
rently being contracted in Europe
could eventually attack and destroy the blockade. With this new
policy in mind, the Navy Department sought reliable shipbuilders
who could produce, in home waters, the needed ironclads within
the shortest possible time. Earlier, several armored vessels had
been under construction at Norfolk with the intent of steaming

Secretary of the Navy Stephen R. Mallory

them through the Albemarle and Chesapeake Canal to the sounds of
North Carolina. With the evacuation of Norfolk and the Gosport
Navy Yard at Portsmouth in the spring of 1862, only the CSS *Richmond* was far enough along to be towed to safety up the James River.
The others had to be destroyed. As a result, by the summer of 1862
additional contracts had been negotiated for the construction of
three ironclads at Wilmington, one at Tarboro on the Tar River, another near Halifax on the Roanoke River, and still another on the
Neuse River opposite White Hall. This last vessel would eventually
be commissioned as the CSS *Neuse*.

The contract for the *Neuse* was finalized on October 17, 1862, between the Navy Department and Howard and Ellis Shipbuilders of
New Bern. Thomas S. Howard and Elijah W. Ellis, were both natives
of Carteret County. The senior partner, Howard, had begun his marine business in New Bern around 1845, and by 1860 his shipyard
employed approximately twenty-five workers. It was during this period that he accepted Ellis, a local turpentine distiller, as a full partner
in the shipyard. Upon the evacuation of New Bern by the Confederates, the two shipbuilders sought safety, it is believed, near High
Point. Regardless of where they relocated, they now had a contract to
build an ironclad warship, the hull of which was to be assigned to an
agent of the Navy Department by March 1, 1863, "complete in all

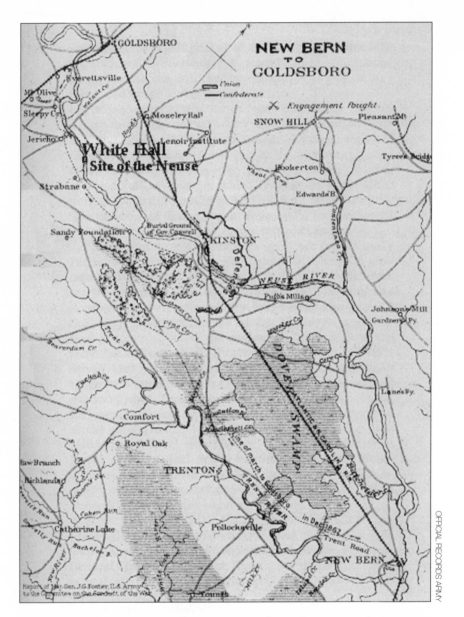

respects ready to receive the engine and machinery, and to put in place and fasten iron plating on said vessel, . . . the iron plates and the bolts for fastening the same are to be furnished by the party of the second part [the Navy Department]."[1]

Howard and Ellis chose for their construction site a sloping piece of ground along the north side of the Neuse River opposite the small village of White Hall (present-day Seven Springs). Lewis Whitfield owned most of the land in the vicinity, and he supplied most of the timber that would eventually go into the *Neuse.* Workers were hired, and soon Whitfield's green timber was being cut and sawed in order to construct the vessel's keel.[2]

A short time after the war, Col. S. D. Pool of the Tenth North Carolina Artillery, penned a graphic description of the area around White Hall:

> White Hall, was, at that time a small hamlet on the Neuse River which was spanned by a substantial county bridge. The river, though much narrower at White Hall, is deep and navigable. On the northern side the river has a gentle sloop to a stream which in 1862, was bordered by a swamp in which there was a somewhat dense growth of tall timbers. A quantity of this timber had been felled and cut into logs, which lay around the bank of the river, and through the swamp. . . . A gunboat was in [the] course of building, and stood, propped on rollers, in the upper end of the swamp, and near the river not far from the bridge. A bridge road ran through and about equally divided the swamp. . . . .The little hamlet of White Hall, built on the southern bank of the Neuse, consisted of two or three stores and warehouses, and a straggling street with some neat dwellings and enclosures. The warehouses were on the bluff which is lofty on the southern side; and some eminencies further from the river, and commanding the much lower level of the northern shore, gave great advantage to the former as a military position. . . . The bluffs were covered with piles of crude rosin, and barrels of spirits of turpentine.[3]

With timber plentiful in the area, preliminary construction proceeded rapidly, and in the first part of November 1862 the keel was laid. Like the *Albemarle,* which was being built on the Roanoke, the *Neuse* was designed by John L. Porter, and his plans called for a wooden flat-bottomed hull that could be simply constructed and assembled by house carpenters. Gilbert Elliott, the young builder of the ironclads at Tarboro and at Halifax, explained how the wooden hulls of these shallow draft vessels were constructed:

The keels were laid and construction was commenced by bolting down, across the center, a piece of frame timber, which was of yellow pine, eight by ten inches.

Another frame of the same size was then dovetailed into this, extending outwardly at an angle of 45 degrees, forming the side, and at the outer end of this frame for the shield was also dovetailed, the angle being about 35 degrees. And then the top deck was added, and so on around to the other end of the bottom beam. Other beams were then bolted down to the keel and to the first one fastened, and so on, working fore and aft, the main deck beams being interposed from stem to stern. The shield was 60 feet in length and octagonal in form.

When this part of the work was completed she was a solid boat, built of pine frames and if chalked would have floated in that condition, but she was afterwards covered with 4 inch planking, laid on longitudinally, as ships are usually planked, and this was properly chalked and pitched, cotton being used instead of oakum, the latter being very scarce and the former the only article to be had in abundance.[4]

To help facilitate the construction of the ironclads in North Carolina, Mallory dispatched Cmdr. James W. Cooke to the area to "assist" in the procurement of machinery and iron that could be rolled into armor plate. Cooke, a native of North Carolina, had been exchanged in February 1862 after his capture at Roanoke Island. In addition to his efforts to obtain machinery and iron, Cooke was to be responsible for outfitting the vessels after they were launched and to act as an adviser between the contractors and the Navy Department in Richmond. He would eventually command the CSS *Albemarle*. After surveying the building sites of the ironclads, Cooke became increasingly concerned about the lack of protection they had in the event of enemy incursions into the interior. This was especially true for the site at White Hall.

Cooke's fears of invasion were well founded, for in the early fall of 1862, Union forces under Gen. John G. Foster began raiding inland from the base at New Bern. To support Foster, Federal gunboats were slowly making their way up the Neuse. So alarmed had Cooke become with these events that, after visiting White Hall, he wrote to

Col. Walter Gwynn, the officer in charge of obstructing the river, expressing his apprehensions. On November 4, 1862, Col. Jeremy F. Gilmer, chief of the Engineer Bureau, replied:

> Colonel Walter Gwynn sends the following extract from a letter of yours to him:
>
> According to the understanding with you in Richmond, I have commenced work at White Hall, and if you think the river [Neuse] cannot be defended in time to protect the work, I will thank you to inform me of the fact through Colonel Gilmer or the Secretary of the Navy.
>
> To which Colonel Gwynn replies in his letter to me:
>
> My opinion is that with a sufficient force the obstructions we are placing in the Neuse River can be defended against any force the enemy are likely to send against it. They, as well as the land defenses, will be completed, I think, in six weeks; but unless the south side of the Neuse is occupied, if the enemy possesses any enterprise at all, they will most assuredly destroy the gunboat which Commander Cooke is building at White Hall. A force stationed at White Hall might,

Initial stages in the construction of the CSS *Neuse*

CSS NEUSE GUNBOAT ASSOCIATION, STEPHEN McCALL, ARTIST

however, prevent such a disaster. You will please communicate this opinion to Commander Cooke.

If further information with regard to troops for defense be desired, it is respectfully suggested that Major-General S. G. French, commanding at Petersburg, be addressed on the subject.[5]

Cooke's fears proved justified in December when a strong Union force advanced along the south side of the Neuse River. While the Federal gunboats, with the exception of one, had turned back because of low water, Foster's troops pushed on toward the important railroad bridge near Goldsboro. One Federal gunboat, the USS *Allison,* was able to advance up the Neuse until she came under fire from Col. S. D. Pool's North Carolina battalion of heavy artillery. As a result of this fire the *Allison* turned back.[6]

Brig. Gen. Nathan G. Evans gathered what few Confederate troops could be found in the area and prepared to meet Foster's 10,000 men on the south side of the river approximately two miles from the Kinston railroad bridge. On December 14, with his North Carolina regiments to the right of the railroad and several South Carolina regiments on the left, Evans's 2,014 men awaited Foster's attack. Lead elements of the Union advance struck the small Confederate force around 9:00 a.m. After a short but bitterly fought battle, the South Carolinians on the left gave way and retreated across the railroad bridge to the north bank. No one informed the North Carolina troops of the retreat, and Evans, believing all of his troops were across the bridge, had it set on fire.

John L. Porter, chief constructor and designer of the *Neuse* and *Albemarle*

NAVAL HISTORICAL CENTER

When the North Carolinians realized what was happening, there was a mad stampede for the burning bridge. Pushing and shoving, gray troops surged through the smoke and flames in a desperate effort to reach the other side. At least

Depiction of the CSS *Neuse* during early construction

four hundred of them arrived too late and were taken prisoner. Union soldiers, forming a bucket brigade, extinguished the flames, while Evans's exhausted remnants retreated west beyond Kinston. The next morning, December 15, Federal troops crossed the Neuse on the charred and blackened bridge and entered Kinston, which they proceeded to loot and ransack. Determined to push on to Goldsboro, Foster late in the day moved his men back across the bridge and took the river road west. The route was now open to Goldsboro, and along the way, White Hall and the partially completed CSS *Neuse*.[7]

General Evans, reinforced by the Forty-seventh North Carolina, kept pace with the Union advance on the north side of the river, and when they approached White Hall, he sent several regiments under Brig. Gen. Beverly H. Robertson to meet them. To avoid a repeat of the Federal crossing at Kinston, Robertson had his men gather all the flammable items that they could find and pile them on the White Hall bridge. On December 16, when the lead elements of the Federal column approached, they found the bridge a mass of flames. Portions of the bridge soon collapsed into the river "and floated down its waters a burning wreck."

Foster, determined to make a show of force at White Hall and then continue on to Goldsboro, wheeled three companies of cavalry and several artillery pieces into position on the south bank and opened fire. Robertson's Tarheels, concealed by heavy undergrowth

Union troops open fire on the partially completed gunboat *Neuse.*

on the north shore, returned a blistering fire that caused many
Union casualties. The Eleventh North Carolina bore the brunt of the
enemy's fire and their historian later wrote: "Posted along the river
bank, from which another regiment had just been driven back, it
was pounded for several hours at short range by a terrific storm of
grape and canister, as well as by musketry; but it never flinched, and
gained a reputation for endurance and courage which it proudly
maintained to the fateful end at Appomattox."[8]

Bluish-gray smoke drifted across the river obscuring visibility for
friend and foe alike. Soon, however, the partially completed *Neuse*
was spotted by Federal gunners. A New York newspaper correspondent traveling with Foster's troops wrote: "We found previous reports
confirmed, in that we discovered a rebel gunboat on the other side of
the river. To destroy the gunboat which was not fully completed, was
one of our principal objects, but to do it in the face of the enemy, concealed in the woods on the opposite bank, was a different matter."[9]

Several Union batteries directed their fire at the *Neuse,* and several rounds struck the unfinished hull. Fortunately, it did not catch fire. With darkness approaching, Union cavalrymen improvised a unique method for accurately maintaining their fire on Confederate positions across the river. A *Harper's Weekly* correspondent reported: "Two thousand barrels of turpentine were seized, piled in an immense heap on the river's bank, and set on fire. Such a bonfire mortal eyes have seldom seen. Vast sheets of billowy flame flashed their forked tongue to the clouds. The whole region for miles around was lighted up. Every movement of the enemy was revealed, and their positions were mercilessly shelled." Several warehouses were also set ablaze.

A Federal major called for volunteers to swim the river and set the gunboat afire. The *Harper's* correspondent related the tale: "To this daring deed, Henry Butler, of Company C, Third New York Cavalry, volunteered." Removing his clothes, Butler "plunged into the wintry waves, and pushed boldly for the opposite shore." Meanwhile Union artillery fired round after round of canister into the Confederate positions in an effort to cover Butler's mission. Reaching the north bank, Butler "ran up the bank to the flaming bridge, seized a [fire] brand and was making for the [gunboat], when several rebels rushed from their sheltered hiding places and endeavored to seize him. Quick as thought he turned, plunged again into the river, and through a shower of bullets returned safely to his comrades."[10]

In the flickering light of blazing turpentine and warehouses, Union gunners now doubled their efforts to destroy the *Neuse.* The *Harper's* correspondent wrote, "Finding we could not well get over to the gunboat, we battered it to pieces with shot and shell." At daylight, Foster's main force arrived on the scene and fighting erupted anew. More shells were fired at the *Neuse,* some hitting her, but later in the day Foster withdrew his weary troops and continued on the River Road to Goldsboro. There, after a spirited contest, one courageous Union soldier managed to set the important Wilmington and Weldon railroad bridge on fire. The damage was only superficial, however, and the line was back in operation within a few days. Wasting little time and believing his operation a success, Foster led his exhausted army back to New Bern.

With the campaign concluded, most Federal commanders were confident that they had destroyed the gunboat at White Hall. In fact, the *Neuse* had been struck only several times, and little damage had been sustained. Shortly after Foster resumed his march to Goldsboro, workmen were busy hammering and sawing on the hull of the unfinished ironclad.

Although the wooden hull was not severely damaged, the battle at White Hall undoubtedly delayed the final completion of the *Neuse*. With plentiful timber in the area, the house carpenters could continue their construction of the hull and framework for the shield at a measured pace. As the rough green timber was cut, it was dragged to the construction site where workmen carefully measured and cut each piece to the length outlined in Porter's plans. The pieces were then notched to fit their adjoining members. This method of building complete frames and bolting them together required a laborious drilling process that took time to accomplish. It was imperative that the holes be drilled and the pieces joined together as quickly as possible to minimize warping of the green timber as it began to cure.

Work continued through the rest of December and January, and in February 1863 Howard and Ellis Shipbuilders were given their third and fourth payments by the Navy Department. Finally in mid-March the hull slid down the ways into the Neuse River. A skeptical Confederate engineer, Henry T. Guion, was not impressed. Guion, who evidently was stationed in Kinston and knew of the many delays and frustrations encountered by the builders, recorded in his journal on March 18: "Howard & Ellis are apparently driving hard upon the gunboat and . . . will finish here [Kinston] in ninety days. . . . I give them till Christmas—we shall see."

Additional carpentry work still remained before the vessel could be towed downriver to Kinston for installation of her armor, guns, and machinery. Once in the water all seams and crevices that showed signs of leakage had to be rechalked while additional work had to be performed on the gundeck and casemate. At last, toward the end of April or the first of May (records are unclear) the *Neuse* was turned over to the Confederate navy, and she was towed eighteen miles downriver to Kinston.

Thomas Howard and Elijah Ellis should have been pleased with their accomplishment. While their contract had called for the com-

pleted hull to be finished by March 1, they had missed that date by
only a few weeks. In addition to the chronic shortage of manpower
and equipment that all Southern construction sites experienced during the war, the builders had also had to contend with enemy action
and damage to the vessel. In spite of these difficulties they had produced a sound boat almost on schedule. Nevertheless, the more difficult task of procuring and installing her iron armor, guns, and
machinery was just beginning.

Upon arrival at Kinston the *Neuse* was anchored at the foot of
Caswell Street, but a few days later she was moved one hundred
yards downstream to what was know as the "Cat Hole." This was a
spot where the river had formed a sharp indentation into the bank,
and was, therefore, ideal for lowering the heavy guns and machinery
into the boat's hull. During the summer and fall, while machinists
drilled the two-inch iron plates as they arrived and bolted them to
the casemate, carpenters (there seemed to be no shortage of them
around Kinston) began fitting out the hull of the ironclad below
deck. Cabins were built for the officers, while quarters and a mess
area were fabricated for the crew. Shell rooms and a magazine were
constructed, and in the forward section a galley was built complete
with a five-burner iron stove that had been made in Baltimore, Maryland. In the midsection, large beams were laid that were intended to

An 1862 map of Kinston showing the Cat Hole where the Neuse was moored support the engine and boilers. Up above on the gundeck, however, events were not progressing nearly as well.

The chronic scarcity of iron plagued all Confederate shipbuilding projects, and the *Neuse* was no exception. The contract with Howard and Ellis was barely two weeks old when the search for iron commenced by the Navy Department. A primary source of iron was the worn out or abandoned railroad lines scattered throughout the South. On October 28, 1862, Mallory had written to Secretary of War George W. Randolph asking that a number of rails belonging either to the Portsmouth and Weldon Railroad or the Norfolk and Petersburg rail line be transferred to the navy. Randolph replied that because of "pressure of the enemy," this would be impossible. On November 4, 1862, Mallory next wrote to Governor Zebulon B. Vance of North Carolina:

> Commander Cooke, sent by me to North Carolina to obtain iron for plating the gunboats being built for the defense of the State, has returned without having accomplished this object. He reports that you have the control of a quantity of railroad iron, and I therefore address myself to you upon the subject.
>
> To enable the boats to resist the guns of the enemy their armor must be at least 4 inches thick, placed at an angle of at least 36 degrees. This armor, from the limited power of our mills, we are compelled to roll into plate 2 by 7 inches and 10 feet long, and to put them on the vessels in two courses. If you will let the Department have the rails and facilitate its transportation to Richmond they will be immediately rolled into plates for the vessels in question and for such other defenses as we may build in the waters of your State.
>
> Commander Cooke will remove the iron if you consent to its transfer and will arrange the compensation according to his instructions.
>
> Please telegraph your reply.[11]

Governor Vance consented and a quantity of rails were obtained and shipped to the rolling mill at Atlanta, Georgia. Still, this was only a beginning. More iron was needed if the *Neuse* and other ironclads being built in North Carolina ever hoped to reach operational status. Mallory and the Navy Department continued to urge the gov-

NATIONAL ARCHIVES

Governor Zebulon B. Vance

ernor to aid in the procurement of railroad iron. In January 1863 the naval secretary received an exasperating letter from Cooke, his agent in North Carolina:

It is impossible to obtain any railroad iron unless it is seized. The Petersburg Rail Road agent says that he must have the old iron on the Petersburg to replace the worn out rails on that road. The Kinston and Raleigh Road require the iron taken below Kinston to replace the iron on the Charlotte & North Carolina Road and those roads are considered a military necessity and the whole subject of railroad iron was laid before the North Carolina Legislature and I am unable to obtain iron.[12]

Mallory had a copy of this letter made and forwarded to Governor Vance. In a tacit comment, the naval secretary added, "The vessels would not have been undertaken had the department not had good reason to believe the railroad iron could be obtained in North Carolina." Vance finally interceded, and in May a quantity of rails was obtained from the Wilmington and Weldon Railroad. A substantial number of unused rails were also obtained from the Wilmington, Charlotte and Rutherford Company, but the majority of these were allocated to the *Albemarle* and the ironclads being built at Wilmington. Most of the iron rails destined for the *Neuse* were shipped to the Schofield and Markham Rolling Mill in Atlanta where they were rolled into two-inch armor plates.[13]

During this period Mallory ordered Lt. William Sharp to command the ironclad at Kinston, and in cooperation with Commander Cooke, to obtain the needed iron to finish the vessel. Sharp was from Virginia and had suffered a severe face wound during the engagement at Fort Hatteras in August 1861. Found unconscious in the fort after its surrender, Sharp's wound was tended by Col. Charles

Heywood of the U.S. Marine Corps, after which the Confederate lieutenant was deemed well enough to travel. Transported north to Fort Columbus on Governor's Island, New York, he was later transferred to Fort Warren in Boston Harbor. Exchanged in November, he had served with the James River Squadron before being sent to Kinston. Sharp's presence as commander of the unfinished *Neuse* lent a sense of stability to the construction project in addition to relieving part of the load being borne by Cooke.[14]

Construction of the *Neuse* progressed at a reasonable pace during the summer and fall of 1863, even though there were frequent delays because of the iron shortage. Carpenters were able to finish the interior below the gundeck, and Chief Mechanic James Fleming from the Gosport Navy Yard was brought in to help install the machinery. The nagging problem, however, was iron. Even after the iron plates were rolled and shipped from Atlanta, it took an enormous amount of time before they finally reached Kinston. The South's inadequate rail system, which was already beginning to show the strains of war, was part of the reason, while an additional obstacle was the priority given to the transportation of munitions and troops for the Confederate army.

As the year 1863 drew to a close, it was becoming painfully obvious that the *Neuse* was behind schedule. It was also plainly evident to those in the Navy Department and to those laboring in Kinston, that the first several months of 1864 would be decisive in commissioning the ironclad into service.

8

THE BUILDING OF THE CSS ALBEMARLE

THE BUILDING, LAUNCHING, AND committing to battle of the CSS *Albemarle* under the most primitive conditions is a story unparalleled. The *Albemarle* was known as the "ironclad that was built in a cornfield," because that is where she was fabricated. Even more remarkable was her builder, Gilbert Elliott. In charge of the entire construction project, Elliott was only nineteen years old when the ironclad's keel was laid. Once commissioned and in the hands of tireless Cmdr. James W. Cooke, the *Albemarle* would help stem the tide of Union invasion and bring a semblance of hope to the besieged citizens of eastern North Carolina. One can only marvel at the magnitude of Elliott's and Cooke's accomplishments given the disastrous conditions prevalent among the sounds and rivers of eastern North Carolina.

As was the case at Kinston and White Hall, Union raids were sporadically launched across the eastern counties of North Carolina from the Federal bases of New Bern, Washington, and Plymouth. Some of these raids had legitimate military objectives, while others were launched, supposedly, to collect supplies. Many times, however, the raids degenerated into pillaging and burning. A Confederate cavalryman who scouted the Trenton-Pollocksville area after one

115

such raid, found utter destruction with only one family remaining. The horseman recalled:

> Many fine dwellings, . . . mostly all destroyed, the Yankees having knocked to pieces those which they could not burn—chairs, sofas, bedsteads, wash-stands, bureaus, and all sorts of furniture are broken up, and scattered broad-cast over the streets and fields. On our road to Pollocksville we passed several of the finest farmhouses I have ever seen, and they were all ruined. I noticed one in particular. The Yankees had destroyed a mill near it, burned the kitchen, broken open the cellar doors, windows, etc., and to "capall" had broken open the plastering and built a big fire between the walls; fortunately it went out, before the house took fire. "To cap all" really, they had killed all the stock on the farm, and the house and yard were full of buzzards, some of them regaling on a dead horse before the front door, and some . . . perching in the parlor and on the peazza. The walls of the house were scribbled on, and [the] writing generally was of a mean character.

While not all Federal troops committed such offenses, it became a common practice among the Union forces in eastern North Carolina. Some of the men in blue seemed to revel in it. In a letter home, a soldier of the Tenth Connecticut stationed at New Bern wrote:

> If you could see the ruin and devastation and utter abandonment of villages, plantations and farms, which but a short time ago was peopled, fenced, and stocked. Homes once comfortable that are now either burned or deserted, barns in ashes all along the roadside, fences destroyed for miles and over thousands of acres, no cows, horses, mules, sheep, or poultry to be seen where ever the Union army advances, and you would see conclusively the destruction for the coming year is to be four fold greater than the past year.[1]

The citizens of these counties appealed to Raleigh and Richmond for troops to drive their tormentors away, but few soldiers could be spared. The home guard, made up of old men and young boys, did what it could, but its efforts, while heroic, amounted to very little. While the plight of the people was distressing in the extreme, more important, the foodstuffs from these agriculturally rich areas was denied to the Confederate commissary. The eastern counties had led the state in the production of beef, hogs, sheep, and various types of grains. Even in the adjoining counties, which were not occupied by the invader, farmers hesitated to plant crops for fear of a Federal raid.

The presence of Union troops in eastern North Carolina was the cause of one additional concern in Raleigh and Richmond. Only a two-days' march from the most western Federal garrison were the tracks of the Wilmington and Weldon Railroad. Along this line, from the seaport of Wilmington north to Virginia, moved the food, supplies, and ammunition that helped keep the Army of Northern Virginia in the field. A disruption of this railroad could have fatal consequences for Lee's army—and the Confederacy.[2]

Like the *Neuse*, the boat being built along the Roanoke that would become the *Albemarle* was designed by John L. Porter and in fact was a sister ship to the one nearing completion at Kinston. The builder of the *Albemarle* was Gilbert Elliott of Elizabeth City. Born on December 10, 1843, Elliott was raised in an atmosphere of naval construction along the Pasquotank River that flowed by Elizabeth City. In fact, his grandfather, Charles Grice, on his mother's side, had been a shipbuilder from Philadelphia and had founded the town.[3] Elliott had been captured while serving as a lieutenant with the Seventeenth

Lt. Gilbert Elliott

NORTH CAROLINA REGIMENTS

North Carolina Infantry when the Federals overwhelmed Hatteras Inlet. While a prisoner of war, he had kept himself occupied by creating drawings of ironclad gunboats. After being exchanged, Elliott was posted to the batteries at Drewry's Bluff on the James River, and taking advantage of his close proximity to Richmond, he sent his sketches to the Navy Department. Porter liked what he saw and made detailed blueprints from Elliott's sketches. Using his influence, Secretary Mallory obtained

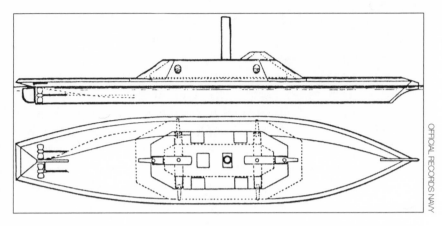

Porter's plans for the *Albemarle* are shown here in profile and two cross sections, one through the casement (*below left*) and the other through the rear deck (*below right*).

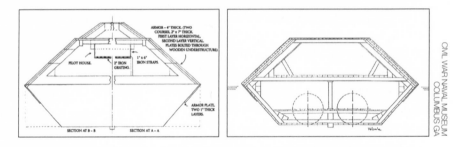

the teenage lieutenant's detachment from the army, and with contracts to build several ironclads of his concept using Porter's plans, Elliott was assigned to special naval duty in North Carolina.[4]

In March 1863, about the time that the hull of the *Neuse* was being launched at White Hall, Elliott moved to Halifax where a small shipyard lay adjacent to the Roanoke River. In spite of the fact that Halifax offered the advantage of being on a rail line, the shipyard was too small to accommodate a vessel the size of the *Albemarle*. Elliott immediately began looking for a suitable location where the construction could begin. Over the past few months he had become acquainted with William Ruffin Smith Jr. and his son, Peter Evans Smith. Both men owned large tracts of property along the Roanoke. Peter Smith owned a large plantation of approximately fifteen thousand acres that bordered the river on the south side and was surrounded by lands owned by other family members.

Late in March, Peter Smith and Elliott surveyed his property for a suitable location. It was extremely important that the site be high enough to ensure its safety during a rise in the river, yet low enough to facilitate the launching of the completed vessel. The spot they chose was a freshly planted cornfield owned by Smith's father on the south bank of the Roanoke near the river crossing known as Edwards Ferry. The village of Hamilton lay about thirty-two miles down river, and the town of Halifax was twenty-two miles upriver.[5]

Elliott assigned Peter Smith as superintendent of construction, and a large steam sawmill (which was later moved to the cornfield) was set up on the adjoining farm of Smith's brother, Benjamin Gordon Smith. Peter Smith had an elaborate forge on his plantation, where almost any tool needed in the construction of the ironclad could be made. In addition, labor was plentiful, for Smith made available many of his plantation workers. As the days lengthened with the coming of spring, the forests and fields of Halifax County resounded with the sounds of the steam sawmill as it cut the great lengths of oak and yellow pine. Once cut, the giant pieces were hauled to the cornfield by oxen and mules, where gangs of laborers began cutting and notching the pieces into something resembling a ship's frame.

Porter's plans called for a hull length of 152 feet between perpendiculars, with a beam of 34 feet at the knuckle, and a depth from the gundeck to the keel of 9 feet. After launching, with her armor and guns installed, she would draw about 8 feet. Porter calculated her

The CSS *Albemarle* under construction

weight as 376 tons. Her bottom was flat, allowing her to navigate areas where the deeper-draft Union vessels could not follow. Progress on the wooden frame proceeded at a fast pace, even though most of the laborers working on her had never seen an ironclad before, much less built one.[6]

Before the main deck beams were fitted, the engine keelson was laid. (See chapter 7 for Elliott's description of how the ironclad's frame was fabricated.) This iron-and-wood framework was secured to the bottom of the hull and used as a bedplate for the engines. From this bedplate, two wooden shaft housings were constructed to carry the propeller shafts from the engines to the rear of the hull and through watertight housings to the propellers. The shafts and three-bladed propellers were fabricated at the Charlotte Navy Yard using machinery that had been removed from the Gosport Navy Yard prior to the fall of Norfolk.[7]

Mindful of the narrow escape of the *Neuse* at White Hall, and fearing a similar advance up the Roanoke from Plymouth, it was decided to launch the hull as soon as possible and tow the boat up the river to Halifax. Here, it was hoped, her armor, engines, and machinery could be installed without fear of enemy interference. Early on the morning of October 6, 1863, taking advantage of high water in the river, Elliott proceeded to launch the vessel. At 3:00 a.m. numerous pine torches cast their flickering light over the shipyard. Leather whips cracked in the night air as teamsters encouraged mules and oxen to pull the heavy *Albemarle* down the greased ways and into the turbulent waters of the Roanoke.[8]

It is reasonable to assume that the hull of the *Albemarle* was launched diagonally upstream where the flow of the current would negate her water surface speed. By doing so, workmen had a few seconds in which to secure her lines to the riverbank. To those in attendance it must have been a gratifying site. Bathed in the light of burning pine torches, the *Albemarle* at last was in her element.

After the war, Cmdr. John Newland Maffitt, captain of the Confederate cruiser *Florida* and numerous blockade-runners, commented: "The building of the ironclad, under all the disadvantages of place and circumstances, was viewed by the community as a chimerical absurdity. Great was the general astonishment when it became known that the indomitable commander had conquered all obstacles and was about to launch his battling. On the appointed day 'Cooke & Company' committed their 'nonesuch' to the turbid waters of the Roanoke, christening her, as she glided from the launching ways, the good ship *Albemarle*."[9]

While the *Albemarle* was being towed the twenty-two miles upriver to Halifax, Elliott was wrestling with the same problem that every builder of ironclads experienced in the Confederacy—the scarcity of engines, machinery, and iron for armor plates. The young builder scoured the North Carolina countryside for scrap iron that could be melted down and rolled into two-inch-by-seven-inch armor slabs. As recounted earlier, negotiations were entered into with Governor Vance for the acquisition of railroad iron for all of the ironclads being constructed in North Carolina. This iron was to come from unused and worn-out rails that were of no value to the rail lines. Even if sufficient quantities were found, however, getting the rails to the rolling mills at Richmond, Atlanta, or Wilmington and back in the form of armor plate over the South's worn-out rail system took enormous amounts of time. In addition, more often than not, naval shipments were shuttled off on some remote siding to make way for urgently needed army supplies.

On January 14, 1864, an order from the Navy Department reached Mallory's agent in North Carolina, Commander Cooke, who at that time was serving on a navy court-martial board: "You are hereby detached from the Naval Court Martial at Wilmington, N.C., and will report to flag officer William F. Lynch, commanding, for the command of the *Albemarle,* at Halifax, N.C., where you will proceed and relieve Lieutenant Johnston."[10]

James Wallace Cooke was born in 1812 in Beaufort, near Cape Lookout on the Carolina coast. By the time he had reached four years, his parents had passed away, and he was being reared by an uncle, Col. Henry M. Cooke. At the age of sixteen, James received an appointment to the U.S. Navy and was placed in training as a midshipman on the USS *Guerierre* (midshipmen were trained aboard ship prior to the establishment of the U.S. Naval Academy in 1845). By 1841 Cooke had attained the rank of lieutenant, but when it looked as though the Old North State would soon leave the Union,

Cooke resigned his commission on May 2, 1861. Two days later he was appointed a lieutenant in the Virginia State Navy, and on June 11, 1861, he was transferred to Confederate service.[11]

During the struggle for Roanoke Island in February 1862, Cooke was in command of the little gunboat *Ellis*. At the close of the battle, with the rest of the Confederate Mosquito Fleet either destroyed or dispersed, Cooke continued to fire at the Federals using the last remaining ammunition from the disabled gunboat *Curlew*. Finally surrounded and boarded, Cooke refused to yield and continued to fire at the boarders with loaded muskets, which were handed up to him from below. Badly wounded in the right arm and with a bayonet wound in the leg, he was finally overpowered and taken prisoner. It was not until September 1863 that he was exchanged and became eligible for active duty. His mission now was to complete the ironclad lying at the small shipyard at Halifax and attack the Federal forces and drive them out of North Carolina.[12]

Cooke asserted his influence in obtaining the necessary armor plate, and finally, on March 7, 1864, the first fourteen carloads of the long gray slabs came slowly rolling into Halifax. Upon the arrival of the armor, workers swarmed over her hull and casemate, drilling and bolting the heavy iron plates into position. It was not long until another problem presented itself. Elliott explained: "The work of putting on the armor was prosecuted for some time under the most disheartening circumstances, on account of the difficulty of drilling holes in the iron intended for her armor. But one small engine and drill could be had, and it required, at best, twenty minutes to drill an inch and a quarter hole through the plates, and it looked as if we would never accomplish the task."[13]

Cmdr. James W. Cooke

NAVAL HISTORICAL CENTER

The conventional method for drilling holes in iron at the time was to grind the metal into a fine powder. Peter Smith began experimenting at his plantation forge, and within a few days returned to Halifax with a "twist drill" that cut the iron into small shavings. Using the twist drill, the amount of time required to drill a hole in the *Albemarle*'s armor was reduced from twenty minutes to four.[14]

When the *Albemarle* left Edwards Ferry, she was still without her engines, boilers, and machinery. A section of her deck had been left incomplete to facilitate the lowering of these bulky items into her hold. There has been much speculation about the true source of the *Albemarle*'s engines. J. Thomas Scharf in his *History of the Confederate Navy* rather grandly states: "The engine was adapted from incongruous material, ingeniously dovetailed and put together with a determined will that mastered doubt, but not without some natural anxiety as to derangements that might occur from so heterogeneous a combination."[15]

While there may be uncertainty as to the engines' origins, once installed, their specifications are fairly well documented. The two noncondensing engines were mounted horizontally, side by side, perpendicular to the keel. Both engines produced two hundred horsepower, and each was connected to its own propeller shaft via a linkage that allowed both engines to transmit their thrust simultaneously through four gears to the propellers. Each engine was steam fed from a cast-iron boiler, which was fired by its own furnace. The two boilers were mounted amidships beneath a single funnel, and the furnaces were mounted aft.[16]

Above all this machinery was the gundeck, which was shielded by the casemate. Elliott wrote that the armored casemate was sixty feet long, octagonal in shape, and that the sides inclined at an angle of 35 degrees. To the twelve-inch-by-thirteen-inch pine beams that formed the walls of the shield was bolted a horizontal layer of five-inch pine planks that were covered by a vertical layer of four-inch oak planks. Prior to installing the armor, six gunports were cut, two on each side, one forward and one aft. The inside of the shield was dressed with a thin layer of smooth planking to protect the crew from splinters. The two-inch-by-seven-inch armor plates were bolted onto the oak planks in two layers, the first laid horizontally, the second vertically. The deck fore and aft of the casemate was covered with a layer of two-inch iron, and a lattice of iron grates formed the top deck

Cmdr. John M. Brooke

in order to provide light and ventilation to the gundeck.[17]

Although Porter's plans did not call for it, sometime during her fabrication it was decided to equip the *Albemarle* for ramming. Elliott described the modification of this bow ram: "The prow was built of solid oak, running 18 feet back, on center keelson, and solidly bolted, and it was covered on the outside with iron plating, 2 inches thick and, tapering off to a 4 inch edge, formed the ram."[18]

The *Albemarle*'s armament consisted of two 6.4-inch double-banded Brooke rifles mounted on pivot carriages, one forward, one aft. Both guns could be worked through a port at its respective end of

Diagram of a Brooke rifle on a pivot carriage such as was used in the CSS *Albemarle*

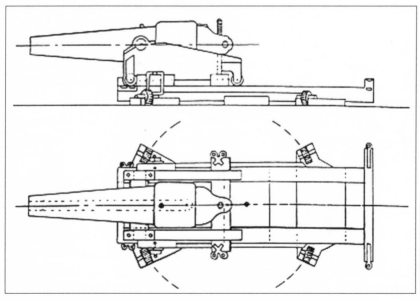

the shield or on either side. Heavy iron shutters, which could be raised or lowered from inside the casemate, covered the ports when the guns were inboard. These rifled guns, designed by John M. Brooke, were the finest naval guns developed during the war.[19]

In the latter part of March 1864, workers swarmed over the iron-clad, attending to the many details of bringing her to operational status. All of the armor was not yet in place, and as a consequence, the drilling machine was run night and day while down below the engineers labored in her cramped engine room, installing the last of her machinery. During this time Cooke anxiously watched as the level of the river began to fall and the Albemarle settled lower and lower in the water as her armor was added. To avoid the risk of her becoming stranded at Halifax, it was decided to move the ironclad downstream. Whether she steamed under her own power or was towed is unknown, but by April 1 she was safely berthed at Hamilton.[20]

As Gilbert Elliott often repeated in his later years, "No vessel was ever constructed under more adverse circumstances."[21]

9

GUN FLASHES ON THE NEUSE

THE BRIGHTLY COLORED AUTUMN leaves were gone. The majestic old shade trees that lined the principal avenues of Richmond were leafless and barren. The winter of 1863 was fast approaching, and cold December winds whistled around the buildings and down the streets of the picturesque Confederate capital on the James River. Almost every day, just before sundown, passersby noticed a tall stately man emerge from the unpretentious white mansion on Clay Street. Unmindful of the cold wind, he would mount his Arabian and set off alone for a mind-clearing ride in the country. The cares and concerns of his office bore heavily upon the Confederate president. He desperately needed to get away from the constant pressure of his position, if only for an hour, to commune with himself and his God.[1]

Occasionally, a young naval officer accompanied Jefferson Davis on his lonely rides. John Taylor Wood, the president's nephew, was assigned to his uncle as an aide. Wood, who had served on the *Virginia* during her battles in Hampton Roads, had been promoted to commander effective August 23, 1863, for "gallant and meritorious conduct" in his small-boat operations on the Chesapeake Bay. As the two rode slowly out of Richmond and into the surrounding Virginia countryside, a weary Davis reviewed the probable future course of the war and discussed with Wood his ideas as to the navy's role. During one of these cold rides, Wood revealed a daring plan to the president.[2]

Ever since the Federals had captured Roanoke Island in February 1862 and had occupied Albemarle Sound, Pamlico Sound, and most of the eastern shore of North Carolina, they had extended their fortifications to include the principal rivers and towns several miles inland. One North Carolina town whose occupation was particularly objectionable, Wood explained, was New Bern. Situated at the confluence of the Neuse and Trent rivers, New Bern had been heavily fortified by the Federal occupying troops, and it continued to provide a base for foraging expeditions against civilians. In addition, Federal excursions that had destroyed the boat being built at Tarboro and almost destroyed the *Neuse* at White Hall the previous December illustrated the dangers that lurked in eastern North Carolina. More important, Wood undoubtedly added that New Bern was only forty-five miles from the all-important Wilmington and Weldon Railroad over which passed most of the supplies for Lee's army in Virginia. If the Union forces from New Bern should attack and cut this railroad line, it would become almost impossible to adequately supply the Army of Northern Virginia.

With Lee's army about to enter winter quarters, Wood believed that enough troops could be temporarily sent to North Carolina. If this force attacked New Bern from the land side, coupled with a naval attack from the river, Wood believed the town could be recaptured. The president responded with "verbal instructions" for Wood to journey to North Carolina, assess the feasibility of recovering New Bern, and report his findings. Undoubtedly, Wood was also ordered to inspect the progress on the *Albemarle* and the *Neuse*. If one or both of these vessels could be completed during the coming winter, they could possibly become the naval element in the anticipated attack on New Bern.[3]

During the first week of January 1864, with the season's first mantle of snow covering the Confederate capital, Wood left Richmond for eastern North Carolina. The young navy lieutenant riding the worn-out rails to Weldon had spent nearly his entire adult life as a

professional military officer. Born
at the army outpost of Fort
Snelling, Iowa Territory (present-
day St. Paul, Minnesota), on August 13, 1830, Wood was the
grandson of Zachary Taylor, twelfth
president of the United States. On
June 10, 1853, he was graduated
second in his class at the Naval
Academy at Annapolis. Making
Maryland his home, he was commissioned a lieutenant in 1855 and
was teaching gunnery and tactics at
the academy when war broke out.
Although his father remained loyal

Cmdr. John Taylor Wood

to the Union and even became assistant surgeon general of the United
States, Wood resigned his commission on April 21, 1861, and traveled
to Richmond to offer his services to the Confederacy.[4]

Upon arriving in North Carolina, Wood probably inspected the
Albemarle and the *Neuse,* and his findings could not have been encouraging. Neither of the vessels, it appeared, could be made operational before spring. By then, any troops dispatched from Lee's army
would be needed for the spring campaigns in Virginia and would be
returning. If the two ironclads could not be completed in time, the
only option was to capture one or more of the enemy's gunboats and
use them to attack the fortifications around New Bern while the
army attacked from the land side. To accomplish this, Wood planned
a night attack employing a force of sailors and marines in small
boats. Hastening back to Richmond he reported his findings and
plans to the president who gave his approval and sent him on to Lee
to discuss the troops that would be needed.[5]

Lee recognized at once the potential for increased supplies that
might be garnered from eastern North Carolina if the Federals could
be driven out. In addition, the security of the railroad was reason
enough to undertake the effort. On January 20, 1864, Lee wrote to
Wood informing him that he was sending Brig. Gen. Robert F. Hoke's
brigade to Kinston and that Maj. Gen. George E. Pickett would be in

command of the operation. Wishing him success, he commended Wood "to the care of a merciful Providence."[6]

Wood spent the final two weeks in January organizing the naval part of the operation. Surgeon Daniel B. Conrad, who accompanied the expedition, wrote afterward:

> In January, 1864, the Confederate officers on duty in Richmond, Wilmington and Charleston were aroused by a telegram from the Navy Department to detail four boats' crews of picked men and officers, who were to be fully armed, equipped and rationed for six days; they were to start at once by rail for Weldon, North Carolina, reporting on arrival to Commander J. T. Wood, who would give further instructions.
>
> So perfectly secret and well guarded was our destination that not until we had all arrived at Kinston, North Carolina, by various railroads, did we have the slightest idea of where we were going or what the object was of the naval raid. We suspected, however, from the name of its commander, that it would be "nervous work," as he had a reputation for boarding, capturing and burning the enemy's gunboats on many previous occasions.[7]

The James River Squadron supplied four cutters, each manned by ten seamen and two officers, under the command of Lt. Benjamin P.

Surgeon Daniel B. Conrad

NAVAL HISTORICAL CENTER

Loyall. Commandant of midshipmen at the Confederate Naval Academy on the *Patrick Henry*, Loyall was to be Wood's second-in-command. The men were armed with cutlasses, revolvers, and a few axes, and each wore heavy clothing, including a pea jacket to ward off the January cold.[8] The sailors were from various ships of the squadron but also included twenty-five marines of Company C under the command of Capt. Thomas S. Wilson. The marines' Enfield rifles soon proved their worth.[9]

To avoid unnecessary attention, Wood instructed Loyall to launch his contingent in the James River and pull downstream to Petersburg where he would meet them. At 9:00 a.m. on the cold Thursday morning of January 28, Loyall and his command left Richmond behind and at a measured gait headed their cutters south. Loyall wrote later, "We reached Petersburg before daylight [next day]. There was a railway train waiting for us, and we hauled our boats out of the water, and, by hard work, loaded them on the flat cars before the people were up and about."[10]

The boats were lashed onto the cars right side up, and once all equipment was loaded aboard, the sailors and marines took their places in the boats. Loyall was amused at the scene: "We started off at once, and it was a novel sight to see a train like that. . . . Jack sitting up on the seats of the boats and waving his hat to the astonished natives, who never saw such a circus before."[11]

Reaching Kinston before daylight on January 31, Wood had the boats unloaded and moved to the Neuse River. Putting Loyall in command, he sent them downstream a few miles where they landed on a small island in the middle of the river and set up camp. Meanwhile, an impatient Wood paced the depot platform waiting for the contingents to arrive from Wilmington and Charleston.[12]

In Wilmington, Lt. George W. Gift had experienced difficulty obtaining the four cutters specified in the orders from Richmond. Finally securing two boats and two heavy launches armed with a twelve-pound howitzer, Gift left for Goldsboro. Here he was to rendezvous with the Charleston contingent under the command of Lt. Philip Porcher. Leaving Goldsboro, their train finally pulled into Kinston at noon on January 31, and Gift along with Porcher found Wood still pacing the station platform. Except for the two heavy launches, the Charleston and Wilmington boats were unloaded and dragged to the river. Eager to join his men at the island, Wood instructed Gift to find a pair of mules, hitch them to the launches, move them to the river, and then join him as soon as possible. Leaving eighty men with Gift, Wood and the remaining sailors pulled out to midstream, and with the sun sinking low on the western horizon, they turned the cutters downriver.[13]

It was almost sunset by the time Wood stepped onto the island where the rest of his men were waiting. Calling the group together, he explained the details of the mission. Dividing the 150 sailors and marines into two divisions, he placed Lieutenant Loyall in command of one and the other under himself.

Surgeon Conrad remembered:

Commander Wood, in distinct and terse terms, gave orders to each boat's crew and its officers just what was expected of them, stating that the object of the expedition was to, that night, board some one of the enemy's gunboats, then supposed to be lying off the city of New Bern, now nearly sixty miles [actually less than thirty miles] distant from where we then were by water. He said that she was to be captured without fail. Five boats were to board her on either side simultaneously, and then when in our possession we were to get up steam and cruise after other gunboats. It was a grand scheme, and was received by the older men with looks of admiration and with rapture by the young midshipmen, all of whom would have broken out into loud cheers but for the fact that the strictest silence was essential to the success of the daring undertaking.[14]

Wood passed out white strips of cotton cloth and instructed each man to tie it around his left arm. The password for the night would be *Sumter.* Everyone now realized that some severe hand-to-hand fighting was in store. Conrad remembered those final moments before casting off on this dangerous mission: "In concluding his talk, Commander Wood solemnly said: 'We will now pray'; and thereupon he offered up the most touching appeal to the Almighty that it has ever been my fortune to have heard. I can remember it now, after the long interval that has elapsed since then."[15]

Lieutenant Loyall also recalled this experience: "It was a solemn and impressive scene . . . just as the shades of evening were falling . . . this unusual assemblage of armed men. Then with muffled oars, a single line was formed, and we pulled with a measured stroke down the stream."[16]

Midshipman J. Thomas Scharf, who would later write a history of the Confederate navy, was in charge of one of the boats. He described the journey down the Neuse:

Bending silently to the muffled oars, the expedition moved down the river. Now, the Neuse broadened until the boats seemed to be on a lake; again, the tortuous stream narrowed until the party could almost touch the trees on either side. Not a sign of life was visible, save occasionally when a flock of wild ducks, startled at the approach of the boats, rose from the banks, and then poising themselves for a moment overhead, flew on swift wing to the shelter of the woodland or the morass. No other

Midshipman J. Thomas Scharf

sound was heard to break the stillness save the constant, steady splash of the oars and the ceaseless surge of the river. Sometimes a fallen log impeded the progress, again a boat would run aground, but as hour after hour passed by, the boats still sped on, the crews cold and weary, but yet cheerful and uncomplaining. Night fell, dark shadows began to creep over the marshes and crowd the river; owls screeched among the branches overhead, through which the expedition occasionally caught glimpses of the sky. There was nothing to guide the boats on their course, but the crews still kept hopefully on, and by eleven o'clock the river seemed to become wider, and Commander Wood discovered that we had reached the open country above New Bern.[17]

Wood and his boats surged on, and in the early morning hours they drew near their objective. Even though they were exhausted from the long pull down the river, the men's spirits rose as they could smell the salt air from the water of Pamlico Sound. Surgeon Conrad noted: "At about half past three o'clock we found ourselves upon the broad estuary of New Bern Bay. Then closing up in double column we pulled for the lights of the city, even up to and close in and around the wharves themselves, looking (but in vain) for our prey. Not a gunboat could be seen; none were there."[18]

Wood searched cautiously looking for a target, but there were no Federal ships in sight. Lieutenant Loyall explained: "We searched in vain to find something afloat, although we got close enough to the wharf to hear talking, probably the sentries on the dock. There was nothing to be done but find some refuge out of sight until next night, but it was hard letting down from the pitch of excitement and expectation we had been under . . . the unbending of the bow that had been strung for action."[19]

With daylight approaching, Wood led his men two to three miles back up the Neuse and entered Bachelor's Creek. Finding a small desolate spot, the boats were pulled into the weeds and carefully hidden in the high grass and brush. With pickets posted to give the alarm, the men threw themselves on the soggy ground and attempted to get some sleep.[20]

As the morning sun began to burn the low-lying mist off the river, the men were startled to see in plain sight of their bivouac a tall crow's nest occupied by a Union lookout on picket duty. By staying well hidden, the presence of the gray sailors and marines went unnoticed by the lookout. Conrad wrote: "Shortly after sunrise we heard firing by infantry. It was quite sharp for an hour, and then it died away. It turned out to be, as we afterwards learned, a futile attack by our lines under General Pickett on the works around New Bern. We were obliged to eat cold food all that day, as no fires were permissible under any circumstances; so all we could do was keep a sharp lookout for the enemy, go to sleep again, and wish for the night to come."[21]

Maj. Gen. George E. Pickett

NATIONAL ARCHIVES

The musket firing that Conrad heard was indeed the sound of the attack launched at daylight by Pickett on the fortifications surrounding New Bern. Leaving Kinston at 1:00 a.m. on February 1, Pickett had divided his forty-five-hundred-man force into three columns. Two brigades were to

attack the Federal fortifications in front of New Bern at sunrise,
while the other force, led by Col. James Dearing, was sent across the
Neuse to attack Fort Anderson opposite the town. Meanwhile, Gen.
Seth M. Barton's command, consisting of twelve companies of cavalry accompanied by artillery, had left the day before and crossed
the Trent River. Their assignment was to prevent Union reinforcements by swinging south of the town and cutting the Atlantic and
North Carolina Railroad between New Bern and Morehead City.
Once that was done, they were to cross the Trent by the railroad
bridge and drive toward New Bern from the south in conjunction
with Pickett's frontal assault.

The Federals offered stiff resistance along Bachelor's Creek, adjacent to where Wood's men were hiding, but Hoke's brigade splashed
across the creek, slammed into the Union troops, and drove them
back toward their fortifications. Soon the heavy guns of the forts were
lobbing shells into the Confederate ranks as Pickett listened anxiously for the sound of Barton's guns to the south. The day wore on,
and still there was no sign of Barton. Late that afternoon two trains
loaded with Federal reinforcements from Morehead City arrived, and
Pickett now knew that Barton had failed to reach his objective. Reluctantly, he issued orders to pull back after dark and return to Kinston.
The land portion of the attack on New Bern was over.[22]

While the abortive Confederate land attack was taking place,
Lieutenant Gift, in Kinston, had found a pair of mules, and with
them, he had dragged the two heavy launches to the river. With forty
men manning the oars in each boat, they sped down the Neuse at
over six knots. Arriving at Swift Creek, about two miles upriver from
Bachelor's Creek, Gift sent a courier to Pickett to inquire about
Wood's whereabouts. When the messenger returned with the information, Gift immediately cast off, rowed the remaining two miles,
and turned into Bachelor's Creek, arriving at Wood's bivouac and
hiding place at sunset. His two heavy launches, each armed with a
12-pounder howitzer and the 85 plus men brought Wood's strength
to approximately 230 men.[23]

Shortly after Gift and his men arrived and with the welcome
shadows of night stretching its protective veil over the river, Wood
called for his swiftest boat and most experienced crew. Together with

Loyall, they pulled noiselessly down the Neuse, taking care to remain within the shadows of the riverbank. Loyall wrote: "We had not gone two miles, when simultaneously we both cried, 'There she is!' We discovered a black steamer anchored close up to the right flank of the outer fortifications of New Bern, where she had come that day."

Staying within the dark shadows of the shoreline, Wood studied the steamer closely with his night glasses. He noted with satisfaction that her low wooden rail would make her relatively easy to board. Loyall continued: "Having located her exactly, we returned to our hiding place, with the understanding that we would attack her between 12 and 4 o'clock in the morning [Tuesday, February 2]."[24]

The Federal vessel that Wood and Loyall had spotted was the USS *Underwriter* commanded by Acting Master Jacob Westervelt. The gunboat was a side-wheel steamer of 325 tons, 186 feet long and 35 feet abeam, and her powerful engines developed 800 horsepower. She had fired the first shot at the battle for Roanoke Island in September 1861 and was considered by the Confederates the most powerful and dangerous gunboat on the sounds of North Carolina. She carried two 8-inch guns, one 30-pound rifle, one 12-pound howitzer, and a crew of twelve officers and seventy-two men.

Assembling his men at 11:00 p.m., Wood went over the attack plan in detail. He explained that the enemy vessel was about one hundred yards from Battery Number Two and not far from Fort Stevenson. The boats would move in double columns with Loyall's division striking the *Underwriter* aft of the giant paddle wheels, while his own section would strike the ship forward. Gift's launches would follow with extra men and be prepared for towing if necessary. Wood reminded them to wear the white armbands and began assigning several marines with Enfield rifles to each boat as sharpshooters. Pistols and cutlasses were strapped on, and ammunition was distributed. Light rain began to fall as the men filed silently to the boats. Looking up at the fast-fading stars, Midshipman Palmer Sanders was heard to mumble, "I wonder, boys, how many of us will be up among the stars by tomorrow morning."[25]

Midshipman Scharf, who refers to Wood by his army rank (Wood had been given the dual rank of colonel of cavalry by Davis on January 26, 1863), wrote a graphic and poignant description of the approach and attack on the Federal gunboat:

> After forming parallel to each other, the two divisions pulled rapidly down the stream. When they had rowed a short distance, Col. Wood called all the boats together, final instructions were given, and this being through with, he offered a fervent prayer for the success of his mission. It was a strange and ghostly sight, the men resting on their oars with heads uncovered, the commander also bareheaded, standing erect in the stern of his boat; the black waters rippling beneath; the dense overhanging clouds pouring down sheets of rain, and in the blackness beyond an unseen bell tolling as if from some phantom cathedral. The party listened—four peals were sounded and then they knew it was the bell of the *Underwriter,* or some other of the gunboats, ringing out for two o'clock.
>
> Guided by the sound, the boats pulled toward the steamer, pistols, muskets and cutlasses in readiness. The advance was necessarily slow and cautious. Suddenly when about three hundred yards from the *Underwriter,* her hull loomed up out of the inky darkness. Through the stillness came the sharp ring of five bells for half-past two o'clock, and just as the echo died away, a quick, nervous voice from the deck hailed, "Boat ahoy!" No answer was given, but Col. Wood kept steadily on. "Boat ahoy! Boat ahoy!!" again shouted the watch. No answer. Then the rattle on board the steamer sprung summoning the men to quarters, and the Confederates could see the dim and shadowy outline of hurrying figures on deck. Nearer Col. Wood came, shouting, "Give way!" "Give way, boys, give way!" repeated Lieut. Loyall and the respective boat commanders, and give way they did with a will.[26]

With the boats only one hundred yards out, the black silhouette of the *Underwriter* suddenly exploded in a wicked crimson line of flame as the Federals opened fire with muskets and pistols. Bending to their oars, their backs to the blazing Federal volleys, the Confederate cutters flew over the water. Stabbing tongues of orange and red suddenly erupted from twenty-five Enfields as Confederate marines, swaying to the motion of the oarsmen, stood in the bows and

THE CONFEDERATE SOLDIER IN THE CIVIL WAR

Confederate sailors and marines launch a night attack on the USS *Underwriter*

bravely returned the fire. Conrad recalled: "Our coxswain [in Wood's boat], a burly, gamy Englishman who by gesture and loud word, was encouraging the crew, steering by the tiller between his knees, his hands occupied in holding his pistols, suddenly fell forward on us dead, a ball having struck him fairly in the forehead. The rudder now having no guide, the boat swerved aside, and instead of our bow striking at the gangway, we struck the wheelhouse, so that the next boat, commanded by Lieutenant Loyall, had the deadly honor of being first on board."[27]

Wood's boats slammed against the side of the *Underwriter* forward of the wheelhouse, and grappling hooks flew through the night air. The second division arrived farther aft, and Lieutenant Loyall recollected:

Our boats struck the vessel just abaft the wheelhouse, where the guards make a platform, an admirable place for getting on board. The ship's armory, where all the small arms were kept, was in a room just there under the hurricane deck, and they did not stop to reload, but loaded guns were handed to the men, as fast as they could fire. It seemed like a sheet of flame, and the very jaws of death. Our boat struck bow on, and our bow oarsman, James Wilson, of Norfolk, caught her with his grapnel, and she swung side on with the tide.[28]

Loyall and Engineer Emmet F. Gill, revolvers and cutlasses in hand, were the first to scramble over the rail, falling in a heap on the slippery rain-soaked surface. Gill, four bullets in his body, was dead before he hit the deck. Before Loyall could rise, four wounded sailors came tumbling down on top of him, while at the same moment Confederate pistols were spitting flame from amidships as Wood and his men scrambled over the side. More boats came crashing against the *Underwriter,* and Lieutenant Gift, who had slowed his launches to avoid ramming the cutters, shouted for Scharf to fire the howitzer. With a loud bang, the little 12-pounder barked and sent a full load of canister whistling into the Union ship's pilothouse. Before Scharf could reload, the launches, too, were against the *Underwriter,* and Gift's men were forcing their way aboard.

Loyall reported: "Now the fighting was furious, and at close quarters. Our men were eager, and as one would fall another came on. Not one faltered or fell back. The cracking of firearms and the rattle of cutlasses made a deafening din. The enemy gave way slowly, and soon began to get away by taking to the wardroom and engine room hatches."[29]

Confederate marines, who were among the first to scramble on board, were grasping their empty rifles by the barrel and wielding them as giant clubs with devastating effect. The deck was slippery from blood and rain, causing men to lose their footing, and as they fell, they wrestled with the enemy, tumbling and rolling in a frightful grapple of death. Wood kept urging his men on. Conrad remembered, "I could hear Wood's stentorian voice giving orders and encouraging the men."[30]

Midshipman Scharf was now in the middle of the desperate fighting and later recalled the scene:

The enemy had by this time gathered in the ways just aft of the wheelhouse, and as the Confederates came up they poured into them volley after volley of musketry, each flash of which reddened the waters around. . . . Cutlasses and pistols were the weapons of the Confederates, and each selected and made a rush for his man. The odds were against the attacking party, and some of them had to struggle with three opponents. But they never flinched in the life-and-death struggle, nor did the gallant enemy. The boarders forced the fighting. Blazing rifles had no terrors for them. They drove back the enemy inch by inch. Steadily, but surely, the boarders began to gain the deck, and crowded their opponents to the companion-ways or other places of concealment; while all the time fierce hand-to-hand fights were going on on other portions of the vessel. Now one of the Confederates would sink exhausted—again, one of the enemy would fall on the slippery deck. Rifles were snatched from the hands of the dead and the dying, and used in the hands as bludgeons did deadly work. Down the companion-ways the attacked party were driven pell-mell into the ward-room and steerage, and even to the coal bunkers, and after another sharp but decisive struggle the enemy surrendered.[31]

Conrad recollected: "In less than five minutes, I could distinguish a strange synchronous roar, but did not understand what it meant at first; but it soon became plain: 'She's ours!' everybody crying at the top of their voices, in order to stop the shooting, as only our men were on their feet."[32]

As the exhausted and bleeding Confederates gathered on deck, the night air was rent with a fierce Rebel Yell. There was little time to celebrate, however. After Wood gave the order to cease fire, he held a hurried conversation with Loyall. If they could raise steam and get the engines running, they could move the gunboat up the Neuse and put her in shape under Confederate colors. Because the *Underwriter* was the largest and most heavily armed vessel on the river, the Confederates would have temporary control of the waters around New Bern. Wood ordered his two engineers to hurry below to see if there was enough steam in the boilers to get the ship under way.

Meanwhile, Surgeon Conrad had begun tending to the wounded: "I examined a youth who was sitting in the lap of another, and in feeling his head I felt my hand slip down between his ears, and to my horror, discovered that his head had been cleft in two by a boarding sword in the hands of some giant of the forecastle. It was Passed Midshipman Palmer Sanders. Directing his body, and those of all the other killed, to be laid out aft on the quarter deck, I went down below, looking for the wounded in the ward-room, where the lights were burning, and found half a dozen with slight shots from revolvers."[33]

While Conrad was tending the wounded below, the engineers reported disappointing news to Wood. The fires in the furnaces were banked, steam pressure was low, and it would take at least an hour to build enough to turn the large paddle wheels. Wood ordered Gift to tow the vessel with his launches, but the ship had been moored so securely that it was estimated it would take another hour to slip the chains that held her fast. At that moment, the *Underwriter* was rocked by the explosion of a shell that crashed into her upper works. The gunners at Fort Stevenson, alerted by the firing, in addition to escaped Federal crewmen, had opened fire on the gunboat.

Scharf recalled, "All the shore batteries then opened fire on the doomed vessel, either careless of or not realizing the fact that their own wounded must be on board; and the captors soon found that a rapid movement would have to be made."[34]

The *Underwriter* had become a trap. As more and more shore batteries opened fire, Wood made his decision to destroy the vessel.

Conrad remembered: "Very calmly and clearly he directed me to remove all dead and wounded to the boats, which the several crews were now hauling to the lee side of the vessel, where they would be protected from the shots from the fort. The order was soon carried out by willing hands."

There was no time to remove the Federal dead, therefore they were left on board. While the wounded and the prisoners were being hurried into the boats, the guns of the *Underwriter* were quickly loaded and pointed toward the Federal fortifications.

Conrad continued:

After an extended search through the ship's decks, above and below, we found that we had removed all the dead and wounded, and then, when the search ended, reported to Captain Wood on the quarterdeck, where, giving his orders where the fire from the fort was deadly and searching, he called up four lieutenants to him, to whom he gave instructions as follows: Two of them were to go below in the forward part of the ship, and the other two below in the after part, where from their respective stations they were to fire the vessel, and not to leave her until her decks were all ablaze, and then at that juncture they were to return to their proper boats and report.[35]

Loyall, who instructed Francis L. Hoge, one of the four lieutenants, to take fire from the furnace and set the ship ablaze, recounted the final act of the drama: "When we had gotten [a] half mile from the ship, Wood pulled up toward our boats and asked if I had ordered the ship set afire. I said: 'Yes,' but it looked as if it had not been done successfully. Just then Hoge came along in his boat and said that he had set fire to her.

Not seeing any flames, Wood ordered Hoge to return to the *Underwriter* and make sure, a dangerous undertaking with every Federal gun that could be brought to bear now firing on the vessel. Loyall reported:

In about ten minutes we saw flames leap out of a window forward of the wheelhouse, where the engineer's supplies were kept, and Hoge pulling away. In a very few minutes the whole expanse of water was lighted up, and you may be sure we struck out with a vim to rendezvous at Swift Creek, about six miles up the river.

In the haste to leave, one of the boats was found to contain twenty Union prisoners and only two Confederate guards. In the confusion of the darkness and exploding shells from the forts, the Federals easily overpowered their captors and escaped to shore. Loyall added, "As we were pulling up we could hear now and then the boom of the guns of the *Underwriter* as they were discharged by heat from the burning ship, and just before reaching our landing place we heard the awful explosion of the sturdy vessel, when the fire reached her magazine."[36]

The rain was falling in torrents as the exhausted Confederates pulled slowly up Swift Creek. From almost every boat could be heard the groans and cries of the wounded. With morning light just breaking over the eastern horizon, the cutters landed on the soggy creek bank, and the injured were gently lifted ashore. Five Confederates had been killed: Engineer Gill, Midshipman Saunders, Seamen

Hawkins and Sullivan, and Pvt. William Bell of the marines. Eleven sailors and four marines had been wounded. The Federals lost nine killed, including the *Underwriter*'s commander, Westervelt, whose body washed ashore a month later. The bodies of the remaining Federal dead burned in the conflagration that consumed the *Underwriter*. Twenty Union sailors were wounded but carried away and cared for by Wood's men, and twenty-six more were taken up Swift Creek as prisoners. Twenty-three of the *Underwriter*'s crew had escaped. The two divisions' cutters bore stark evidence to the ferocity of the Federal's fire with each one averaging fourteen white plugs to seal the jagged bullet holes.

Later that afternoon, a solemn funeral service was held on the banks of Swift Creek. With Lieutenant Loyall reading the church service, five comrades in navy gray were lowered into North Carolina soil. That night and for the next two nights, the Confederates pulled against the strong current of the Neuse and arrived at Kinston on February 5. There they waited while Wood proceeded on to Richmond. Loyall sent the Wilmington and Charleston contingents home, and finally, on February 9, Wood telegraphed orders for the remainder to return to Petersburg.[37]

The objective to capture New Bern had failed, owing in part to the lack of aggressiveness by Pickett and the failure of Barton to cut the rail line. The Confederate navy, and indeed the entire country, was elated over the destruction of the Federals' most powerful gunboat in the sounds of North Carolina, accomplished under the very guns of the Union fortifications. While the Confederate Congress passed a resolution offering its gratitude to Wood and his command, perhaps the highest compliment was given by Union Admiral Porter: "This was rather a mortifying affair for the [Union] navy, however fearless on the part of the Confederates. This gallant expedition was led by Commander John Taylor Wood. It was to be expected that with so many clever officers, who left the Federal navy, and cast their fortunes with the Confederates, such gallant action would often be attempted."[38]

10

THE ALBEMARLE ATTACKS

NOTWITHSTANDING THE FAILURE TO recapture New Bern, Confederate authorities were still hopeful that they could take back portions of eastern North Carolina. With this in mind, Gen. Braxton Bragg in Richmond issued detailed orders on April 17, 1864, for Brig. Gen. Robert F. Hoke to assemble a force for the recapture of Plymouth. Bragg suggested that Hoke solicit the cooperation of Cooke and the *Albemarle,* and soon thereafter the general paid a visit to the navy commander at Hamilton. Initially the *Albemarle*'s commander was hesitant to commit his unfinished vessel to the anticipated assault, for while her engines and boilers were in place, they were still not connected. Much of the armor still lay stacked on her deck, awaiting the services of the drilling machine, and Cooke pointed out that few crew members had been assembled. Hoke promised that additional mechanics would be sent from the army and outlined the importance of the ironclad's role in the coming campaign. Additionally, he pledged his assistance in obtaining the necessary sailors to man the warship. Encouraged by Hoke's optimism, Cooke declared that if the promised mechanics and crewmen materialized, he would have the vessel ready in fifteen days.[1]

Time for striking a blow in North Carolina was running out, for once the roads dried and the giant blue host began to move in Virginia, Hoke would be forced to return his troops to the Army of Northern Virginia. Cooke was determined, therefore, to do all in his power to assure the attack's success. The additional mechanics arrived, and with their help, the work progressed at a breakneck pace.

NATIONAL ARCHIVES

Brig. Gen. Robert F. Hoke

On April 17, 1864, a cryptic telegram was received at the Navy Department in Richmond: "The C.S. Steamer *Albemarle* was placed in commission this day at 2 o'clock P.M. The officers ordered to her hitherto awaiting her completion will be entered on your books as on duty afloat from this date inclusive. I am very respectfully, J. W. Cooke, Commanding C.S.N."[2]

All afternoon workers scurried about loading last-minute supplies and stores and hurriedly stashing below. Coal had been taken on earlier, and steam had been raised, but the banging and hammering emanating from the engine room indicated that all was still not quite ready in that department. The last of the iron plates was carried aboard, and portable forges were set up on the *Albemarle*'s flush decks. A line was secured to a flat, and additional forges and extra materials were loaded aboard it. By 3:00 p.m. all appeared to be ready. Cooke ordered all lines cast off, and a small steamer nudged the bulky ironclad into the waterway. Because of the swiftness of the current, along with the many twists and turns in the river, Cooke directed that the ironclad steam stern-first down the stream and ordered that heavy chains be dragged from her bow. With the red-and-white national ensign snapping in the breeze, the *Albemarle* began her slow and careful journey down the Roanoke. As Cooke had promised Hoke just fifteen days earlier—she was on her way.[3]

The *Albemarle* had not gone far before the steamer *Cora*, carrying the twenty experienced sailors promised by General Hoke, caught up with her. These navy men, which increased the crew to fifty, were badly needed, for the only crewmen on board were Tarheel volunteers from Hoke's North Carolina Brigade. At 5:00 p.m. Cooke stopped briefly at Williamston where equipment and nonessential workers were put ashore. Several blacksmiths and machinists were retained on board, and they continued to hammer and bang away on the unfinished areas of the ironclad as she continued on her journey toward Plymouth.

Scharf paints a picturesque description of this trip down the Roanoke: "On the turtle-back numerous stages were suspended, thronged with sailors wielding huge sledge-hammers. Upon the pilot house stood Captain Cooke giving directions. Some of the crew were being exercised at one of the big guns. 'Drive in spike No. 10!' sang out the commander. 'On nut below and screw up! In vent and sponge! Load with cartridge,' was the next command. 'Drive in No. 11, port side—so. On nut and screw up hard! Load with shells—prime!' And in this seeming babble of words the floating monster glided by."[4]

Evening shadows began to fall across the river, but Cooke pushed on, knowing that Hoke and his troops were depending upon the *Albemarle*'s support. Soon the river was shrouded in total darkness, and the pilots had to keep a sharp lookout to prevent the big ironclad from running aground. Suddenly there came a clanging sound from the engine room.

Dragging chains behind her, the *Albemarle* descends the Roanoke River.

Cooke explained: "At 10 o'clock on the night following, a portion of the machinery broke down. The damage consisted in the wrenching up of the bolts which fastened the main coupling of the center shaft. Having taken the precaution to carry a portable forge down with me in a flat, we were enabled to repair damages and get underway after about six hours' delay. Having proceeded some distance down the river the rudder head broke off, and another delay of four hours was sustained. But despite these difficulties, I anchored 3 miles above Plymouth on Monday night at 10 o'clock."[5]

Meanwhile, Hoke's command had left Tarboro on April 15, and by 4:00 p.m. on April 17, it had arrived within five miles of Plymouth where they routed a company of Union cavalry and captured several of the enemy's pickets. The following morning Hoke launched several attacks in earnest against the well-entrenched Federals surrounding Plymouth. The approximately twenty-five hundred Union troops fought stubbornly, and by late in the day little progress had been made by the gray-clad troops. At approximately 6:00 p.m., Hoke's own brigade assaulted Fort Wassells while fourteen pieces of artillery poured fire into Fort Williams. Night fell and the sky was illuminated by the light of streaking shells. A Richmond correspondent wrote:

> The sight was magnificent—the screaming, hissing shells meeting and passing each other through the sulphurous air, appeared like blazing comets with their burning fuses, and would burst with frightful noise, scattering their fragments as thick as hail.

Confederate troops managed to claw their way to within two hundred yards of the enemy's works, but there they were stopped by intense Federal fire. Union soldiers lobbed hand grenades over the parapet and into the midst of Hoke's troops while artillery and heavy shells from four gunboats tore through the Confederate ranks. The storm of shot and shell was too much, and by 1:00 a.m., the bleeding Southern forces were compelled to withdraw.[6]

The constant and accurate fire from the Federal vessels stationed in the river behind the town was particularly devastating to the Southern troops. The warships that caused such carnage were the

NAVAL HISTORICAL CENTER

The USS *Miami,* flagship of the Federal fleet at Plymouth

Miami and the *Southfield,* plus two smaller vessels, the *Whitehead* and the *Ceres.* Lt. Cmdr. Charles W. Flusser was the Federal officer in charge of the flotilla at Plymouth, and he flew his flag from the largest gunboat, the USS *Miami.* Flusser had been hearing rumors for months about the "Rebel" ram under construction up the river, and now, as he sat in his cabin on the *Miami* late at night on April 18, he knew the rumors were about to come true. Writing a short dispatch to his superior, Rear Adm. Samuel Phillips Lee, he said: "We have been fighting here all day. About sunset the enemy made a general advance along our whole line. They have been repulsed. . . . The Ram will be down tonight or tomorrow. I fear for the protection of the town."[7]

Gilbert Elliott had accompanied the *Albemarle* down the Roanoke, and later he wrote about her arrival above Plymouth: "She came to anchor about three miles above Plymouth, and a mile or so above the battery [Fort Grey] on the bluff at Warren's Neck, near Thoroughfare Gap, where torpedoes, sunken vessels, piles, and other obstructions had been placed. An exploring expedition was sent out, under command of one of the lieutenants, which returned in about two hours, with the report that it was considered impossible to pass

The *Albemarle* on her way to Plymouth

the obstructions. Thereupon the fires were banked, and the officers and crew not on duty retired to rest."[8]

Elliott does not identify the lieutenant by name, but the author believes that his reluctance to do so indicates that it may have been John Lewis, who deserted Confederate service in January 1865.

With no "official" duties to perform, a restless Elliott probably paced the gundeck while the crew, exhausted from thirty-two hours of constant work since leaving Hamilton, threw themselves on the deck near their stations to rest. It had taken enormous sacrifice and effort to come this far, and with success nearly in their grasp, Elliott could feel it slipping away. Something had to be done.

Having accompanied Captain Cooke as a volunteer aide, and feeling intensely dissatisfied with the apparent intention of lying at anchor all that night, and believing that it was "then or never" with the ram if she was to accomplish anything, and that it would be foolhardy to attempt the passage of the obstructions and batteries in the day time, I requested permission to make a personal investigation. Captain Cooke cordially assenting, and Pilot John Luck and two of the few experienced seamen on board volunteering their services, we set forth in a small lifeboat, taking with us a long pole, and arriving at the

obstructions proceeded to take soundings. To our great joy it was ascertained that there was ten feet of water over and above the obstructions. This was due to the remarkable freshet then prevailing; the
proverbial "oldest inhabitant" said, afterwards, that such high water
had never before been seen in the Roanoke River. Pushing on down
the stream to Plymouth, and taking advantage of the shadow of the
trees on the north side of the river, opposite the town, we watched
the Federal transports taking on board the women and children who
were being sent away for safety, on account of the approaching bombardment. With muffled oars, and almost afraid to breathe, we made
our way back up the river, hugging close to the northern bank, and
reached the ram about 1 o'clock, reporting to Captain Cooke that it
was practicable to pass the obstructions provided the boat was kept
in the middle of the stream. The indomitable commander instantly
aroused his men, gave the order to get up steam, slipped the cables in
his impatience to be off, and started down the river.[9]

Commander Cooke undoubtedly stood in the pilothouse with
the helmsman and perhaps John Luck. Squinting through the narrow slits of the cupola's armored walls, they waited impatiently for
the cables to be slipped. An almost full moon illuminated the water
and reflected off a thin mist that hung low over the river. Finally, the
anchor crew came running back from the bow and clambered
through the forward gunport. The port shutter slammed closed.
Down in the engine room, the signal gong clattered to life, ordering
all ahead slow. Sluggishly the big ironclad began to move, and the
helmsman spun the wheel to point the sharp prow toward the middle of the river.

No more stern first. No more heavy chains dragging from the
bow. Steam hissed in the Albemarle's boilers, her frame vibrated
slightly from the steady thump of the engines, as twin screws drove
her forward. Soon the obstructions were reached. Carefully the
helmsman guided the ironclad through the middle of the line of debris and sunken wrecks while each crewman held his breath. Within
a few seconds the line was passed, and not a scrape was heard. Again
the gong in the engine room rang—this time for all ahead full—and
quickly the Albemarle began to pick up speed.

Suddenly, a flash of light flooded through the viewing slits in the pilothouse followed by a demonic howl as a heavy shell screamed low overhead. Fort Grey had opened fire. Rifle balls clattered against the slanted armor as unseen muskets joined in. Elliott noted: "Protected by the iron-clad shield, to those on board the noise made by the shot and shell as they struck the boat sounded no louder that pebbles thrown against an empty barrel."[10]

Most likely the Brooke rifles were swung to starboard, but Cooke ordered the gunport shutters kept closed. Silently the *Albemarle* glided past the Federal fortification in the moonlight, not bothering to respond to Union fire. Cooke had more serious business downriver.

Within a few minutes of passing the obstructions, the *Albemarle* approached the town of Plymouth, which lay on the south side of the river. Lookouts were posted, one on the bow, and one in the top-side forward hatch. Situated on the right flank of the Federal fortifications and adjacent to the river was Battery Worth with a 200-pounder Parrott gun. Although the Roanoke was only two hundred yards wide at this point, the darkened ironclad steamed silently by without attracting a shot. Once opposite Plymouth, Cooke ordered the gunport shutters opened. Crewmen heaved on large levers that, through a chain device, swung the heavy iron shutters down to one side. Cool air coursed through the casemate and helped dispel some of the heat generated from the furnaces below.[11]

Suddenly one of the lookouts gave a shout. Past the town and only a short distance down the river, he could see the running lights of two approaching steamers. Cooke ordered the large Brooke rifles charged with solid shot, and in less than a minute, the lanky Tarheels had the big guns loaded, run out, and ready to fire.

The two vessels approaching up the middle of the Roanoke were the *Miami* and the *Southfield*. Commander Flusser had lashed the two gunboats together with heavy spars and loose chains in anticipation of snaring the *Albemarle* between them and pounding her to destruction with their broadsides.

At first, in the fading moonlight, Cooke failed to notice the chains, but when he did, he took decisive action. Instructing his helmsman to steer close to the north side of the river, he rang the engine room for full speed. Steadily the vessels approached one another. The *Miami* and the *Southfield,* because of their deeper drafts, kept to the middle of the river; the *Albemarle* hugged the north shoreline. Cooke squinted through the viewing slits and waited. Then, upon a sharp command, the helmsman spun the wheel to starboard, swinging the bow straight toward the two oncoming enemy vessels. Black smoke poured from the ironclad's funnel as her engines pounded. At a thirty-degree angle and at full speed, the Confederate ironclad charged the startled Union warships. Within seconds the *Albemarle* was upon them.

Federal officers screamed commands to their divisions, and several guns opened fire. The *Albemarle's* port knuckle scraped by the port bow of the *Miami,* and at almost the same instant, with an explosive crash, the Confederate ironclad slammed into the starboard bow of the *Southfield.* The side of the Federal ship exploded in a mass of splintered and broken wood as the prow smashed through her forward storeroom. With a fearful grinding and screeching sound, the ram of the *Albemarle* finally came to rest in the fire room, ten feet inside the *Southfield's* hull.[12]

Immediately, the *Southfield* began to sink. At the moment of impact, the *Albemarle's* engines were thrown into reverse, and they labored to back her away, but she failed to move. The shriek of escaping steam mixed with the shouts, curses, and screams of the Federal sailors as they scrambled to escape the doomed ship. Above this crescendoing noise was the creaking and groaning of the *Southfield's* timbers as they strained against the pressure. Suddenly the early morning twilight exploded in flames as the *Miami* opened fire

NAVAL HISTORICAL CENTER

The *Albemarle* slams into the *Southfield.*

at point-blank range. When the *Albemarle* struck the two enemy vessels, the forward chains were torn apart, and now the *Miami* was almost parallel to the Confederate ironclad with her port broadside guns opened a thunderous fire against the armored casemate.

Blue-clad sailors clawed their way toward the *Southfield's* stern where they could scramble over the rail and onto the *Miami*. Some threw themselves into the water while others hastily lowered a small boat. The *Southfield* was going down rapidly, but with her weight on the *Albemarle's* bow, the entrapped Confederate vessel was going down with her.

As the *Albemarle's* stem was pressed lower and lower, anxious gun crews could only wait, their weapons useless at the inclined angle. In the engine room, frenzied engineers and firemen worked desperately to increase the power of the engines. The *Albemarle* shook and vibrated while her twin screws churned the Roanoke waters to foam, but still she would not budge.

All the while, thunderous explosions crashed against the iron shield as the *Miami* continued to fire her eight heavy guns from just a few feet away. In his zeal to destroy the *Albemarle*, Commander Flusser on the *Miami* rushed forward to assist with a 9-inch Dahlgren on the bow. Pulling the lanyard himself, he sent a spinning shell with a two-second fuse slamming against the *Albemarle*. It rebounded off the iron casemate, arched up and back over the *Miami*, where it exploded directly over the Dahlgren. The courageous Flusser was virtually torn apart.[13]

Lt. Cmdr. Charles W. Flusser

LIBRARY OF CONGRESS

Cooke, fearing an attempt by the Federals to board the *Albemarle,* sent his Tarheels onto the roof where they opened an intense rifle fire against the gun crews on the *Miami*. Reloaded muskets were handed up through the iron grating as fast as the empty ones were passed below. During this melee, one of the *Albemarle's* crew fell

NAVAL HISTORICAL CENTER

After sinking the *Southfield,* the *Albemarle* pursues the *Miami.*

dead, a pistol ball through his skull. The *Southfield* was almost on the bottom, and the *Albemarle*'s bow was still firmly wedged in her side. The Confederate ironclad was herself half submerged while her pounding engines continued to labor in reverse. Alarmed crew members watched as water began to pour through the forward gunport. Finally, the *Southfield* touched bottom and rolled to port, freeing the *Albemarle*'s ram. In a swell of cascading water, steam, and smoke, the ironclad's bow shot to the surface like a cork. Confederate sailors scrambled down from the roof and to the gundeck where they opened fire on the *Miami* with the forward Brooke rifle.[14]

William N. Welles, the *Miami*'s executive officer, had second thoughts about engaging the Confederate vessel now that she was free from the *Southfield.* Reversing his engines on the double-ender boat, he fled downstream toward the protection of other Federal vessels in Albemarle Sound. Cooke ordered the ironclad's boats lowered, and eight Union sailors were plucked from the cold waters of the Roanoke. As the tinge of light in the eastern sky announced the coming of daybreak, the naval battle of Plymouth was over.[15]

With daylight breaking, Cooke stood atop the casemate and surveyed the scene around Plymouth. No Federal vessels were in sight.

The waters around the North Carolina town were once again controlled by the Confederate navy. Cooke was at a loss, however, as to his next course of action, for he had no idea what General Hoke's plans were. Later he wrote: "Not having heard anything from the army, I laid about one mile below the town, anticipating an attack on the town, and at 11 o'clock a.m., being again at a loss to know what course to pursue, Mr. Elliott again volunteered and took Pilot Hopkins with a boat's crew and proceeded down to the mouth of the river and up a creek in the rear of Plymouth, distant from the boat by water about 12 miles. He communicated with General Hoke and sent me dispatches."[16]

During the day on April 19, Hoke's troops made little progress, but the *Albemarle* trained her guns on Battery Worth, and through the afternoon and all during the night, the Confederate vessel maintained a slow but steady fire on the Federal fortification. On the following morning Hoke launched a coordinated attack from the east along the river while the *Albemarle* anchored off Jefferson Street with

This wartime map of Plymouth highlights the site of the sinking of the *Southfield* in the upper right-hand corner.

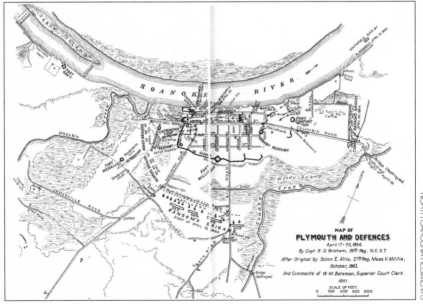

MAP OF
PLYMOUTH AND DEFENCES
April 17-20, 1864.
By Capt. R. D. Graham, 56th Reg, N.C. S.T.
After Original by Solon E. Allis, 27th Reg, Mass. V. Militia,
October, 1863.
And Comments of W. M. Bateman, Superior Court Clerk.
1901.

SCALE OF FEET.
0   500   1000 1500 2000

an unobstructed view of Fort Williams. The ironclad's gunners and their large Brooke rifles methodically shot to pieces the key to the Federal defenses. The steamer *Cotton Plant,* which had followed the *Albemarle* down from Hamilton, joined in the assault, utilizing sharpshooters who were posted on her deck behind protective iron plates. At 10:00 a.m. a white flag appeared over Fort Williams, and Brig. Gen. Henry W. Wassells accepted terms presented by Hoke and surrendered all Federal forces at Plymouth.[17]

On April 20, Secretary Stephen R. Mallory wrote to the Confederate Congress: "The signal success of this brilliant naval engagement is due to the admirable skill and courage displayed by Commander Cooke, his officers and men, in handling and fighting his ship against a greatly superior force of men and guns."[18]

The *Albemarle's* work, however, was just beginning.

11

FRUSTRATION AT KINSTON

WHILE THE *ALBEMARLE* WAS receiving her baptism of fire in front of Plymouth, workmen at Kinston were still struggling to complete the CSS *Neuse*. Some machinery for her engines had arrived in January 1864, and there was much expectation in Richmond at that time that both ironclads would soon be finished. So much so in fact that on January 2, General Lee wrote to President Davis: "The time is at hand when, if an attempt can be made to capture the enemy's forces at New Berne, it should be done. I can now spare troops for the purpose, which will not be the case as spring approaches. . . . A bold party could descend the Neuse in boats at night, capture the [enemy's] gunboats, and drive the enemy by their aid from the works on that side of the river, while a force should attack them in front. . . . The gun-boats, aided by the iron-clads building on the Neuse and Roanoke, would clear the waters of the enemy and capture their transports, which could be used for transportation."[1]

Davis replied to Lee's letter and informed him that it was impossible for the *Neuse* and the *Albemarle* to be finished in time to aid in the attack on New Bern. A disappointed Lee responded on January 20:

I have delayed replying to your letter of the 4th until the time arrived for the execution of the attempt on New Berne. I regret very much that the boats on the Neuse and Roanoke are not completed. With their aid I think success would be certain. Without them, though the place may be captured, the fruits of the expedition will be lessened and our maintenance of the command of the waters in North Carolina uncertain. I think every effort should be made now to get them into service as soon as possible. You will see by the enclosed letters to Generals [George E.] Pickett and [William H. C.] Whiting the arrangements made for the land operations. The water expedition I am willing to trust to Colonel [John Taylor] Wood. If he can succeed in capturing the gunboats I think success will be certain, as it was by aid from the water that I expected Hoke to be mainly assisted.[2]

As recounted earlier, although Commander Wood was able to capture the USS *Underwriter,* the attack on New Bern was a failure. Many felt that the principal reason for this failure was the unfinished state of the two ironclads, particularly the *Neuse.*

With the failure to retake New Bern, the need to finish the *Neuse* as quickly as possible was becoming painfully evident. In February Hoke reported: "I have but 95 carpenters and mechanics and 50 laborers from my command to work on the gunboat, and they will soon have it completed. The material I have made arrangements to have brought forward, and by the 1st of March I hope to have both of the ironclads ready for work, with which there can be no doubt of success."[3]

Shaken by the failure to capture New Bern, and determined to hasten the completion of the *Neuse,* Mallory in February dispatched Lt. Robert D. Minor to Kinston "to hasten the completion of the gunboat." Minor's instructions called for him to employ as many mechanics as he thought necessary, regardless of the cost, and to work "night and day" to get the ironclad finished. Minor, who was from Virginia, had served on the CSS *Virginia* during the two-day battle of Hampton Roads and more recently had been in charge of the ordnance works in Richmond. On February 16, after spending two days inspecting the *Neuse* and interviewing her commander, Lt. William Sharp, Minor forwarded his report to Secretary Mallory:

Lieutenant Commander Sharp has a force of one hundred and seventy
men employed upon her, including nineteen men from the Naval Station on the Peedee, four from Wilmington and 105 detailed temporarily by Brig. Gen. Hoke from his Brigade now in camp in this vicinity. As
you are aware the steamer has two layers of iron on the forward end of
her shield, but none on either broadside, or on the after part. The carpenters are now bolting the longitudinal pieces on the hull, and if the
iron can be delivered more rapidly . . . with some degree of regularity,
the work would progress in much more satisfactory manner. The boiler
was today lowered into the vessel and when in place, the main deck
will be laid in. The river I am told is unprecedently low for the season
of the year. I am satisfied that not more than five feet can now be carried down the channel, and as the steamer when ready for service, will
draw between six or seven feet, it is very apparent that to be useful, she
must be equipped in time to take advantage of the first rise. I have advised and directed the immediate construction of four camels, to be
used to move the ship on her way down the river. Mr. A. F. Tift left here
for Augusta, Georgia on Monday to hurry forward the remainder of the
iron plates—two car loads of which arrived prior to his departure.
Agents have been sent to various points to collect material. At my sug-
gestion Lieutenant Sharp has adopted the plan of working his men
from 7 a.m. until 7 p.m. with an intermission of one hour for dinner,
and with relief parties who will work from 7 p.m. until 3 a.m. Lieutenant Sharp informs me that General Hoke has already commenced
the removal of the obstructions in the river, but from my inspection of
them today I am [sure that it will take two or three weeks] to open the
channel. Lieutenant Sharp also informs me that he is organizing his
crew—twenty-eight are now on board, and he will make up the whole
number of men allowed the vessel from those in the army who are accustomed to a seafaring life and have volunteered. I have advised and
since directed the immediate construction of a covered lighter of sufficient capacity to carry two days coal and twenty days provision for the
steamer. If the material is delivered here as rapidly as I hope I believe
the steamer will be ready for service by the 18th of next month.[4]

An analysis of Minor's report supplies an interesting picture of
the progress, or lack thereof, on the construction of the *Neuse*. It was

NAVAL HISTORICAL CENTER

Lt. Robert D. Minor

obvious that numerous difficulties would have to be overcome if the warship was to be completed by the "18th of next month," not the least of which was acquiring the needed crew members. While Minor reported that the twenty-eight men now on board would be supplemented by volunteers from surrounding army units, precedent had shown that most Confederate army commanders were very re-luctant to transfer any of their men to the navy. Even the army work force, which was composed of units from the Sixth, Twenty-first, Forty-third, Fifty-forth, and Fifty-seventh North Carolina regiments, plus a few from the Twenty-first Georgia, was only available as long as their units were in the area.[5]

Minor mentions that on the day of his writing the boiler was low-ered into place. The boiler, engine, and attached machinery suppos-edly came from the Baltimore and Ohio locomotive No. 34, built in 1844, although a Federal report indicates that the boiler came from "Pugh's Mill" in New Bern. Whatever the case, her boiler was in place, and mechanics were busily working on connecting her engines.[6]

Sometime toward the latter part of February 1864 (records are un-clear), Mallory ordered Lt. Benjamin P. Loyall, who had just returned from the expedition to capture the USS *Underwriter,* to replace Sharp as the *Neuse's* new commander. Loyall's instructions were to finish the ironclad as quickly as possible and then assume her command. The Virginia lieutenant would find this a Herculean task. On March 9 he wrote to Minor: "The *Neuse* floats not, the first course of iron is com-plete, the second fairly begun, the Guns are in and mounted and I think will work well. But the ignorance and greeness of my conscripts is inconceivable. They surely would make an old tar swear his head off. The *stop* is at Wilmington, where there are several car loads of iron waiting transportation. We have been working slowly for the past few days from want of iron and I don't know how it can be helped."[7]

Loyall was discovering what other shipbuilders within the Confederacy had already experienced, namely that a lack of transportation facilities, or their worn-out condition, was seriously hampering the completion of the *Neuse*. Several days later, on March 11, 1864, Mallory appealed to Secretary of War James A. Seddon:

> I beg leave to call your attention to the enclosed extracts from letters of Flag Officer [William F.] Lynch and Lieutenant Loyall, C. S. Navy, dated the 8th instant, and respectfully request that instructions may be given to have the iron plates referred to transported to Kinston and Halifax at the earliest moment. The gunboats at those points are completed with the exception of the iron plating, and the mechanics are delayed in their work waiting for it. The work upon these vessels has been delayed for months by the want of transportation, and now that they are very near completion I respectfully urge that no further delay on this account may be had, for unless completed at an early day the detention of the boat at Kinston by the fall of Neuse River will be disastrous and may cause her destruction. The subject is of so much importance that I suggest the detail by the Quartermaster-General of an officer specially charged with it.

On March 12, 1864, Seddon forwarded the letter to Quartermaster Gen. A. R. Lawton "for inquiry and remarks." On March 15 Lawton replied to Seddon, "At present forage and food necessary for our armies in the field demand our entire transportation." Lynch added:

> Fourteen car-loads of plate iron arrived last evening, and for a week past we have had two car-loads waiting transportation to Kinston and Halifax. The whole rolling capacity of the road, except passenger trains, has been monopolized by the army, and I fear the completion of the gun-boats at those places will

James A. Seddon

NATIONAL ARCHIVES

be delayed. Besides my own occasional visits to the depot, a reliable officer is detailed to be there twice every day and apply for and report the prospects of obtaining transportation. The rights of the Navy are not respected, its wants are utterly disregarded, and it is in the power of an acting assistant quartermaster to cause our transportation to be set aside at will. The importance of speedily completing the ironclad on the Neuse and Roanoke does not seem to be comprehended.

Loyall notified Mallory: "Flag Officer Lynch telegraphs me today that he cannot procure transportation for me from Wilmington. We are in want of it here."[8]

Even if the army had not monopolized the rail lines, it would have been difficult to coordinate the delivery of all the materials necessary for the speedy completion of the ironclads in North Carolina. There existed no central location for the stockpiling of supplies, and shipbuilding sites were for the most part in remote and out-of-the-way places. Most Southern railroads had been laid to facilitate the shipment of cotton and tobacco from the inlands to the coast and not for interstate transportation. Iron plates coming from Richmond, for example, had to traverse a roundabout series of railroads before arriving at the *Neuse* construction site.

In spite of all the ensuing difficulties, by mid-March the ironclad was nearing completion. Most of her officers had been assigned and were being lodged in a private residence a short distance from the construction site until quarters below the gundeck were completed. Efforts were under way to assemble an experienced crew, but seasoned sailors were almost nonexistent and most men would have to come from local army units. One of the officers, Lt. Richard H. Bacot, wrote to his sister on March 19 concerning the progress of the vessel and his impression of the North Carolina landsmen they had on board:

Her iron fixin's are not done, her engines are not ready, her quarters and storerooms are not ready, and last but not least, the river is falling about 12 inches a day & we will have to trust to Providence for another rise when the vessel is finished; finally to complete our misery we have a crew of long, lank, "Tar Heels" (N.C.'s from the "Piney woods"). Our guns are mounted and we drill the crew every morning at 5:30 o'clock. We have one or two good men, but I am afraid the others can never learn anything about a gunboat. You ought to see them in the boats! It is too ridiculous. They are all legs & arms & while working at the guns their legs get tangled in the tackles. . . . They are always in the wrong place & in each other's way.[9]

Minor's original estimate that the boat would be completed by March 18 was proving to be overly optimistic. By the end of that month she was still unfinished. While Hoke had supplied a large detail of men to work on the vessel, they were kept waiting for the most part for lack of iron plates. By the end of the month the ironclad was still not armored, and during the first week in April another problem arose. In exasperation, Loyall wrote to Minor: "There has been a flare up with the mechanics employed here. . . . Mr. Howard . . . declares that they understood you to authorize a man employed four hours at night should receive a day's wages for the work. A new paymaster was ordered here, and, when the mechanic's rolls were being made up, he called upon me for authority to pay double for Sunday, and double for four hours of night work."[10]

Loyall was in a bind. Four of his best mechanics walked off the job because of the dispute. To the paymaster, the Neuse's new commander explained that the wage arrangements had been made by Lieutenant Sharp before he had assumed command. At Loyall's urging, the paymaster wrote to John L. Porter in Richmond in hopes he could set the record straight. Porter replied that it was government policy that if a mechanic worked on a Sunday he was to be paid two days' wages. Each hour worked at night should be paid at time and a half. Foreman Howard now entered the fray on behalf of the mechanics and claimed they were promised eight hours pay for four hours of night work.

With the Neuse already behind schedule, an exasperated Loyall gave in and agreed to their demands. He was not happy, however, and in writing to Minor expressed his exasperation: "Confound them, they should all be enrolled and made to work at government prices with rations, or go into the army."[11]

He added: "You have no idea of the delay in forwarding iron to this place—it may be unavoidable, but I don't believe it. At one time twenty one days passed without my receiving a piece. . . . Every time I telegraphed to Lynch he replies, 'Army monopolizing cars.' It is all exceedingly mortifying to me."[12]

On April 16 Loyall wrote that the *Neuse* would be operational in about a week, even if all of her iron armor was not in place. The ironclad's commander was not very impressed with his ship, however, and his next letter to Minor reflected his lack of confidence in her: "The vessel will draw nearly 8 feet of water when complete. Mark what I say, when a boat built of green pine & covered with four inches of iron gets under fire of heavy ordnance, she will prove anything but bomb proof. This vessel is not fastened & strengthened more than a 200-ton schooner. Her upper deck is 2-in. pine, with light beams, & is expected to hold a pilot house. I should not be surprised if said pilot house was knocked off, there is very little to hold it on."[13]

Unfortunately, Loyall's pronouncement that the *Neuse* would be "ready in a week" would prove to be too late, for three days prior to this announcement, Lee sent word that he would soon need Hoke's troops to prepare for the spring campaign. Hoke's campaign to regain control of the North Carolina sounds was well under way, however, and as already related, with the help of the *Albemarle*, Plymouth was recaptured on April 20, 1864. The general next turned his attention to New Bern and sent instructions to Loyall to get under way with the *Neuse* and participate in the attack.

The ironclad's commander was determined to support the attack and had his crew up early on the morning of April 22, 1864. After a hasty breakfast, everyone, even the lanky Tarheels, hastened to their assigned stations in preparation for casting off. The engineers raised steam all morning, and wisps of black smoke could be seen curling upward from her short stack into the cloudless sky. Even now, with her departure looming, hammering could still be heard from below as workmen hurried to complete some last-minute construction.

When all was ready, Loyall issued his orders. Lines were cast off fore and aft; bells rang in the engine room. In response engineer John T. Tucker opened the valves to start the engines. Thick black smoke billowed upward from her funnel while excess steam hissed from escape valves. The two large propellers began to turn, and as

The CSS *Neuse* hard aground

they increased in speed they churned the waters of the river causing mud and debris to bubble to the surface. Slowly, the ironclad began to move. The helmsman spun the wheel to direct the bow away from the wharf and toward the middle of the stream. A few onlookers on-shore cheered and waved while the steady throb of the engines drove the ironclad forward at an ever-increasing rate of speed. With the navy jack at her stem and the national ensign at her stern, the CSS *Neuse*, after all of the delays, was finally headed for battle.

Everything seemed to be going well when about a half mile down the river there was a terrible crunching sound. The *Neuse* shuddered to a sudden stop, sending some crew members bowling over one an-other. She had run aground on a sandbar. Bells rang again in the en-gine room, and the engines were quickly reversed. As the crew rushed aft to lighten the bow, the twin propellers churned up mud and gravel from the river bottom as they labored to back the ironclad off the sandbar. The crew worked desperately to free the vessel, for all were aware that the river was falling rapidly. By nightfall Loyall had to admit it was hopeless. The *Neuse's* bow was four feet out of the water.

Several days later, a bitter Lieutenant Bacot was writing to his sister:

I have bad news to tell you this time. Even worse than I anticipated when I wrote last week . . . there was scarcely enough [water] for us to cross the obstructions; we nevertheless started down last Friday and had proceeded about a half mile when we grounded on a sand bar. . . . The stern of the vessel is afloat, but the bow is 4 feet out of the water. We will have to wait for a freshet again and that will probably take place in July or August. I assure you our disappointment was great when we found we could not get off; the troops were here and ready to join us in an attack on Newbern and we were all expecting to take the city and sink the gunboats without much trouble . . . it does seem hard to be so sorely disappointed after expecting so much.[14]

By the first of May it had become obvious that the *Neuse* could not be freed from the sandbar without a substantial rise in the river. Gen. P. G. T. Beauregard, who had assumed command of the newly created Department of North and South Carolina on April 23, wanted Hoke to continue with his operations against New Bern. As a result, Hoke launched his attack on May 4, 1864. The following day, however, he received orders from Richmond to discontinue the operation and entrain his troops immediately for Virginia. Ulysses S. Grant was showing signs of beginning his spring offensive, and Hoke's regiments were needed as reinforcements for the Army of Northern Virginia.

Gen. P. G. T. Beauregard

The delay of the *Neuse* and the turning back of the *Albemarle* had cost the South the possibility of driving the invader out of North Carolina. The two ironclads still posed a definite threat to Federal forces, however. Union officers were convinced that the *Albemarle* would venture down the Roanoke again, and as soon as the Neuse River rose, the *Neuse* would also attack them. As one Federal general wrote from his headquarters in New Bern, "The ram is no myth. Rest assured of that."[15]

By the last of May, thanks to heavy spring rains, the Neuse River began to rise and soon the ironclad slipped off the sandbar. Slowly she returned to her berth at Kinston. With the North Carolina countryside now stripped of army troops, there was little the *Neuse* could do.

Again, Bacot wrote his sister: "The workmen are again on board making music with their sledge-hammers driving the bolts in the iron overhead. All the troops have left for Virginia and the place is exceedingly dull."[16]

On May 2, a cavalryman in Company K, Third North Carolina Cavalry, summed up the frustration, and the "might have beens," in a letter to his wife: "It is a great misfortune that we have managed so badly without the boat at Kinston. Could it have been completed a month ago and carried down the river . . . and the *Albemarle* come up the river, we would have had easy work taking New Bern and very probably saved hundreds perhaps thousands of valuable lives."[17]

12

STORM OVER ALBEMARLE SOUND

THE CAPTURE OF PLYMOUTH had an enormous morale-boosting effect on the inhabitants of eastern North Carolina. Several counties were now free of the Northern intruders, and farmers could plant their spring crops. No more would the dreaded hoofbeats be heard in the middle of the night, signaling the arrival of Union troops bent on pillaging and burning. In addition to the capture of 2,500 men, 28 pieces of artillery, 500 horses, 5,000 stands of small arms, and 700 barrels of flour by the army, Cmdr. James W. Cooke was pleased to find 200 tons of clean anthracite coal for his bunkers. Both Cooke and Gen. Robert F. Hoke firmly believed that their victory at Plymouth was the first step in the long-awaited effort that would finally drive the Federals out of eastern North Carolina.[1]

The *Albemarle*'s commander was thankful for the experienced sailors sent to him by Hoke, and in his report to Secretary Stephen R. Mallory, he acknowledged: "I had only 20 seamen, those sent from Charleston, and without them I should have been almost powerless. The damage to the *Albemarle* was slight, only nine bars [of] iron being broken, and she now lies at Plymouth undergoing repairs and completion."[2]

The capture of Plymouth led to the Federal withdrawal from Washington, North Carolina, at the mouth of the Tar River. Hoke laid siege to the town, but the Union forces withdrew before the Confederates could storm the fortifications. Washington felt the wrath of the retreating blue troops, as evidenced by a day-and-night frenzy of robbery, rape, and burning. A Federal report later admitted some of the shameful atrocities: "Government stores, sutler's establishments, dwelling houses, private shops, and stables suffered alike. Gangs of men patrolled the city, breaking into houses and wantonly destroying such goods as they could not carry away. The occupants and owners were insulted and defied in their feeble endeavors to protect their property." When Confederate troops entered the town, they found a "ruined city . . . a sad scene—mostly . . . chimneys and heaps of ashes to mark the place where fine homes once stood, and the beautiful trees which shaded the sidewalks, burnt, some almost to a coal."[3]

Leaving the Sixth North Carolina behind to garrison Washington, Hoke pushed his forces toward the large Federal base at the confluence of the Neuse and Trent rivers. If New Bern could be recaptured, the Federals would indeed be driven out of North Carolina. Once again, Hoke called upon his good friend Cooke for assistance. If the *Albemarle* could join forces with the *Neuse*, which had been completed and was lying up the Neuse River at Kinston, the capture of New Bern would be assured. To reach New Bern, however, the Confederate ironclad would have to first traverse the Albemarle Sound from west to east, turn south, and steam past Union-occupied Roanoke Island into Pamlico Sound, continue southwest to the mouth of the Neuse, and from there ascend the obstructed river to New Bern. The total distance by water was approximately 190 miles. In spite of the distance involved and the Federal warships that patrolled the sounds, Cooke agreed to help.[4]

Meanwhile, the *Albemarle* was not idle. Writing to John Taylor Wood, Cooke explained:

> I returned this evening from an expedition in the Sound to the mouth of the Alligator River where I departed on Thursday last [April 28] to bring a small steamer, barge and schooner captured by some of our men, loaded with some 3 or 4 thousand bushels of grain and lumber.

On Friday [April 29], on entering the sound I . . . chased three of the enemy's gunboats and a transport, but was unsuccessful in over-hauling them. I am induced to believe . . . the reports they carried of my presumed attack . . . caused the evacuation of Washington, N.C.

I was able to bring off the steamer. The other two vessels [were] up the river and my boat [was] unable to ascend. We have succeeded in raising the *Bombshell,* and expect to have her ready by Wednesday [May 4]. The *Southfield* we will not be able to raise at present, but in-tend to attempt to get her gun off.[5]

By May 4, 1864, therefore, Cooke had three armed vessels in his armada: *Albemarle, Cotton Plant,* and now *Bombshell.* During the af-ternoon on April 19, prior to the *Albemarle's* arrival at Plymouth, the USS *Bombshell* had steamed up the Roanoke near Fort Grey to recon-noiter but was holed several times below the waterline by Confeder-ate artillery. Struggling back to Plymouth, she arrived just in time to sink as she was being tied to the wharf. After Herculean efforts, the *Bombshell,* with her three guns, had been raised, and was now under the command of Lt. Albert G. Hudgins.[6]

During the first few days of May, workmen swarmed over the three vessels of the Confederate flotilla, repairing damages and load-ing supplies for the trip to New Bern. The *Bombshell,* armed with four guns and carrying extra supplies and provisions, was to act as a ten-der to the *Albemarle* while the steamer *Cotton Plant* had a detachment of troops on board and, according to Cooke, would go as far as the Alligator River. Whether or not they intended to accompany the ex-pedition to New Bern is unclear.

At noon on May 5 the three vessels, with the *Albemarle* in the lead, left Plymouth in convoy and steamed for the mouth of the Roanoke where it empties into Albemarle Sound. By 2:00 p.m. they had reached the large body of water, and Cooke reported that he im-mediately discovered six Union vessels lying about four miles dis-tant. They were the *Ceres,* a small gunboat with two 20-pounder Parrott rifles, the *Commodore Hull* with six guns, the eight-gun double-ender *Miami,* and the army transport *Trumpeter.* The two ad-ditional vessels that Cooke presumably saw—for records testify that they participated in the coming engagement—were the gunboats

The USS *Commodore Hull*

Whitehead and *Isaac N. Seymour.* The Federal warships had arrived at
the entrance to the Roanoke that morning with the intention of de-
ploying torpedoes in the main river channel. With the appearance of
the little Confederate flotilla, they hauled off and steamed rapidly
down the sound.[7]

Cooke ordered pursuit and signaled the *Bombshell* and the *Cotton
Plant* to turn around and retrace their course back up the Roanoke.
The *Cotton Plant* read the signals and obeyed, but for some reason the
Bombshell continued to keep company with the ironclad. Referring to
the retreating Federal warships, Cooke noted: "They immediately got
underway, and stood down the sound E. N. E., until we had run
about 16 miles, when three more gunboats, double-enders, of a much
more formidable class, carrying from ten to twelve guns each, made
their appearance."[8]

Cooke knew beforehand from an informant that the Union fleet
had been reinforced by three additional vessels, but he was still ignorant as to what type they were until that afternoon when they filled
the view of his marine glass.

Steaming rapidly to their comrades' assistance was the 974-ton,
ten-gun *Mattabesett* and the fourteen-gun *Wyalusing.* The *Mattabesett*

carried four 9-inch Dahlgren smoothbores, two 100-pounder Parrott rifles, two 24-pounders, one 12-pounder heavy smoothbore, and one 12-pounder rifle; the *Wyalusing* was armed with four 9-inch Dahlgrens, four 24-pounder howitzers, two 100-pounder Parrotts, two 12-pounder rifles, and two 12-pounder smooth bores. The third vessel was the *Sassacus,* which was armed with four 9-inch Dahlgrens, two 100-pounder Parrotts, two 24-pounder howitzers, one 12-pounder rifle, one 12-pounder heavy smoothbore, and two 20-pounder Dahlgren rifles. All three vessels, in addition to the *Miami,* were double-enders—side-wheel steamers with a rudder fore and aft. In addition to being able to steam equally well in either direction, they were fast and very maneuverable.[9]

The Federal fleet was under the command of Capt. Melancton Smith, who flew his pennant from the *Mattabesett* and who had directed his commanders to pass their ships as closely as possible to the *Albemarle* without damaging their wheels. While passing the ironclad in the opposite direction, they were to deliver their broadsides at point-blank range, round the Confederate warship's stern, and make another pass. The smaller gunboats were to add their fire to that of the double-enders and guard against any other enemy vessels that might be in the area.

The fleeing Union ships fell into line with the approaching heavy Federal warships and, in accordance with Smith's preconceived plan, now raced toward the *Albemarle* in a double column of eight vessels, a half mile apart. Cooke stood in the pilothouse, squinting through the viewing slits, as the silhouettes of the approaching enemy grew larger and larger. Later he reported: "Perceiving the unequal contest in which we were compelled to engage, I immediately prepared for action."[10]

Executive officer Francis M. Roby shouted out his orders, and

Capt. Melancton Smith

PORTER, THE NAVAL HISTORY OF THE CIVIL WAR

the already loaded giant Brooke rifles were quickly pivoted; the forward gun to starboard, the aft gun to port. Levermen heaved on heavy iron bars linked to chains, and with a resounding clang, the gunport shutters were swung open. The Brookes were trundled out, and with primers inserted, the gun captains signaled that they were ready to fire. Down below, additional crew members lined the passageways, ready to pass shot and shell from the magazine. Once the ammunition reached the gundeck, powder boys, one of whom was Benjamin H. Gray, a black lad of only twelve years, rushed it to the guns. Forward, surgeons George Foote and Frederic Peck took their stations in the wardroom, where they prepared their instruments for the expected arrival of the wounded. In the engine room, sweating coal heavers continued to shovel fuel into the blazing fires while the engineers busied themselves over the engines and machinery. Any failure in this department would result in almost certain destruction. With dry throats and pounding hearts, the men of the *Albemarle* prepared themselves for battle.

The Federal commander had planned to pass his double column of vessels on either side of the approaching ironclad, but when the *Albemarle* came within firing range, Cooke ordered a sharp sweeping turn to starboard, foiling Smith's plans. The arc of the *Albemarle's* turn positioned the Confederate ironclad parallel to the starboard side of the lead Federal vessel *Mattabesett*. Steaming now in the same direction as the Union ships, the *Albemarle's* aft gun opened fire. It was 4:40 p.m. The first shot from the *Albemarle* streaked low over the water and found its mark, destroying a launch along with miscellaneous davits and spars and wounding several of the *Mattabesett's* men. Before the Union boat had time to reply, a second shot from the aft Brooke rifle tore through the double-ender's rigging.[11]

The Union warship finally responded. The starboard side of the *Mattabesett* virtually exploded in smoke and flames as her large guns opened fire on the *Albemarle*. At a range of only 150 yards her heavy iron and steel-tipped solid shot slammed into the ironclad's casemate, where it shattered and exploded into thousands of jagged and spinning shrapnel. Inside, on the *Albemarle's* gundeck, sweating sailors, stripped to the waist, reeled from the concussion as deadly wooden splinters, knocked loose by the impact, knifed across the deck. Fortu-

NAVAL HISTORICAL CENTER

The *Albemarle* is surrounded by the *Wyalusing* (*on the left*), the *Sassacus* (*in the center*), and the *Mattabesett* (*on the right*). The CSS *Bombshell* is to the far right.

nately, the iron plating held and no shots broke through to the interior. Momentum carried the *Mattabesett* past the *Albemarle,* and the Federal vessel now rounded her bow in a turn to starboard. As she crossed the ironclad's stem, Cooke shouted for Roby to "Give the Yankee the bow gun!" The forward gun crew finally had their opportunity, and with a roar, they sent two well-directed shots crashing into the Federal, dismounting one gun and injuring many of her crew.[12]

By this time the *Bombshell,* which was following at some distance in the *Albemarle*'s wake, had opened fire on the *Mattabesett,* causing considerable confusion aboard the Federal vessel. Several guns on the *Mattabesett* returned the fire, punching holes through the Confederate's wooden hull.

By 4:50 p.m. the *Wyalusing* and the *Sassacus* had passed the *Albemarle* on her port side, and they too rounded her bow, all the while pouring thunderous barrages against her iron casemate. The *Albemarle* was now surrounded. The casemate, hot as an oven from the blazing furnaces below, was filled with retching smoke. Confederate sailors coughed and gagged as they struggled to load and fire. Suddenly, struck by one of the Federal shells, the muzzle of the aft gun shattered in a shower of sparks and hissing fragments. The undaunted gun crew rammed another round down the broken and jagged barrel, heaved the gun out, and continued firing. The noise inside the casemate was deafening. Solid bolts and explosive shells pummeled the *Albemarle*. Officers screamed and shouted their orders, but could not be heard above the racket. Fortunately, nothing had broken through the casemate walls so far, but more than half the crew suffered with bleeding ears and noses because of the fierce concussions.[13]

After her engagement with the *Mattabesett,* the *Bombshell* continued to maneuver and fire while following the *Albemarle,* and now the *Sassacus* became the gunboat's target. Opening with her 20-pounder Parrott and three rifled howitzers, the *Bombshell* continued to annoy the Union vessel until the *Sassacus* retaliated with a horrific broadside that crashed into the Confederate gunboat, hulling her in three places. With his vessel completely at the mercy of the Federal double-ender, Lieutenant Hudgins ordered her colors struck, and the little gunboat quickly surrendered.[14]

While the *Sassacus* was accepting the *Bombshell's* capitulation, Cooke maintained a steady headway with the *Albemarle,* all the while surrounded by the Federal double-enders. Their heavy shells

Chart of the action in Albemarle Sound

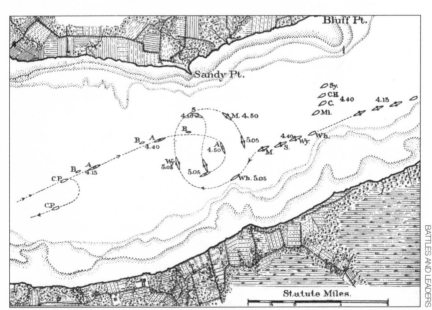

continued to batter the ironclad, but miraculously, the *Albemarle's* two guns continued to hammer away at her antagonists. Thick gray smoke from the guns, mixing with the black smoke from the throbbing engines, made it almost impossible to see anything outside the casemate, and sweating Confederate gunners were forced to aim at the flashes of the enemy's guns. Whenever a port was uncovered, rifle and pistol balls poured through the opening, splintering the wood backing and ricocheting dangerously throughout the gundeck. Cooke had another concern. With so many shot holes in the smokestack, the draft was affected, and steam pressure was beginning to drop.[15]

Dealing with the *Bombshell* had caused the *Sassacus* to drift about three hundred to four hundred yards away from the *Albemarle*. The ship's log noted: "During this time, the ram had kept up an intermittent fire on us and the other vessels, and had swung around presenting her broadside to us, when seeing that we had room to gather headway, and a good opportunity to strike her, [we] rang four bells again and started for her [at] full speed, working our battery as long as we could train, and pouring into him solid and chilled-end shots."[16]

Plumes of spray curled from both sides of her bow, and smoke poured from her stack as her big side-wheels drove the 1,173-ton *Sassacus* straight for the side of the *Albemarle* at almost twelve knots. From his station inside the pilothouse, Cooke could see her coming. She was headed for his starboard beam, just where the aft end of the casemate joined the hull. Fearing that the *Sassacus* might be carrying a spar torpedo, alarm bells were rung, and the men rushed to their escape positions near the hatches. Cooke shouted for full steam ahead, and someone else sang out, "Stand by small arms and repel boarders!" Eight men ran out the damaged aft gun and, with only seconds to spare, sighted it on the onrushing Federal. Frantically, the helmsman spun the wheel to meet the collision, but it was too late.

At 5:05 p.m., with an explosive buckling of wood and scraping iron, the *Sassacus* slammed into the *Albemarle*. Confederate sailors were thrown from their feet and hurled against the side of the casemate. Oil lamps in the passageways below went out, and water poured through the starboard ports as the *Albemarle* heeled over to an alarming angle. Cooke, standing in the forward hatch, was hurled roughly to the deck, and although badly shaken, he seemed otherwise uninjured. Some of the men feared the ironclad was sinking and left their stations, but Master William P. Hamilton and his crew clawed their way back to the Brooke rifle that they had aimed. With the jagged muzzle only a few feet away from the *Sassacus,* Hamilton couldn't miss. Surgeon Edgar Holden on board the Union vessel saw it coming: "Through the starboard shutter, which had been jarred off by the concussion, I saw the port of the ram not ten feet away. It opened, and like a flash of lightning I saw the grim muzzle of a cannon, the gun's crew naked to the waist and blackened with powder; then a blaze, a roar and the rush of the shell as it crashed through, whirling me around and dashing me to the deck."[17]

The commander of the *Sassacus,* Lt. Cmdr. Francis A. Roe, wrote in his report:

> The collision was pretty heavy and the ram careened a good deal, so much so that the water washed over her deck forward and aft the casemate. At one time I thought she was going down. I kept the engine going, pushing, as I hoped, deeper and deeper into her, and also hoping it might be possible for some one of the boats to get up on the opposite side of me and perhaps enable us to sink her, or at least to get well on to her on all sides. I retained this position for a full ten minutes, throwing grenades down her deck hatch and trying in vain to get powder into her smokestack, and receiving volleys of musketry.[18]

The "volleys" of musketry were being fired by Frank P. O'Brien and Mortie Williams, who had precariously positioned themselves on top of the casemate. In spite of the shattered bow of the *Sassacus* pushing the starboard side of the *Albemarle* under water, Cooke managed to maintain headway with the ironclad. The frenzied gun crews, ankle deep in water, tried desperately to load and fire the Brookes, but the severe slant of the deck prevented them from aiming the guns. Down below, in the darkened furnace room, firemen labored to keep the fires burning. With so many shot holes in the funnel, the draft was dying, and engineers watched apprehensively as the steam pressure in the gauges dropped. Gradually the *Albe-*

marle was being forced around and toward the starboard side of the *Sassacus*. Seeing this, Cooke ordered pilot Hopkins to throw the tiller hard aport. This action swung the *Albemarle's* stern to port, and the bow of the *Sassacus* began to slide aft. At this moment Cooke ordered all ahead slow, and within a few seconds, the *Albemarle* was free.

Continuing in a starboard arc, Cooke found that he was nearly parallel to the *Sassacus* and only a few feet away. The forward gun had already been pivoted to starboard, and angry Confederate gunners heaved vigorously on the tackle. The gun slammed against its forward stops, and almost instantly, with a thunderous roar, it fired. The muzzle of the gun was so close the blast scorched the paint on the *Sassacus* as the shot tore through the Union ship, smashing frames, bulkheads, and exploding the starboard boiler. Instantly the shrill scream of escaping steam and boiling water drowned out the roar of the guns as the scalding vapor enveloped the entire vessel. Every man in the fireroom was grievously scalded, and one coal handler was killed instantly. For several minutes the *Sassacus* was totally enveloped in smoke and steam; Cooke was convinced she was sinking.

On board the stricken Federal warship, Surgeon Holden remembered: "The shouts of command and the cries of scalded, wounded,

At almost twelve knots, the *Sassacus* slams into the *Albemarle*.

NAVAL HISTORICAL CENTER

NAVAL HISTORICAL CENTER

When the *Sassacus* rammed the *Albemarle,* water poured through the starboard aft gunport. Hamilton's crew struggled back to their gun and fired point-blank into the Federal ship.

and blinded men mingled with the rattle of small-arms that told of a hand-to-hand conflict above. The ship surged heavily to port as the great weight of the water in the boilers was expended, and over the cry, 'The ship is sinking!' came the shout, "all hands, repel boarders on starboard bow!'"[19]

Cooke ordered the *Albemarle* alongside, and about twenty-five men assembled on the forward deck with pistols and cutlasses in hand. Seeing that the decks, spars, and other open areas on the *Sassacus* were crowded with armed sailors and marines, Cooke wisely ordered his men back inside the casemate. Continuing to fire gamely at the *Albemarle,* the *Sassacus* drifted down the sound, her engines continuing to run for a few minutes on vacuum alone. Soon they stopped, and being completely disabled, she anchored off Bluff Point. The *Albemarle,* her steam pressure barely turning the screws, continued to labor up the sound toward the mouth of the Roanoke at five knots while her exhausted gunners maintained a sporadic fire against the remaining Union vessels.

Once the *Sassacus* had drifted out of the fight, the *Miami*, with her bow-mounted torpedo, attempted to ram the *Albemarle*, but a well-placed shot from the ironclad nearly disabled her rudder, and she became unmanageable. Before breaking off her attack, however, the *Miami* unleashed a tremendous broadside utilizing all of her guns. The damaged *Miami* dropped anchor, but next came the *Wyalusing*, and then the *Commodore Hull*, each vessel pounding the slow-moving *Albemarle* at no more than a ship's length.[20]

It was now past 6:30 p.m., and evening shadows began to stretch across the waters of the sound. The *Albemarle* continued her painful course toward the sanctuary of the Roanoke River, all the while subjected to the harassing fire of the trailing Union vessels. Cooke realized that if the ironclad became dead in the water, the Federal vessels would close in, ram, and destroy her. But with the riddled smokestack, the once blazing fires were quickly becoming smoldering heaps of ashes. Steam pressure in the twin boilers was so low she was barely making five knots, and this speed was dropping. To make matters worse, the tiller ropes had parted, and while the ironclad steamed an erratic course, mechanics worked feverishly in the dark hull to splice the ropes back together.

Her deck enveloped in steam, the severely damaged *Sassacus* rounds the stern of the *Albemarle* as the Union warships struggle to head down the sound.

NAVAL HISTORICAL CENTER

It was absolutely imperative that, somehow, steam pressure be raised. If coal would not burn, they would try wood. Cooke passed the order to all hands, and axes and sledge hammers were wielded against bulkheads, doors, cabin furniture, interior casemate planking, and any interior structure that could be knocked loose. The shattered pieces were fed into the furnaces but would not burn for lack of a draft. Steam pressure was down to where the propellers were barely turning, when some enterprising individual suggested casting the ship's supply of bacon, ham, and lard onto the smoldering embers. Knowing that these materials needed no upward draft to burn, sailors raced to the ship's pantry and began carrying armloads of the foodstuffs to the fire room. Soon, to the cracking sound and the tantalizing aroma of sizzling ham and bacon, the needles in the steam gauges began to quiver upward. With steam pressure rising, her twin screws were again driving her forward, and Cooke directed that the course be maintained to the mouth of the Roanoke.[21]

By 7:30 p.m. the *Albemarle* had reached the entrance to the river, and Cooke ordered her brought about. The Confederate ironclad sat motionless on the dark waters of the sound. Steam hissed gently from her escape valves as the sweet-smelling scent of bacon wafted across the evening breeze. Facing her in the lowering shadows, but hesitant to continue the attack, were the *Ceres* and the *Commodore Hull*. Farther down the sound Cooke could see at anchor the lights of the *Miami,* the *Wyalusing,* the *Whitehead,* and the *Mattabesett.* As the *Albemarle* sat facing her antagonists, the bow port shutter clanged open, and the forward Brooke rifle trundled out. Suddenly, with a thunderous roar, it belched forth a shaft of flame and sent a final parting shot streaking in the direction of the Federal vessels. The Union guns did not reply. Sluggishly, agonizingly, the ironclad turned against the current and began pushing slowly up the Roanoke toward Plymouth. Progress was difficult, for a piece of armor plate had been knocked loose from her bow and now hung down into the water, counteracting the movements of the rudder. Finally, at 2:00 a.m., the battered and still smoking *Albemarle* was tied to the dock at Plymouth. The battle of Albemarle Sound was over.[22]

13

WILMINGTON AND THE CAPE FEAR

THE THUNDERING GUNS HAD fallen silent over Albemarle Sound for only a day when, during the late afternoon of May 6, 1864, the CSS *Raleigh* dropped her anchor in the chill waters of the Cape Fear River below Wilmington. The frowning ramparts of Fort Fisher, which towered off the port side, were lined with curious soldiers seeking a closer look at the Wilmington Squadron's latest ironclad. Peering over the torpedo boom on the bow, her skipper, 1st Lt. J. Pembroke Jones, could see the breakers across the bar, and several Federal warships beyond. Two small wooden gunboats, the CSS *Equator* and the CSS *Yadkin,* had also anchored near the *Raleigh.* Behind the Confederate vessels, several sleek blockade-runners, heavily laden with cotton bales, awaited an opportunity to escape the port. Jones was impatiently waiting for darkness to spread its mantle over New Inlet, at which time he intended to launch an attack upon the Union warships offshore. Whether in support of the operations of the *Albemarle* and the offensive against New Bern, or perhaps the beginning of escort operations for departing blockade-runners, Jones's intent is unknown. It would be the only offensive action taken by the Confederate navy in defense of Wilmington.

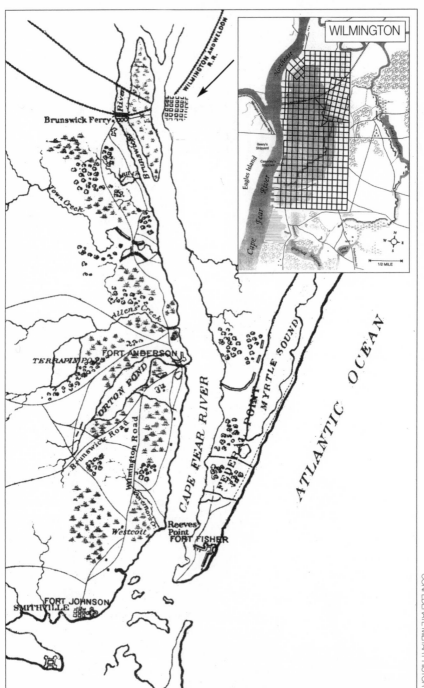

WILMINGTON

WILMINGTON ANDWELDON R.R.

Brunswick Ferry

Town Creek

Allens' Creek

TERRAPIN PO

FORT ANDERSON

ORTON POND

Brunswick Road

Wilmington Road

Westcott

Reeves
Point
FORT FISHER

FEDERAL POINT

MYRTLE SOUND

CAPE FEAR RIVER

ATLANTIC OCEAN

FORT JOHNSON
SMITHVILLE

Northeast

Eagles Island

Beery's Shipyard

Cassidey's Shipyard

Cape Fear River

1/2 MILE

Not long after the opening of hostilities, it became evident to the government in Richmond, as well as to state officials in Raleigh, that Wilmington would occupy a position of paramount importance in the new nation's struggle for independence. By early 1863 Wilmington, situated twenty miles upstream from the mouth of the Cape Fear River, had become the most important and accessible port for blockade-runners. Its relative close proximity to the war front in Virginia and the difficulty of blockading the two entrances to the river made it an ideal port for the fast steamers coming from the Bahamas or Bermuda. Old Inlet to the south and New Inlet to the east were separated by Smith Island, and with the ten-mile-long island dividing the two inlets, Federal blockaders had to cover an arc of approximately fourteen miles.

In an effort to keep the blockaders at bay and to protect the runners when entering and leaving Wilmington, the Confederate army had constructed numerous earthen fortifications at the mouth of the river and along the eastern and western shores. The most prominent of these was massive Fort Fisher, situated at the tip of what formally had been called Federal Point but renamed, for obvious reasons, Confederate Point. The Confederate navy would play an important role in the defense of Fort Fisher near the end of the war, but it is the building of the Wilmington Squadron, including two ironclads, the CSS *Raleigh* and the CSS *North Carolina,* that is of interest here.

With the disasters that befell eastern North Carolina in 1861 and 1862, Wilmington and the Cape Fear region were included in the plan to build warships that could defend the inland waters of the state. While much confidence was placed in the forts downriver, especially Fort Fisher then under hurried construction, it was acknowledged that a naval force would be necessary in the event the Federals were able to force their way upriver. This possibility took on added significance when Adm. David G. Farragut forced his way past the forts guarding New Orleans on April 24, 1862. The only naval vessels at Wilmington of any significance at the time were the *Uncle Ben,* a converted tug, and the *Arctic,* which had previously served as the lightship stationed near Frying Pan Shoals. With these facts in mind, when the contracts were negotiated for the *Albemarle,* the *Neuse,* and the unnamed ironclad on the

Tar River, contracts were also signed for two ironclads to be constructed at Wilmington.

Two weeks after the climactic battle in Hampton Roads between the *Virginia* and the *Monitor,* Secretary Stephen R. Mallory sent specific "instructions relative to gunboats" to Cmdr. William T. Muse, commander of Confederate naval forces at Wilmington. In June 1862 the keels for two ironclads were laid.[1]

Although the Tarheel State's largest seaport was smaller than all other deep-water ports along the Confederate coast, Wilmington and the defense thereof was vital not only to North Carolina but to the whole Confederacy. With the loss of New Orleans and Norfolk and the tightening blockade around such ports as Savannah, Charleston, and Mobile, Wilmington took on added importance. By the middle of 1863 Wilmington would be the only port where blockade-runners had a reasonable chance of eluding the blockaders.

Wilmington had never earned the reputation of a shipbuilding center, but in the years prior to the war numerous vessels for the Cape Fear River trade had been built here. Close to twenty-seven

Site of the Cassidey Shipyard in Wilmington as it appears today and (inset) a nearby historical marker

HENRY HARRIS

small ships had been constructed between 1815 and 1860, seven of these being steamers. By the beginning of the war, two shipyards were deemed capable of building warships for the Confederate navy.[2]

One of these was the shipyard of James Cassidey, a native of Massachusetts who had been building boats at his yard at the foot of Church Street for almost twenty years. On behalf of the Confederate navy, Cassidey began work on a Richmond-class ironclad—to be commissioned as the CSS *Raleigh*—in June 1862. The second and larger shipyard was owned and operated by brothers W. L. and B. W. Beery and situated across the Cape Fear on Eagles Island. Beery's shipyard—which would construct the Richmond-class ironclad CSS *North Carolina* and the gunboat *Yadkin,* plus several torpedo boats, and had another ironclad, the CSS *Wilmington,* on the ways at the end of the war—would most often be referred to as the Navy Yard.

Unlike the construction sites at Edwards Ferry and White Hall, Wilmington enjoyed the presence of one of the most modern iron foundries in the state. The Hart and Bailey ironworks included copper, machine, and pattern shops as well as a foundry. During the war

Present-day view of the Beery Shipyard site on Eagles Island as seen from the Wilmington side of the Cape Fear River and (*inset*) a nearby historical marker

R. THOMAS CAMPBELL (INCLUDING INSET IMAGES)

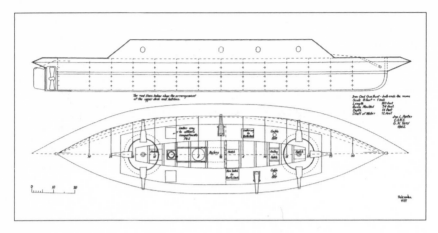

John L. Porter's plans for a Richmond-class ironclad were the blueprint for both the CSS *North Carolina* and the CSS *Raleigh*.

they cast wrought iron stern posts, port shutters, stanchions, davits, and torpedo spars in addition to machinery parts such as gauges, steam pipes, couplings, spikes, screws, bolts, nails, and steel washers. Hart and Bailey was one of the limited number of shops in the Confederacy that could forge heavy propeller shafts, producing shafts for the *North Carolina* and modifying those for the *Yadkin*. Evidence indicates that it may have also built the engines for the *Yadkin* plus miscellaneous parts such as boiler iron, grate bars, flues, flue plugs, and smokestacks. Hart and Bailey also manufactured torpedoes and drilled the iron plates that were then shipped to the *Neuse* at White Hall.

Another prominent facility at Wilmington was the foundry established by Thomas E. Roberts. The Roberts Foundry built many of the same items as Hart and Bailey but was especially involved with the building and installation of the machinery in the *Raleigh*. In addition to the *Raleigh*, the Roberts Foundry also drilled and fitted many of the iron plates for the *Neuse*. Certainly with the manufacturing facilities available, the task of building ironclads at Wilmington looked very bright. Such, however, proved not to be the case.[3]

Of all the Confederate navy squadrons, information concerning the Wilmington Squadron is the most elusive. Very few Southern navy reports referring to the Wilmington area have survived, and one is left to speculate as why the Confederate navy had such a poor record in regard to ironclad construction at this location. Most historians agree that the *North Carolina* and the *Raleigh* were two of the most poorly constructed ironclads in the Confederacy. One is at a loss to explain why shipbuilding here was so mediocre compared to the comparatively superlative qualities of the *Albemarle* and the *Neuse* that were constructed under much more primitive circumstances. One is led to the conclusion that the shipyards of Cassidey and Beery did not exercise the same standards of quality control that Gilbert Elliott and the partners Thomas S. Howard and Elijah W. Ellis applied to the construction of the *Albemarle* and the *Neuse*.[4]

The shortage of acceptable materials, especially seasoned timber, seemed to affect shipbuilding at Wilmington more than elsewhere in North Carolina. A ready supply of seasoned lumber was generally not available anywhere in the Confederacy, and the hulls of Southern ironclads, out of necessity, had to be constructed from green timber. Much of the seasoned timber that was available at the beginning of the war was burned when the Confederates evacuated Norfolk in May 1862. As a result, both the Beery and Cassidey shipyards used green timber in all of their construction throughout the war. This greatly affected the Wilmington ironclads, particularly the *North Carolina*. Soon after the *North Carolina* was launched the hull timbers began to warp and split. Generous amounts of oakum and cotton

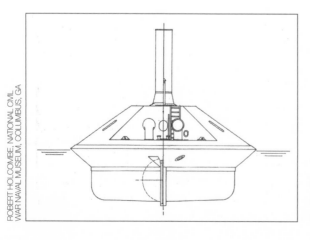

ROBERT HOLCOMBE, NATIONAL CIVIL WAR NAVAL MUSEUM, COLUMBUS, GA

This drawing of Porter's Richmond-class design offers a split rear (*left half*) and front (*right half*) view.

were used in a vain attempt to seal her leaks. Finally, pumps had to be manned constantly just to keep the ironclad afloat.[5]

Like the *Albemarle* and the *Neuse*, the *Raleigh* and the *North Carolina* were designed by John L. Porter. They were, however, larger than their North Carolina cousins, designed along the lines of what historians have defined as the Richmond class. Each was 172 feet 6 inches in length, 34 feet abeam, and had a draft of approximately 12 feet. Their displacement was around 850 tons, and their woefully inadequate speed was between five and six knots. Their armored 105-foot casemates were protected by 4 inches of iron plates, and because of their larger size, both carried six guns rather than four. Surviving records are not clear, but it is believed that the *North Carolina* carried two 7-inch Brooke rifles in forward and after pivots and two 6.4-inch Brookes in broadside. The *Raleigh* was armed with a 9-inch smoothbore, probably in the aft pivot position, and a 7-inch Brooke rifle in the forward position. Like the *North Carolina,* the broadside guns were 6.4-inch Brooke rifles. Both vessels were designed to be powered by two engines driving a single propeller.[6]

In spite of facilities such as Hart and Bailey, Roberts Foundry, and others, the Wilmington ironclads suffered from the same shortages of construction material and skilled labor as other Confederate ironclads. Supplies of green timber near Wilmington were soon exhausted, and the navy experienced great difficulty transporting needed timber from forests inland. In addition to the transportation problem, when timber did arrive, much of it was commandeered by the army for the building of fortifications around Wilmington. The Beery shipyard obtained much of its timber from an area west of Wilmington near Laurinburg. One of the brothers wrote, "We find it extremely difficult getting it elsewhere, as upon the watercourses the timber cannot be had."[7]

In addition to the supply of timber, another problem for the Wilmington shipyards appeared in the fall of 1862. Soon after the blockade-runner *Kate* docked at the city wharves, a shipyard worker was mistakenly diagnosed as having jaundice. He soon died, and within a short time fifteen workers near the yard were also dead. Authorities then realized to their horror that the *Kate* had brought dreaded yellow fever to Wilmington. A mass exodus to the countryside ensued, including most, if not all, of the carpenters and mechanics working on the *North Carolina* and *Raleigh*. Between October 20 and the middle of November, 710 people died from the epidemic. Even though cold weather put an end to the outbreak by the end of November, most ship carpenters did not return until January, further delaying the progress on the two ironclads.[8]

While seasoned timber was not to be had, iron needed for the fabrication of machinery and machine parts, on the other hand, was more easily obtainable for the Wilmington facilities than other construction sites in North Carolina. Iron ore and coal were mined along the Deep River Basin in the central part of the state and transported to Wilmington via the numerous watercourses that led to the city. This lessened the burden on the rail system, but there were never enough barges or flats to facilitate the timely transport of these raw materials to Wilmington. In addition, the output of the Deep River mines was never that great, and what they did produce was quickly absorbed by military and naval construction. Nevertheless, the Wilmington foundries such as Hart and Bailey and the Thomas Foundry operated consistently throughout the war.

The supply of iron needed for the fabrication of armor plate, however, was never sufficient and caused significant delays in the completion of the *Raleigh*. The navy contracted for and purchased used rails for the purpose of rolling them into armor plate from the Wilmington and Weldon as well as the Wilmington and Manchester Railroads. Two-inch armor plate was rolled from these rails at the Tredegar Iron Works in Richmond and Scofield and Markham's Iron Works in Atlanta, but the *Albemarle,* and to a lesser extent the *Neuse,* received much of this iron. Nevertheless, during the early part of 1863, the *North Carolina* finally began receiving some of her armor plate, but additional armor that was destined for the *Raleigh* was instead diverted to Charleston in response to a buildup of Federal forces there.

Capt. William F. Lynch, who was now in command of all of the naval defenses of North Carolina, sent a staff officer to meet with the superintendent of the Wilmington Charlotte and Rutherfordton Railroad in an effort to expedite the shipment of rails to Atlanta. The railroad promised much but little was accomplished. In exasperation

Lynch wrote Governor Zebulon B. Vance urging that the North
Carolina chief executive use his influence to force the railroad to
comply. Finally the company shipped the rails, but as a consequence
of this dawdling the completion of the Wilmington ironclads was seriously delayed.[9]

A skilled labor shortage was another disadvantage that affected
both the Beery and Cassidey shipyards. The two yards competed
with other areas within the Confederacy for skilled shipbuilders and
competed with each other. Although both facilities offered higher
wages than other locations in the South, they failed to attract the
necessary workers. Their failure was due in part to the seasonal
threat of yellow fever. When the epidemic struck in the fall of 1862,
the labor force at the Cassidey yard fell by 65 percent, and 70 percent
of the workers at the Beery shipyard fled the city. Even with the advent of cold weather, many skilled workers hesitated to return.

In spite of the enormous difficulties in acquiring men and materials, the ironclads slowly neared completion. Worn-out engines
from the *Uncle Ben* were removed and installed in the *North Carolina.* In a letter to Governor Vance on May 14, 1853, Lynch reported
that the *North Carolina* had been launched, her battery was aboard,
and she was ready for her officers and crew. The Beery-built ironclad
was officially commissioned into the Confederate navy on June 10,
1863. The presence of Wilmington's first ironclad eased Lynch's concerns regarding the defense of the Cape Fear, and he ordered Cmdr.
William T. Muse to take the *North Carolina* downriver to Smithville
where it could cooperate with the forts guarding the two inlets into
the river.

The *North Carolina*'s maiden voyage in July, however, was not
without incident. In spite of pilot Thomas Garrison's best efforts,
the twelve-foot draft of the *North Carolina* was too great for the
Cape Fear River, and the ironclad soon ran aground. The tide was
running out, and with darkness approaching, the armored warship
became stranded for the night. The next morning, as the river rose,
she finally floated free, and Muse continued his slow course down
the river.

Her maiden voyage would not be the first time the *North Carolina* would run aground in the Cape Fear. Her deep draft was simply

too much, and subsequent trips up and down the river usually resulted in several groundings. In addition, numerous leaks soon appeared as the green timbers of her hull began to warp, and crewmen reported difficulty working the guns due to the unevenness of the gundeck. The situation became so serious that, in December, Lynch ordered the removal of the deck armor forward of the casemate in an effort to keep the vessel from "hogging," that is, to bow up in the middle and sag at the ends. In a letter to Muse on December 27, he wrote: "I have sent Superintendent [Hugh] Lindsay with a gang of mechanics for the purpose of taking up the plate-iron on the deck forward of the shield, for the purpose of bringing the ship near an even keel. Be pleased to give them every facility and let them have their dinners on board."[10]

In spite of her limitations, the *North Carolina* continued to occupy her position opposite Smithville during the summer and fall and into the new year of 1864, thus adding measurably to the defenses of Wilmington. At last, the Wilmington Squadron of the Confederate navy had a respectable presence in the Cape Fear region.[11]

Meanwhile, work was progressing slowly on the squadron's second ironclad, which languished in the Cassidey yard for lack of armor plate. Lynch had determined that the *Albemarle* and *Neuse* were of a higher priority, and much of the iron plate rolled for the *Raleigh* had been diverted to them.

Progress was so behind schedule that Brig. Gen. William H. C. Whiting, district commander, wrote on April 21, 1863, to Secretary of War James A. Seddon: "Please ask the Secretary of the Navy if he will lend me the armament of the *Raleigh, especially* the Brooke rifles, until she is ready to use them. She will not be ready for at least three months and during that time I may be attacked and these guns would be of incalculable service in the defense."

On April 25 Mallory answered the general: "Knowing your want of heavy guns, I would have sent you the *Raleigh's* battery before had it been ready; but two of the guns designed for her are anywhere near ready. They will be sent with ammunition and equipments in a few days. They are 11,000-pound, double-banded Brooke 6.4-inch guns, whose penetration, as shown by our iron targets, equals that of the 7-inch. Their bolts weigh 90 pounds."

Whether Whiting received his guns or not is unknown. Sometime during the spring of 1864, the CSS *Raleigh* was finally completed, and in April she was commissioned with 1st Lt. J. Pembroke Jones of Virginia appointed as her commander. Jones had seen service on the James River at Richmond and at Savannah where he had commanded the floating battery *Georgia* and the Richmond class ironclad *Savannah*.

Now that the *Raleigh* and the *North Carolina* were operational, Lynch felt he had an opportunity to prove the usefulness of the navy at Wilmington. The squadron had been much criticized for its inability to drive off the blockaders and its incapacity to protect blockade-runners when entering or leaving the port. Lynch hoped to utilize a squib-class torpedo boat being built at the Beery yard to attack the blockaders, but it and an army boat were both destroyed on April 26 when a fire broke out in the government cotton yard on Eagle Island. After consuming numerous warehouses, twenty-five railroad cars, and large quantities of baled cotton, the flames spread to the Beery yard, destroying the saw mill, a quantity of cut timber, and the two torpedo boats.[12]

While the *North Carolina* with her weak engines and leaky hull could not be used in offensive operations, the newly completed *Raleigh* offered Lynch that opportunity. Obtaining a crew for the *Raleigh*, however, presented a problem. Lynch solved this by pulling most of the men from the *North Carolina*, leaving her with only a skeleton crew, barely enough to work one gun. Lynch and Jones spent approximately two weeks training the men on the *Raleigh*, and once the final ordnance stores arrived, they were ready.

The two Confederate commanders watched impatiently on the late afternoon of May 6 as the sun sank below the western horizon. Calling down to the engine room, Jones ordered the engineers to begin raising steam. Behind the *Raleigh* several blockade-runners also began preparations for departure. Some had been waiting several days for the right conditions. By previous arrangement two small gunboats, the *Yadkin* and the *Equator,* would accompany the *Raleigh* on her attack against the Federal blockaders. With darkness now settling over New Inlet, Jones and Lynch were ready.

A little after 8:00 p.m., utilizing red, green, and white lights set

NAVAL HISTORICAL CENTER

The CSS *Richmond* was the first of its type. The *North Carolina* and *Raleigh* were similar in design.

by Fort Fisher, the *Raleigh* crossed the bar at New Inlet, and Jones ordered a course straight for the USS *Britannia* offshore. The *Britannia* was a 495-ton side-wheel steamer mounting one 30-pounder rifle, two 12-pounder rifles, and two 24-pounder rifles. The captain of the Federal warship, Lt. Samuel Huse, had been watching the Confederate ironclad, and in his report gave a vivid description of the *Raleigh*'s initial attack:

> At about 8:30 she turned directly for this ship, in company with another vessel, and ran at full speed. I fired several rockets and fired my 30-pounder Parrott at her, but she kept on directly after us. I ran for the buoy, firing at her with [our] 24-pounder howitzer. She then commenced firing at us; the first shot put out our binnacle lights, and the next went a little over the starboard paddle box, sounding very like a 100-pounder Parrott shot when it tumbles. We now burned a blue light, [for assistance] when the enemy fired again. Our course was changed three times, hoping to elude him, but he followed and gained on us considerably, being within about 600 yards when we passed the buoy, at which time we hauled up short N. E. and think he went on E. S. E., as we shortly after heard a gun in that direction.[13]

The *Britannia* had run into shallow water in order to escape. Jones wisely broke off the engagement and turned to look for other blockaders. He was in no hurry. The confusion caused by the attack on the *Britannia* was enough to allow the blockade-runners to escape, and Jones would be more cunning in the selection of his next target. Even though the night was very dark with no moon, several Federal warships could be discerned silhouetted against the eastern horizon, and Jones ordered a slow advance toward the nearest.

She proved to be the USS *Nansemond,* a 335-ton side-wheel steamer commanded by Ens. J. H. Porter with one 30-pounder and two 24-pounder rifles. Around 11:45 p.m. the *Nansemond* discovered the ghostly shape of the Confederate ironclad lying only a few hundred yards off her bow. The Federal warship got under way and advanced toward the shape, believing it might be a blockade-runner attempting to escape. When only a few yards away, the *Nansemond* flashed a light that Jones answered by displaying a white light. This was not, however, the agreed Federal signal for the night, and Porter became even more suspicious. Jones quietly ordered full speed ahead, and as the *Raleigh* crossed the *Nansemond*'s bow the Federal captain had to put his helm hard astarboard to avoid collision. The Federal flashed the challenge light again, and Jones this time, adding to the suspense, flashed a red light. By this time the *Raleigh* had turned and was headed directly for the Union ship. Porter flashed his light a third time, then convinced that this was an enemy, he ordered one of his 24-pounder howitzers to fire.

First Lt. J. Pembroke Jones

VIRGINIA HISTORICAL SOCIETY

Suddenly there was a crimson flash on the bow of the approaching "blockade-runner," blinding those on the *Nansemond* looking in her direction. Within seconds a 6.4-inch Brooke rifled bolt whistled low over the Federal's walking beam and splashed hissing into the ocean beyond. With the *Raleigh* now less than five hundred yards away and closing rapidly, a second shot soon followed, this one too whining just over the startled Federal warship. Porter was no coward, and he banged away with his lonely howitzer while the two ships approached one another in opposite directions. As they passed, Porter stood by the rail and could clearly see the outline of the *Raleigh's* casemate and the white water thrown up by her churning propeller. Before the Federal commander could turn his ship, the *Raleigh* loosed another thunderous shot, it too being aimed high. With that, she disappeared into the gloom of the Atlantic darkness.[14]

Jones had stealthily brought the *Raleigh* within easy range of the enemy, but his crew's lack of experience and the excitement of the moment had caused the shots to be wild. He had missed a great opportunity.

The USS *Howquah,* commanded by Acting Master J. W. Balch, had been busy all night steaming to and from each gun flash and rocket sighting, but so far she had seen nothing. Finally, at 4:25 a.m., just as the eastern sky began to lighten with the coming dawn, Balch spotted the *Raleigh* on a bearing of "N. W. by N. in a line with Fort Fisher (burning soft coal), distant 1¼ miles." Jones, too, had noticed the *Howquah,* and with black smoke pouring from the ironclad's funnel, he had the *Raleigh* steaming directly toward her at more than six knots. The *Howquah* turned, firing as she did, and ran for the open sea, just as the *Raleigh* unleashed a screaming shot from her bow pivot. The shell exploded into the sea just off the Union ship's starboard quarter. Jones swung the *Raleigh* left and right to give his broadside guns a shot. One final shot tore through the *Howquah's* smokestack, leaving a gaping and jagged hole.[15]

By now other Federal warships were racing to the scene and firing from long range, their shots, however, falling short. Marine Lt. Henry M. Doak was in charge of the *Raleigh's* starboard guns and recorded in his memoirs his remembrance of this moment:

During the engagement a fifteen-inch shell exploded on or just over a seven-inch iron grating over my post between my two guns—inciting a momentary fear that Atlas had carelessly dropped this planet. Receiving an order for my starboard gun to stand by for the next light, I threw a shell into Ft. Fisher and was promptly ordered under arrest by Admiral Lynch. Capt. Pembroke Jones, commanding the *Raleigh* convinced the Flag Officer that the next light had gone by, leaving Ft. Fisher showing the next light by the time I received the order. I was promptly restored to duty.

In the dense gloom I barely missed the stern of Capt. Steele's blockade runner, *Will-o'-the-Wisp,* which only escaped through its extraordinary speed. We had cleared the offing of fifteen wooden blockaders. At daybreak they formed a circle and bore down upon us. A few shots from our long-range rifle guns soon showed the folly of attacking a great well-armed ironclad. Next day Admiral Lynch notified the British consul that we had raised the blockade. It did us no good—the British government having at that time other views of international law—a fact I failed to realize until a much later reading of British law. We had done all we proposed—and our prow was turned homeward.[16]

Slowly Jones turned the ironclad's head back toward the bar and the entrance to the river. As the *Raleigh* approached, the *Yadkin* and *Equator* stood ready to escort her into the safety of the Cape Fear. With the national ensign at her stern and the navy jack snapping at her bow, the *Raleigh* returned triumphantly to the cheers of soldiers gathered along the shore. As she passed over the bar and turned upriver, she was greeted by a booming nine-gun salute from Fort Fisher. Evidence indicates that as many as six blockade-runners— *Edith, Index, Lucy, Thistle, Will-o'-the-Wisp,* and *Young Republic*—may have successfully escaped, and one, the *Annie,* had safely arrived during the commotion caused by the *Raleigh's* operation.[17] Jones and his crew must have been extremely proud.[18]

The bright spring morning of Saturday, May 7, 1864, was a crowning moment for the Confederate navy in the waters of eastern North Carolina. At Plymouth the *Albemarle* was undergoing repairs after sinking a Union warship, assisting in the recapture of the town, and causing severe damage to several other Federal warships in Albemarle Sound. While she had been forced to return to Plymouth, she still presented a serious threat to Federal forces and a deterrent to further Union incursions along the Roanoke River. Near Kinston the *Neuse,* momentarily aground on a sandbar in the Neuse River, awaited the arrival of the spring freshet. The water was rising, and it was just a matter of days until she would be free. Incapacitated as she was at the moment, she still presented a serious threat and an obstacle to Union plans in the region. And at Wilmington, the *North Carolina* stood guard off Smithville, and the *Raleigh* had scattered and disrupted the Federal blockading fleet. Within a few days, weeks, and months, however, all of this would change. But considering the shortage of materials, the scarcity of skilled shipbuilders, and numerous other adversities, the Confederate navy by the morning of May 7, 1864, had achieved nothing short of miracles in the waters of eastern North Carolina.

14

THE LOSS OF THE IRONCLADS

A FTER SUCCESSFULLY, IF ONLY momentarily, scattering the Federal blockading fleet on May 6–7, 1864, off Wilmington, the *Raleigh* returned through New Inlet and turned downriver. Then tragedy struck.

Whether by sheer accident or gross carelessness, she ground to a crunching halt on a sandbar. As the water level in the river continued to fall, her bow remained fast on the sandbar while her stern floated free. The weight of her armor not being supported amidships was too much for her green timber, and her keel snapped. In an instant, the pride of the Confederate navy at Wilmington was a broken wreck. A few days later a visitor to the scene remarked, "She was very much sunken at the stern, lifting her bow considerably . . . altogether she had the appearance of a monstrous turtle stranded and forlorn."

So much time and Herculean effort had gone into her construction, so many workers had struggled day and night with inadequate means and materials to finish her, so successful in her first foray to disrupt the blockading fleet—and all for nothing. Only the leaky and worm-eaten *North Carolina* and a couple of small gunboats remained of the Wilmington Squadron. J. Pembroke Jones and William F. Lynch must have been overcome with embarrassment, grief, and frustration.

Jones requested a court of inquiry, and on June 6 the court, sitting at Wilmington, published its findings:

> The court having inquired into all the facts connected with the loss of the C. S. S. *Raleigh* in the waters of North Carolina, have the honor to report the same, together with our opinion upon the points in which it is required by the precept.
>
> In the opinion of the court, the loss of the *Raleigh* can not be attributed to negligence or inattention on the part of anyone on board of her, and every effort was made to save said vessel. We further find that the *Raleigh* could have remained outside the bar of Cape Fear River for a few hours with apparent safety, but, in the opinion of the court, it would have been improper; and, in view of all the circumstances, "her commanding officer was justified in attempting to go back into the harbor when he did."
>
> It is further the opinion of the court that the draft of water of the *Raleigh* was too great, even lightened as she had been on this occasion, to render her passage of the bar, except under favorable circumstances, a safe operation, particularly as her strength seems to have been insufficient to enable her to sustain the weight of armor long enough to permit every practicable means of lightening her to be exhausted.[1]

Salvage work began soon after the *Raleigh*'s grounding. Her guns were removed and transported to Wilmington. Divers were able to remove her boilers, which were shipped to Columbus, Georgia, where they were installed in the repaired gunboat CSS *Chattahoochee*. The ironclad's engines and propeller shaft, however, remained deep in the broken hull and were never retrieved. Workers salvaged as much of her armor plate as possible, but much toward the stern and along her knuckle had to be left behind. It was a crushing blow for Lynch and the Wilmington Squadron. Mallory rushed chief constructor John L. Porter to Wilmington with orders to spare no expense to construct a new and better ironclad. Lynch's squadron now consisted of the immobile *North Carolina* and several small

wooden gunboats, hardly enough
to offer a serious challenge if the
Federals should attempt a push
into the Cape Fear.

Sadness had also stalked the
decks of the *North Carolina*. On
April 8, just as the *Raleigh* was becoming operational, the *North
Carolina*'s beloved captain, William
Muse, died of typhoid fever. Ship's
surgeon William W. Griggs had reported several cases of the dreaded
disease between March and May,
and one sailor had died just ten
days before Muse. Engineer Charles

Cmdr. William L. Maury

S. Peek wrote that Muse was "loved and respected by all who knew
him."

Mallory sent Cmdr. William L. Maury to replace Muse. Maury
had just returned to the Confederacy after successfully commanding
the commerce-raiding cruiser CSS *Georgia*. Maury created a favor-
able impression on the *North Carolina*'s crew, and soon he was as
much admired as Muse had been.

By the summer of 1864 it was plainly evident that the old *North
Carolina* would not last much longer. Some insight into her condition is provided by engineer E. Alexander Jack, who had been assigned to the *North Carolina* soon after her completion. Jack had
seen extensive service during the war, having served on the CSS *Virginia* during the battles in Hampton Roads and had also made the fa-
mous fighting voyage down the Mississippi on the CSS *Arkansas*.
Long after the war, sometime between 1900 and 1904, Jack wrote a
brief memoir, part of which dealt with his service on the *North Carolina* and her demise:

> I went on board the *North Carolina* as acting chief engineer. My duties
> there were light, for she did little steaming, and was hardly in a condi-
> tion to keep afloat, as the torpedo [worms] had already begun to cut
> her hull. At any rate, we never crossed the bar to attack the enemy, but

stood ready to resist them if they should attempt to enter the river. It was on this vessel that I came nearer than ever before or afterwards, to losing my life. A new assistant engineer was sent on board, and I took him into the engine room to show him how to handle the engine. While handling it myself, I thoughtlessly reached under a moving part, which, descending, caught me in the shoulder, and pressed me down and back upon the floor, so that the engine shaft revolved by the nape of my neck, the eccentric scraped my left ear, and the bar that had thrown me down, pressed upon my breast bone so hard that it broke the skin, and fortunately then took its upward stroke. I got up, stopped the engine and went to bed in a state of nervousness that I have never since experienced. Mr. [Robert S.] Herring, the 3rd assistant [engineer] mentioned, was doing his best to stop the engine, but instead his efforts kept it going. If he had let the handle go that he was pulling on, the engine would have stopped. That was no fault of his though, but due solely to the peculiarity of the mechanism. No one who saw my predicament thought that I would escape alive. I even heard the firemen exclaim, "My God he is killed."

I got over my fright soon and Mr. Herring learned how to work the engine. But the old boiler and the old hull were fast wasting away, and after a while it became necessary to put the vessel ashore to keep her from sinking, and steam had to be kept on the boiler constantly to pump her out. I represented the necessity of having an auxiliary boiler so that the large one might be cleaned and examined, but for some time no attention was paid to my recommendation. At last I prevailed and a boiler was bought and sent down, but before it could he placed in position and connected with the steam pump the large boiler gave out in the furnace so that the fires were put out. Nothing now could keep the ship from filling, and soon we had to abandon her.[2]

Engineer E. Alexander Jack

ALAN B. FLANDERS

The ironclad sank at her moorings in September 1864, with only a portion of her superstructure visible above water. Engineer Charles S. Peek wrote to his family: "The old *North Carolina* is no more. She [was] full of water before I left. The men are now employed taking iron from her." Capt. Robert F. Pinkney, who had succeeded Lynch as naval commander for the Wilmington area, left a small detachment as a guard on board during the month of October, but for all intents and purposes, the *North Carolina's* career, such as it was, was over. During the spring of 1864 the state of North Carolina could boast of four ironclads that stood ready to defend her eastern perimeter. Now, only two remained.

☆   ☆   ☆

On May 6, 1864, as the *Raleigh* steamed down the Cape Fear River preparatory to her attack on the Union blockaders, the morning light at Plymouth revealed to early observers a damaged but still very much intact *Albemarle*. After returning from her battle with the Federals in Albemarle Sound, a careful count disclosed forty-four indentations in her iron plating where enemy shots had found their marks. Several plates were cracked or broken, and one had been purposely cut away on the return trip up the river when it hampered her steering. Five of her gunport shutters were missing, as was the flagstaff, although the colors had been saved. The aft Brooke rifle, which was damaged in the fight, would have to be replaced, but the most serious damage, as events had proven, was to her smokestack that was so riddled that it became totally useless. While externally the ironclad certainly displayed the effects of her three-hour ordeal, the exhausted officers and crew, sleeping late in their hammocks on shore, bore testimony that John H. Porter's design had served them well. Aside from numerous cuts and bruises, there was not one causality among the *Albemarle's* crew.[3]

As the morning sun rose over the broad waters of Albemarle Sound, a frustrated Capt. Melancton Smith surveyed his injured Federal command. While his eight warships had prevented the *Albemarle* from continuing to New Bern, they had failed miserably in their combined attempts to destroy her. In addition, the Federal commander was impressed by the *Albemarle,* as evidenced by a candid paragraph in his official report:

> The ram is certainly very formidable. She is fast for that class of vessel, making from 6 to 7 knots, turns quickly, and is armed with heavy guns as is proved by the 100-pounder Brooke projectile that entered and lodged in the *Mattabesett,* and a 100-pounder Whitworth shot [?] received by the *Wyalusing,* while the shot fired at him were seen to strike fire upon the casemate and hull, flying upward and falling in the water without having had any perceptible effect upon the vessel.[4]

While workmen swarmed over the *Albemarle* to remove and replace her damaged plates, Cmdr. James W. Cooke completed his report to Cmdr. Robert F. Pinkney, who, prior to his command at Wilmington, commanded Cooke's district. Aware that the ironclad's success was entirely dependent upon her crew, he wrote:

> I can not speak too highly of the officers and crew, especially of the following-named men, viz, John Benton, James Cullington, J. B. Cooper, H. A. Kuhn, John Smith, H. P. Hay, Thomas Wroten, John Steely, and T. Nichols. The pilot, J. B. Hopkins, deserves great credit for the manner in which he maneuvered the vessel, and bringing her safely back to port. Since the engagement I have ascertained by flag of truce that there was no one hurt on the *Bombshell.*[5]

It was perhaps fortuitous that the *Albemarle* did not make it to New Bern, for just as Robert F. Hoke's forces arrived outside the fortifications, he received an urgent message to immediately entrain his troops for Richmond. The spring campaign in Virginia was about to begin and Lee needed every available man. Before leaving on May 7 Hoke wrote a farewell letter to Cooke:

> Thank God for your safe return. A great relief is given me by the reception of your letter as I am ordered to another field. I have just written Commodore Pinkney that I had taken the River Road and had command of the river and the enemy completely surrounded when I had my orders to proceed to another field which I deeply regret, but

the summer's work can still be accomplished and I hope with the aid
of the Almighty to do it as soon as my troops are not wanted elsewhere. The Almighty is certainly with you in your movements. Take
care of Plymouth.[6]

Meanwhile, the Federals were extremely anxious to obtain any
information concerning the condition of the *Albemarle*. On or about
May 12 a small-boat reconnaissance was undertaken up the Middle
River that roughly parallels the Roanoke at a distance of five or six
miles. After a fatiguing four-hour tramp through the snake-infested
swamp that separates the two rivers, the Federal party finally arrived
at 5:00 p.m. on the north bank of the Roanoke opposite Plymouth.
Ensign Peacock, leader of the expedition, reported the following:

> The ram is lying at the coal yard wharf, at the lower end of town,
> with smokestack down and a number of men engaged upon the re-
> pairs. The vessel seems to have been lightened, as he appears much
> higher out of the water forward and aft than when we engaged him
> in the sound, but the sides of his casemate are even now touching
> the water.
>
> We could not see that the roof plating was at all broken or dis-
> placed, and nothing of the stack of the *Southfield*, which would have
> been visible if the vessel had not been raised or her smokestack re-
> moved to supply one for the *Albemarle*. The last suggestion seems to
> be most probable.[7]

On May 17 another reconnaissance revealed that the *Albemarle*'s
repairs, including a new smokestack, appeared completed, and
Smith, intent on destroying the ironclad without bringing on a general engagement, devised a cautious plan. Convinced that the Confederate vessel could be destroyed by torpedoes floated down the
river then guided against her hull by a small team of men, Smith
asked for volunteers.

On Tuesday, May 24, Cooke took the newly repaired *Albemarle*
on a trial run to the mouth of the Roanoke. Standing out in the
sound was the *Whitehead,* which fired one long-range shot at the
ironclad. Cooke chose not to respond.

In the afternoon of May 25 five crew members from the *Wyalusing* set out in a small boat and paddled up the Middle River. Tied securely in the bottom of the skiff were two 100-pound torpedoes. Toward evening they reached the spot where the previous reconnaissance patrols had left the river to cross the swamp. Leaving one man in charge of the boat, the remaining four began the difficult trek through the marsh carrying the two torpedoes on a stretcher. After an exhaustive and frightening tramp in the blackness across the Carolina swamp, they arrived at the Roanoke, a little distance above Plymouth. Carefully and quietly the four assembled their gear. When all was ready, Charles Baldwin and John Lloyd pushed out into the stream with a line and swam to the other side. Allan Crawford and John Laverty remained on the north bank to detonate the torpedoes upon a signal from Baldwin. Once on the Plymouth side of the river, the two torpedoes, which were connected by a bridle, were pulled across.

By 11:00 p.m. all was quiet along the river. Only the katydids, singing in the tall cypress trees lining the river's bank, broke the silence. Downstream a few lights still twinkled from Plymouth. Cautiously, Baldwin pushed out into the stream, guiding the now armed torpedoes before him. Lloyd remained behind, hidden along the bank, playing out a line attached to Baldwin. The plan was to guide the torpedoes using the bridle, so that they would pass on either side of the vessel's bow. At that moment the switches on shore would be thrown, electrically detonating the explosives. Slowly, floating with the current, Baldwin drifted downstream. When within only a few yards of the target, a sentry on a wharf shouted a challenge, followed by the sharp crack of a musket. Another shot rang out, followed quickly by several more, which churned the water around Baldwin's head. Lloyd, hearing and seeing the firing, cut the guiding line, threw away the ignition coil, and swam the river to the north side. Baldwin, too, made good his escape, and the party hurriedly made their way back to their boat on the Middle River.

The plan was a good one and was well executed by the Federal sailors. There were two mistakes, however. Baldwin allowed himself to be spotted by the sentry, and the "ironclad" toward which he guided the torpedoes was a schooner anchored in the river.[8]

On June 4 Cooke was informed that he had been promoted by
the president with the consent of Congress to the rank of captain for
"gallant and meritorious conduct" displayed in the actions of April
and May. For some time, however, Cooke had been experiencing
failing health, and for this reason he requested to be relieved from
command of the *Albemarle*. On June 17, 1864, his request was
granted, and Cmdr. John Newland Maffitt of the CSS *Florida* fame
was ordered to Plymouth to take command of the ironclad.[9]

Maffitt's assignment to the *Albemarle,* no doubt, raised the anxiety level of the Federal commanders in North Carolina. As a former
blockade-runner captain and commander of the commerce-raider
Florida, Maffitt had established himself as a fighter who was not
afraid to take risks. Secretary Mallory's verbal orders to Maffitt—to
"attack the enemy's fleet in the sound with the *Albemarle*"—were
well received by the ironclad's new commander, but there were many
in the area of eastern North Carolina who disagreed. Plymouth,
Washington (NC), and all the surrounding counties were free of invading Northern soldiers thanks, in part, to the *Albemarle*. With
most Confederate troops now en route to Virginia, she was all that
was preventing the Federals from returning and again overrunning
the eastern portion of the state. It was not worth the risk of losing
her in a confrontation with the Federal fleet in the sound, they argued, when her mere presence at
Plymouth was enough to keep the
enemy at bay.

Cmdr. John Newland Maffitt

Brig. Gen. Laurence S. Baker,
commanding the Second District,
Department of North Carolina,
wrote to Maffitt on July 6. His concluding remarks were a plea for
caution: "I have no doubt that in
event of an attack by you, the most
desperate efforts will be made to
destroy your boat, and thus open
the approach to Plymouth and
Washington. I hope, Captain, you
will appreciate the importance of

the matter which has induced these suggestions, and pardon the liberty taken."[10]

While Confederate authorities argued over the best method of employing the *Albemarle,* the ram continued to languish at her dock during the hot and humid summer of 1864. Occasionally Maffitt took her to the mouth of the river to observe the enemy and to show the flag. Often a small boat would accompany the ironclad and would proceed to drag for torpedoes while the *Albemarle* stood guard. Each time, the Union vessels, which were stationed in the sound to watch for the *Albemarle,* raised steam and hastened eastward, hoping to draw the ironclad into open water and toward the rest of the fleet, but Maffitt refused the bait. The sultry summer days, with no activity and no diversions, produced boredom and a feeling of isolation among the crew. To add to the oppressive atmosphere, the news from the war fronts was not encouraging. In Virginia, Lee's thin gray line was being savagely pressed back around the defenses of Richmond and Petersburg. In Georgia, Atlanta was besieged, and considering the dwindling Confederate manpower supply, there seemed to be no way of stopping William T. Sherman's relentless drive. As the wearisome month of August gave way to September along the meandering Roanoke River in eastern North Carolina, the *Albemarle* received another commander.

Lt. Cmdr. Alexander F. Warley

SCHARF'S HISTORY OF THE CONFEDERATE NAVY

Maffitt was urgently needed to command the blockade-runner *Owl,* and his orders were cut on September 9, 1864. On that same day a telegram reached Lt. Cmdr. Alexander F. Warley at Charleston, ordering him to report immediately to Pinkney for assignment to the command of the *Albemarle.* Warley had earned distinction as the courageous commander of the ram CSS *Manassas* during the battle of New Orleans in April 1862. Later he commanded the ironclad CSS *Chicora* at Charleston, and at the time of his assignment to the *Albemarle,* he was skipper of the *Water Witch,* a gunboat that had been captured from the Federals in Ossabaw Sound, Georgia.

Warley was not at all impressed with his new command: "When I took command of the Confederate States ironclad *Albemarle,* I found her made fast to the riverbank nearly abreast of the town of Plymouth. She was surrounded by a cordon of single cypress logs chained together, about ten feet from her side. There was no reason why the place might not be recaptured any day; the guns commanding the river were in no condition for use, and the troops in charge of them were worn down by fever, and were undrilled and worthless."[11]

On September 23 Warley took his new command eight miles downstream to the entrance of the sound to reconnoiter. The Federal gunboat *Valley City,* which was on picket duty, fired one long-range shot and then withdrew down the sound. Warley did not reply and refused to be lured into open water to face the combined vessels of the Union fleet. Confederate sailors, unaware of the political pressures to safeguard the *Albemarle* at all cost, no doubt grumbled that their new commander was no more aggressive than the previous one.[12]

While the *Albemarle* suffered through the late summer heat and the constant change in commanders, the Federal navy was devising yet another plan to attempt her destruction.

In September, Lt. William B. Cushing proposed two plans to Rear Adm. Samuel Phillips Lee, commander of the Federal North Atlantic Squadron. Because no Federal ironclad could cross the bar at Hatteras Inlet due to their deep draft, the navy could not bring an armored vessel into the sounds to challenge the *Albemarle* on equal terms. It became necessary, therefore, to attempt to destroy the Confederate warship through a surprise night assault by a small attack force. The first scheme involved sending approximately one hundred men overland through the swamp, carrying rubber boats. Once they reached the Roanoke opposite Plymouth, they would launch the boats, storm and board the *Albemarle,* cut her loose from the dock, and float her down to the mouth of the river, where she would be taken in tow by a Federal warship. The second plan, favored by Cushing, was to attack the Confederate ram at her dock with two small steam-driven tor-

NAVAL HISTORICAL CENTER

Lt. William B. Cushing

pedo boats. The Federal navy had been much impressed by the activities of the Confederate torpedo boats at Charleston and other locations, and Lee ordered Cushing to Washington to present his plans to the Secretary of the Navy Gideon Welles. The department, desperate to see the *Albemarle* destroyed, agreed to Cushing's second plan and sent him to New York to find suitable boats.[13]

Cushing wrote:

Finding some boats building for picket duty, I selected two and proceeded to fit them out. They were open launches, about thirty feet in length [other accounts place the length at forty-five to forty-seven feet], with small engines and propelled by a screw. A 12-pounder howitzer was fitted to the bow of each, and a boom was rigged out, some fourteen feet in length, swinging by a goose-neck hinge to the bluff of the bow. A topping lift, carried to a stanchion inboard, raised or lowered it, and the torpedo was fitted into an iron slide at the end. This was intended to be detached from the boom by means of a heel-jigger leading inboard, and to be exploded by another line, connecting with a pin, which held a grape shot over a nipple and a cap.[14]

While bringing the launches to Norfolk, Cushing lost one along the way. He continued on with one boat and finally rendezvoused with the fleet in Albemarle Sound on October 24. Nine days earlier, on October 15, a final reconnaissance had been made across the swamp by Master's Mate John Woodman. Arriving at the landing site on the Middle River at daylight, Woodman and a companion made their way across the morass, arriving opposite Plymouth at 10:00 a.m.

I had a good view of the rebel ram *Albemarle,* he wrote. She was moored alongside the wharf, head downstream, apparently having no

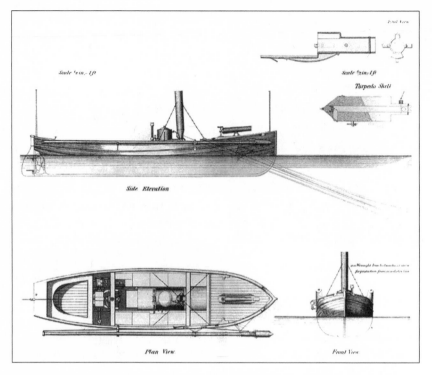

U.S. Navy Department plans for the screw picket boat (with a diagram of the spar torpedo in the upper right-hand corner) used in Cushing's attack on the *Albemarle*

steam. On her port side, which was towards the stream, there are timbers extending from the wharf and lapping on her prow and stern one
quarter her length from each end, one half her side being protected
by piles, the other half being unprotected. At 10:30 a.m. I proceeded
down the river toward the *Southfield* and arrived opposite her at
noon. The *Southfield* is in the same position as last I saw her—except
her smokestack being removed. There are two vessels forward, one
on each side and two aft, one on each side, having timbers extended
across for the purpose of raising the *Southfield*. The work seems to be
abandoned for the present.[15]

Commander Warley had done all that he could to guarantee the
safety of the *Albemarle,* but his resources were limited.

The crew of the *Albemarle* numbered but sixty, too small a force to allow me to keep an armed watch on deck at night and to do outside picketing besides. . . . The officer in command of the [army] troops was inclined to give me all assistance, and sent a picket of twenty-five men under a lieutenant; they were furnished with rockets and had a field piece. This picket was stationed on board a schooner about [a] gunshot below the *Albemarle,* where an attempt was being made to raise a vessel [the *Southfield*] sunk at the time of Commander Cooke's dash down the river.

When all was ready on the dark, rainy night of October 27, 1864, Cushing and his tiny crew entered the Roanoke with their steam launch and headed upriver toward Plymouth. Towed behind was a cutter with armed sailors on board; their mission, if they were hailed, was to capture the Confederate pickets on the schooner before they could give the alarm. The launch's engine had been boxed over and warped in tarpaulins so she made scarcely any noise at all. Just before 3:00 a.m. Cushing stealthily approached the ghostly shapes of the schooner and the sunken *Southfield.* Silently the launch, with the cutter in tow, passed the pickets with no challenge being heard. Cushing briefly toyed with the idea of storming the *Albemarle* with his twenty men, all armed with revolvers, cutlasses, and hand grenades, but sud-

An artist's depiction of Cushing's torpedo boat under way

denly a hail was shouted from the deck of the ironclad. Cushing quickly ordered the cutter to cast off, return downstream, and capture the pickets. More hails followed, mixed with the shouts from officers, all demanding to know the identity of the vessel in the river. Without warning, a huge bonfire was ignited nearby on the shore, casting its lurid light on the approaching torpedo launch.

Warley described the scene:

> It was about 3:00 a.m. The night was dark and slightly rainy, and the launch was close to us when we hailed and the alarm was given—so close that the gun could not be depressed enough to reach her; so the crew were sent in the shield with muskets, and kept up a heavy fire on the launch as she slowly forced her way over the chain of logs and ranged by us within a few feet. As she reached the bow of the *Albemarle*, I heard a report as of an unshotted gun, and a piece of wood fell at my feet.
>
> Calling the carpenter, I told him a torpedo had been exploded, and ordered him to examine and report to me, saying nothing to anyone else. He soon reported "a hole in her bottom big enough to drive a wagon in." By this time I heard voices from the launch: "We surren-

Cushing detonates the spar torpedo against the side of the *Albemarle*.

der," etc., etc. I stopped our fire and sent Mr. [Master James C.] Long, who brought back all those who had been in the launch except the gallant captain [Cushing] and three of her crew, all of whom took to the river. [Two of the four drowned, while Cushing and one other man escaped.] Having seen to their safety, I turned my attention to the *Albemarle* and found her resting on the bottom in eight feet of water, her upper works above water.[16]

Of the twenty-two ironclads put into service by the Confederate navy, the "Ironclad of the Roanoke," the CSS *Albemarle,* was the only one the Federals were able to destroy. Even this success, however, was not by the massed firepower of Union naval guns but by the courage and audacity of one lone individual—Lt. William B. Cushing. Regardless of how she was lost, the *Albemarle,* along with the protection she offered for the people of eastern North Carolina, was now resting in the mud on the bottom of the Roanoke. Warley continued his description:

After her destruction, failing to convince the officer in command of the troops that he could hold the place, I did my best to help defend

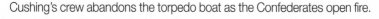

Cushing's crew abandons the torpedo boat as the Confederates open fire.

The *Albemarle* sits on the bottom of the Roanoke River.

it. Half of my crew went down and obstructed the river by sinking the
schooner at the wreck, and with the other half, I had two 8-inch guns
commanding the upper river put into serviceable order, re-laid platforms, fished out tackles from the *Albemarle,* got a few shells, etc.,
and waited. I did not have to wait long. The fleet steamed up to the
obstruction, fired a few shells over the town, steamed down again,
and early next morning, rounding the island, were in the river and
opened fire.

My two 8-inch guns worked by Mr. Long and Mr. [Master B. F.]
Shelley did their duty, and I think did all that was done in the defense
of Plymouth. The fire of the fleet was concentrated on us, and one at
least of the steamers was so near that I could hear the orders given to
elevate or depress the guns. When I felt that by hanging on I could
only sacrifice my men and achieve nothing, I ordered our guns
spiked and the men sent round to the road by a ravine. The crew left
me by Captain [John Newland] Maffitt were good and true men, and
stuck by me to the last.[17]

Plymouth fell to the enemy on October 31, and Washington,
North Carolina, soon thereafter. Once again, the people of eastern
North Carolina groaned under the heel of the invader. But for a

while at least, the CSS *Albemarle* had provided them with a short reprieve. With the loss of the *Albemarle*, however, only one ironclad, the *Neuse*, remained operational in the state of North Carolina.

☆ ☆ ☆

To compensate for the lack of an adequate naval force on the Cape Fear River at Wilmington, Gen. William H. C. Whiting ordered the construction of an immense battery at the southern tip of Confederate Point where it could command the entrance of New Inlet. The army commander considered the position, which would become known as Battery Buchanan, as a substitute for the lost navy ironclads, stating that the battery "was only ordered when I lost all hope of aid in defense of the 'Rip bars' by the *North Carolina* and *Raleigh.*" The battery was to be commanded and manned entirely by naval personnel and armed with navy guns. Whiting notified Cmdr. Robert F. Pinkney that the "command will be exclusively naval, as much so as if the defensive force was in a ship of war at anchor off the Rip."

Construction began in September, and by October two 10-inch Columbiads had been temporarily mounted. By November 1864 Battery Buchanan was complete and ready for its naval garrison.

Battery Buchanan stood at the southern end of Confederate Point.

Ultimately the battery's armament consisted of two 7-inch Brooke rifles and two 11-inch smoothbores. Except for skeleton crews to man the gunboats *Caswell, Equator, Yadkin,* the receiving ship *Arctic,* and the torpedo boat *Squib,* which had been transported from Richmond, Pinkney ordered the majority of naval personnel at the Wilmington station transferred to the battery. Commanded by Lt. Robert F. Chapman, the battery would play an important role in the coming Federal attacks against Fort Fisher.

Lt. Robert F. Chapman

When the Federal invasion fleet appeared off Fort Fisher on December 23, 1864, Pinkney transported all available naval personnel to the battery on board the *Yadkin.* There they reported for duty to Chapman. He sent a detachment of twenty-nine men under Lt. Francis M. Roby to Fort Fisher where they manned the two Brooke rifles that had been removed from the *Raleigh* and mounted between the Mound Battery and the sea face. On December 24 the Federals unleashed their massive bombardment of the Confederate bastion. Roby's crew fought hard the first day, garnering praise from their

Plans for the torpedo boat CSS *Squib,* which was sent by rail to Wilmington

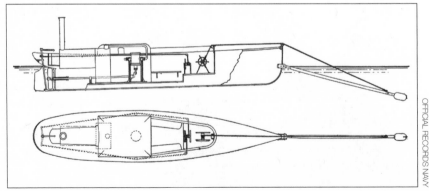

army comrades. One officer remarked, "Our sailors behaved with great coolness, as we had no relief crews, they had tiresome work."

On the second day, both Brookes exploded, wounding fifteen sailors but miraculously killing none. Battery Buchanan was also kept busy, as Chapman reported: "At 2:30 a number of boats were lowered from the ships of the fleet and approached the battery. I think they were dragging for torpedoes. We opened fire on them from one gun, and at the fourth discharge sunk one of their boats; the others quickly withdrew."

When the enemy finally withdrew on December 26, nineteen of the twenty-nine men in Roby's detachment, sent from Battery Buchanan, were dead or wounded. After the battle the navy received high praise for its role in combating the immense Union fleet. Few believed, however, that the two-day battle had settled the fate of Fort Fisher or Wilmington. After reorganizing and refitting, the Federals would be back.[18]

Pinkney's greatest concern was manpower. Savannah had fallen on December 23, and the Navy Department ordered all officers and men of the Savannah Squadron to retreat to Wilmington where they could bolster the defenses of Battery Buchanan. On January 1, 1865, fifty-one officers and men arrived at Wilmington after an arduous overland march; among them were nine black sailors who were included in the assignment to Battery Buchanan. At last Pinkney had sufficient manpower to meet the expected coming attack.

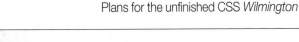

Plans for the unfinished CSS *Wilmington*

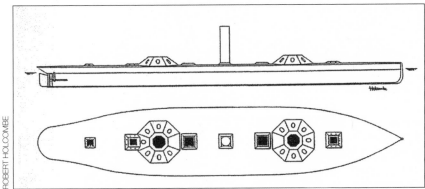

ROBERT HOLCOMBE

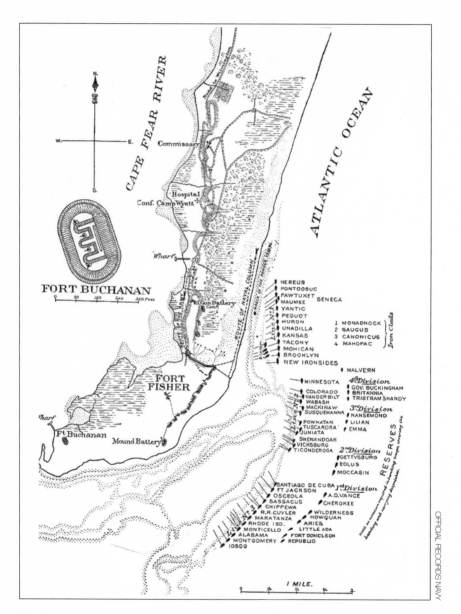

War Department chart of the final Federal attack on Fort Fisher. The layout of Battery Buchanan is shown in the inset.

NAVAL HISTORICAL CENTER

The Federal fleet bombarding Fort Fisher on January 15, 1865

On January 12 the Federal fleet reappeared off Fort Fisher. Again the Union forces unleashed a terrific bombardment, and again sailors and marines from Battery Buchanan fought side by side with their army comrades. Battery Buchanan was less involved in this second and final attack, and after hours of hand-to-hand combat, Fort Fisher was finally overrun, Chapman turned the guns of the battery on friend and foe alike. When the remnants of the fort's garrison retreated to Battery Buchanan, they found the battery deserted and the guns spiked. Chapman had pulled his men out at the last minute and escaped across the river. What was left of the Fort Fisher garrison surrendered around 10:00 p.m. The port of Wilmington was closed, but her navy squadron would live to fight another day.

The retreating navy crews were directed to occupy Batteries Meares and Campbell along the west bank of the Cape Fear River. The Federals consolidated their gains on February 19 and began their push toward Wilmington. On February 20 Union gunboats shelled Batteries Meares and Campbell. Weary Confederate sailors responded with several ineffective shots and then pulled out. Wilmington was evacuated. While docks, warehouses, and immense

R. THOMAS CAMPBELL

Present-day view of Battery Buchanan

numbers of baled cotton were set ablaze, the Beerys methodically set fire to everything in the navy yard on Eagle Island, destroying records, drawings, buildings, and the unfinished *Wilmington*.

At the Cassidey yard the scene was the same. The navy scuttled the remaining small vessels and joined the retreat northward along the Wilmington and Weldon Railroad. The Wilmington Squadron and its defense of that area of eastern North Carolina was over.

The loss of Wilmington would have an ominous impact on the CSS *Neuse*. During the month of May 1864 the ironclad had been freed from the sandbar upon which she had grounded on April 27 and safely moored back at her dock in Kinston. By the beginning of June all structural modifications to the ironclad had been completed, but because of the lack of infantry support the *Neuse* remained inactive at her berth. On August 24 the ironclad experienced a change in command. Commander Loyall was ordered to report the Naval Academy's school ship, the CSS *Patrick Henry*, where he was to assume the duties of commandant of midshipmen. In his place the department sent Cmdr. Joseph H. Price, a native of Wilmington who had seen service with the Savannah Squadron and had participated in the expedition to capture the USS *Water Witch* in June 1864.

The arrival of Price did nothing to change the circumstance surrounding the *Neuse*. She still lay at the "cat hole" at Kinston. Life for the crew aboard was light and boring, with the only diversions being an occasional junket in town. Second Lt. Richard H. Bacot wrote to his sister in July: "The Gunboats (as we are called here) have concluded to have as nice a time as possible and find plenty of amusements. We have the exclusive use of a tin-pin alley, where we exercise our muscles every morning. We pitch Quoits after dinner and have various diversions for the evening; such as boating, visiting, walking."[19]

By early November the river had risen sufficiently to allow the ironclad to descend, but without troops to provide infantry support, there was little the *Neuse* could accomplish. In December, with Sherman's army drawing closer to Savannah and Grant's army laying siege to Richmond and Petersburg in Virginia, the situation for the *Neuse* had not changed. On December 12 one crewman wrote: "I learned this morning that the Yankees taken [sic] Tarboro about two days ago. I want to fight the Yankees with our gun boat but they is afeared [sic] to come in shooting distance. . . . I expect the Yankees will undertake Kinston. If they do they will take it I think, but I don't

Cmdr. Joseph Price

think they can take our boat easy. We would die for it rather than give it up. We would blow it up rather than they should have it."[20]

After the fall of Fort Fisher, every available soldier in North Carolina was rushed to Wilmington. This negated any possibility of the *Neuse* launching an attack downriver against New Bern. On January 16, Bacot wrote: "The urgent necessity for troops at Wilmington prevents our having a land force to cooperate in an attack on Newbern. It would do my heart good to help take that place. . . . I say fight Yankeedom forever if we have to bushwhack & live in the swamps. We've gone too far to back down & I glory in our cause. . . . We are not yet whipped & our people are not discouraged."[21]

On March 6 a Union force of thirteen thousand men, commanded by Gen. Jacob D. Cox, left New Bern with the objective of joining Sherman's troops near Goldsboro. Confederate Gen. Robert F. Hoke's division, after retreating from Wilmington, assembled in the vicinity of Kinston with the intent of attacking Cox's advancing forces. On March 8–10 near Wyse Fork (also known as Southwest Creek), three miles east of Kinston, Hoke and elements of the Confederate Army of Tennessee fought a series of sharp engagements with Cox's troops but were defeated. With Hoke's repulse, Gen. Braxton Bragg ordered the evacuation of Kinston and a general retreat toward Goldsboro, including specific instructions for Commander Price and the CSS *Neuse:* "Captain Price, C.S. Navy, commanding the C.S.S. *Neuse,* is

The CSS *Neuse* fires on Union cavalry

BOTH: CSS NEUSE GUNBOAT ASSOCIATION, STEPHEN McCALL, ARTIST

desired to cover Major General Hoke's movement, and if practical, before sacrificing his vessel, to move down the river by diversion, and
make the loss of his vessel as costly to the enemy as possible."[22]

During the night of March 10 all Confederate troops crossed the
Neuse River and took up their march for Goldsboro. Union forces
did not push their pursuit. Several Federal commanders were very
concerned about the *Neuse* and petitioned New Bern via telegraph to
have a steamer equipped with a torpedo that could ascend the river
and destroy the ironclad.

Finally, Union troops began moving into Kinston on the morning
of March 12. Commander Price ordered the *Neuse* to get under way
and move to the center of the river. Soon enemy cavalry appeared on
the southern riverbank, and the *Neuse's* two Brooke rifles roared,
sending their shells crashing into the midst of the Union horsemen.

Several shots were fired, after which Price ordered the ironclad set
on fire and the crew to abandon ship. The *Neuse* had the dubious

The CSS *Neuse* is abandoned and scuttled.

honor of being the last ship to fire its guns in defense of eastern North Carolina. Lieutenant Bacot described the last moments: "All the troops had withdrawn from Kinston & the Yankees 18,000 strong came upon us & not having any prospect of being relieved before our provisions gave out & being in a narrow river where we could not work the ship under fire, after shelling the Yankee Cavalry for a little while, we removed our powder & stores & burnt the vessel."

As her crew marched away, the *Neuse* became engulfed in flames with black smoke pouring from her open gunports. Soon there was a massive explosion as the fire reached her magazine, and the Confederacy's last ironclad in North Carolina sank quickly to the bottom.[23]

15

SOME FINAL THOUGHTS

L OOKING AT THE CONFEDERATE navy's record in eastern North Carolina and viewing their accomplishments—or lack thereof—from
hindsight, one might be tempted to conclude that they failed to protect the eastern portion of the state from invasion. Such a conclusion
would be in error. On the contrary, after the disastrous losses along
the Outer Banks and Roanoke Island, the growing strength of the
Southern navy in the waters of North Carolina contributed signifi-
cantly to the defense of North Carolina.

In any analysis of the navy's role in the state, one must be careful not to isolate that role from the rest of the war. In other words,
it is essential that any student of the naval war be thoroughly famil-
iar with the other events transpiring throughout the Confederacy.
Only in this context can one begin to understand the severe hard-
ships, limitations, and frustrations under which the Confederate
navy undertook the defense of eastern North Carolina. When
viewed in this broader scope, one can begin to appreciate just how
much was truly accomplished.

When privateers and vessels of the North Carolina navy began
sailing out of Hatteras Inlet and attacking Northern shipping, it

225

served only to hasten the arrival of a Federal invasion fleet. While at the time there seemed valid reasons for utilizing the protective waters of Pamlico Sound for such operations, the state no doubt could have used the extra time to strengthen the fortifications at Hatteras Inlet. As some pointed out at the time, these attacks served only to call attention to the danger lurking there for Northern commerce. Still, considering the remoteness of the inlet on the Outer Banks, there was probably little hope of defending it against a determined enemy assault. The real disaster, therefore, was the fall of Roanoke Island.

With inadequate time and insufficient manpower, there was never any real hope of holding Roanoke Island. As fast as North Carolina could muster its sons into military service, they were marched off to the various fronts in Virginia and Kentucky where they were desperately needed. Precious few troops remained to defend Roanoke Island. While William F. Lynch and the Mosquito Fleet did the best they could with their ragtag fleet of converted tugboats, they never came close to matching the firepower of the Federal vessels. The Mosquito Fleet's destruction at Elizabeth City could probably have been avoided, or at least delayed, if Lynch had dispersed his vessels up the various rivers and tributaries.

With Roanoke Island lost and the Mosquito Fleet destroyed, the whole of Albemarle and Pamlico sounds and the rivers flowing into them were at the mercy of the enemy. It was only after these disasters that the Confederate government in Richmond awoke to the real danger that now presented itself in North Carolina. If a determined enemy advanced inland, they could overrun all the eastern counties, a major breadbasket for the state, and possibly advance on Raleigh itself. If the Union had taken North Carolina out of the war, the front in Virginia would have become untenable.

With events in eastern North Carolina initially ignored because of pressing military needs elsewhere, Secretary of the Navy Stephen R. Mallory devoted his energy to shoring up the naval defenses of the Tarheel State. With North Carolina's sons constantly marching off to the distant war fronts, it became the role of a few strategic fortifications and the navy to convince the Union forces that any further advance into the state would be extremely costly. At stake was the all-important supply line of the Wilmington and Weldon Railroad.

Fortunately for the Confederacy, Federal commanders also experienced difficulty in convincing their government in Washington that they should commit adequate numbers of troops and resources to the region.

By the latter part of 1863 the gunboat-and-ironclad program was starting to have the desired effect. With armored vessels completed or nearing completion at Wilmington and on the Roanoke, Tar, and Neuse rivers, the Confederate navy was finally able to pose a respectable threat to the Federal forces. Cruising offshore at Wilmington or ensconced behind their fortifications at such places as New Bern, Washington, and Plymouth, Union commanders knew that they would have to face the Brooke rifles of the Southern navy if they ventured inland. While the ironclads that were completed had many flaws—especially those at Wilmington—it is amazing, given the circumstances, that they were constructed at all. Considering the lack of raw materials and skilled labor, the building of any respectable armored warships in North Carolina constituted a minor miracle. The very presence of these vessels, their prowess always overblown by the Federals, worked as a deterrent against further invasion.

The career of the *Albemarle* is a case in point. Constructed by a nineteen-year-old builder in a cornfield, she earned the admiration of the entire Confederacy and the fear and respect of her adversaries. The *Albemarle* sank one Union warship, severely damaged several others, and was the deciding factor in the recapture of Plymouth and the Federal evacuation of Washington, North Carolina. After she was torpedoed and her threat to the Federals eliminated, Union forces quickly regained the areas they had lost. One can only surmise as to what would have happened if the *Albemarle* and the *Neuse* could have joined forces in the sounds.

The role of the navy at Wilmington, however, was disappointing. The facilities there for the construction of warships, while not on a par with those found in other port cities such as Charleston, Savannah, and New Orleans, were far superior to the hacked-out fields along the banks of the Roanoke and Neuse rivers. Yet for various reasons the Wilmington yards lagged behind in ironclad construction. Some of this was unavoidable, for iron plates, engines, and machinery were diverted to other projects. But even when completed, the *Raleigh* and *North Carolina* were disappointments when compared to the other Richmond-class ironclads such as *Chicora, Palmetto State, Richmond,* and the *Savannah.* Nevertheless, in the spring of 1864 the Federals knew that if they succeeded in forcing their way past Fort Fisher, they would have to contend with two formidable Confederate ironclads on the Cape Fear River before they could reach Wilmington.

As with many aspects concerning the epic saga of the Southern states' bid for independence, the desperate struggle endured by the Confederate navy in North Carolina was long, bitter, painful, and sometimes humiliating. But with all of the disasters during those four long years of terrible war that befell the Confederate armies, it should be remembered that behind them, it was the Confederate navy that defended—and held—the eastern portion of North Carolina.

APPENDIXES

1. Confederate Forces at Roanoke Island
2. Officers and Crew of the CSS *Albemarle*
3. Officers and Crew of the CSS *Neuse*
4. Officers and Crew of the CSS *North Carolina* and/or the CSS *Raleigh*
5. Capture of the USS *Underwriter*
6. The Confederate States Navy Yard at Charlotte, N. C., 1862–1865
7. The Ram *Albemarle:* Her Construction and Service
8. The Confederate Ram *Albemarle*

APPENDIX 1

CONFEDERATE FORCES AT ROANOKE ISLAND

Roanoke Island, Brig. Gen. Henry A. Wise

TROOPS:

2nd North Carolina, Battalion, Lt. Col. Wharton J. Green
8th North Carolina, Col. H. M. Shaw
17th North Carolina (3 companies), Maj. G. H. Hill
31st North Carolina, Col. John V. Jordan
48th Virginia, Maj. H. W. Fry
69th Virginia, Lt. Col. Frank P. Anderson

NAVAL FORCES, Flag Officer William F. Lynch

CSS *Seabird* (flag steamer), Lt. Patrick McCarrick
CSS *Curlew,* Lt. Thomas T. Hunter
CSS *Ellis,* Lt. James W. Cooke
CSS *Beaufort,* 1st Lt. William H. Parker
CSS *Raleigh,* 1st Lt. Joseph W. Alexander
CSS *Fanny,* Lt. James L. Tayloe
CSS *Forrest,* Acting Master James L. Hoole
CSS *Black Warrior,* Master Frank M. Harris

APPENDIX 2

OFFICERS AND CREW OF THE CSS ALBEMARLE

Roanoke River and Albemarle Sound, 1864

OFFICERS

NAME	RANK	FROM
Cooke, James W. (Commanding 1/14/64–6/9/64)	Cmdr.	NC
Maffitt, John N. (Commanding 6/9/64–9/9/64)	Cmdr.	NC
Warley, Alexander P. (Commanding 9/9/64–10/28/64)	1st Lt.	SC
Roby, Francis M.	1st Lt. (Exec. Officer)	AL
Lakin, Edward	1st Lt.	
Lewis, John	1st Lt.	
Roberts, William W.	1st Lt.	NC
Elliott, Gilbert	1st Lt. (CSA)	NC
Hamilton, William P.	Master	SC
Long, James C.	Master	TN
Shelly, B. F.	Master	SC
Burbage, Thomas J.	Acting Master	
Freeman, Robert	Acting Master's Mate	
Hill, James C.	Acting Master's Mate	
Pitt, Lorenzo	Acting Master's Mate	
Discher, Henry	3rd Asst. Engineer	MO
Hardy, William H.	3rd Asst. Engineer	VA
Robinett, James T.	3rd Asst. Engineer	
DeLeon, Perry M.	Asst. Paymaster	SC
Hopkins, James B.	Pilot First Class	
Hobbs, George W.	Pilot	
Luck, John	Pilot	
Shipley, Walter	2nd Class Pilot	
Foote, George A.	Asst. Surgeon	NC
Peck, Frederic	Asst. Surgeon	NC
Dand, William	Gunner	England
McDonald, Hugh	2nd Class Gunner	LA
Fentress, George D.	Carpenter	

CREW

Alrid, Shubal	Landsman	Cullington, James	Captain of the Forecastle
Anderson, J. T.	Landsman		
Andrews, J.	Captain of the Hold	Daniel, J. T.	Ordinary Seaman
Anthony, J. C.	Landsman	Davis, John	Landsman
Atcock, Ambrose	Landsman	Dunton, Joseph	Landsman
Autrey, D. H.	Landsman	Eno, R. H.	Ordinary Seaman
Aveia, W. H.	Landsman		
Avent, J. J.	Landsman	Flinn, James	Landsman
Avent, J. W.	Landsman	Fountain, Cofield	Landsman
Ball, Erasmus	Landsman	Fulford, J. M.	Ordinary Seaman
Barber, Simeon	Landsman		
Barker, Caleb	Coxswain	Game, J. T.	Landsman
Barton, John	Landsman	Gibson, A.	Landsman
Beal, Wilson	Landsman	Gibson, H. M.	Landsman
Belcher, James	Ordinary Seaman	Gray, Spence	Quartermaster
		Griffin, John	Landsman
Benton, John	Boatswain's Mate	Hardy, Peter	2nd Class Boy
Beveridge, B.	Quartermaster	Harrison, John	Landsman
Blout, Miles	Landsman	Hatly, Hardy	Landsman
Breedlove, J. P.	Landsman	Hay, H. P.	Captain of the Hold
Brown, J.	Captain of the Hold	Hays, W. H.	Landsman
Burgess, William	Seaman	Hayward, Benjamin	2nd Class Boy
Cain, J. H.	Landsman	Henderson, James	2nd Class Boy
Capps, G. D.	2nd Class Fireman	Hight, H. C.	Landsman
		Hobbs, C. L.	Seaman
Carter, J. A.	Landsman	Hobbs, G. W.	Quartermaster
Childs, Charles	1st Class Fireman	Holmes, William	Landsman
		Hooten, George	2nd Class Boy
Clark, Nat	Landsman	Horne, G. W.	Landsman
Clifton, W. J.	Landsman	Humble, Alfred	Landsman
Close, John	1st Class Fireman	Ives, Edward T.	Landsman
		Johnston, M. N.	Landsman
Cole, William	Captain of the Maintop	Johnston, T. P.	Ship's Steward
		Jones, Felix	Landsman
Cooper, A. B.	Yeoman	Jones, Wiley	Landsman
Crews, Robert T.	Landsman	Kate, Thomas A.	Landsman

King, Alfred — Quarter Gunner

Kuhn, H. A. — Coxswain

Lancaster, L. H. — Landsman

Layard, W. S. — Landsman

Lindsey, E. R. — Landsman

Lynum, M. A. — Landsman

Massey, Simon — Landsman

McAdams, Francis — Landsman

McClaron, Benjamin — 2nd Class Fireman

McDaniel, W. J. — Landsman

Mitchell, B. B. — Landsman

Mitchell, John W. — Landsman

Morton, Edward — Ordinary Seaman

Mullins, John — Seaman

Nichols, Thomas — Landsman

Noah, Amos — Landsman

Nobles, J. A. — Seaman

O'Neil, William — Landsman

Payne, M. — Ship's Cook

Pratt, William — Gunner's Mate

Reynolds, J. W. — Master at Arms

Ricketts, George — Landsman

Rouzee, C. W. — Surgeon's Steward

Sanders, J. T. — Landsman

Sikes, Franklin — Seaman

Simmons, W. S. — Landsman

Simpson, Isaac — Landsman

Smithwick, J. R. — Ordinary Seaman

Snowden, J. B. — Captain of the Hold

Sorrell, W. M. — Landsman

Stafford, John — 2nd Class Fireman

Stancil, Moses — Landsman

Steeley, J. W. — Boatswain's Mate

Stuart, A. — 1st Class Fireman

Taylor, Edward — Quartermaster

Troutman, Samuel — Landsman

Turner, J. D. — Landsman

Waid, James — Captain of the After Guard

Walker, William L. — Landsman

Weeks, T. P. — Landsman

White, Charles — Landsman

White, John — Captain of the After Guard

White, Samuel W. — Landsman

Wilkins, John — Landsman

Williams, Ezekiel — Ordinary Seaman

Williams, Lewis — Landsman

Wilson, John L. — Landsman

Wilson, Robert — Landsman

Wilson, William — Landsman

Winfield, Henry — Landsman

Woodell, Jerry — Landsman

Wright, John — Landsman

York, Franklin — Landsman

APPENDIX 3

OFFICERS AND CREW OF THE CSS NEUSE

March–October 1864

(*Source:* Muster Rolls of the Confederate Navy Department,
Record Group 45, National Archives, Washington DC)

OFFICERS

NAME	RANK	FROM
Bacot, Richard H.	2nd Lt.	SC
Edwards, Robert E.	3rd Asst. Engineer	VA
Farrell, James E.	Master's Mate	
Field, Thomas	Gunner	
Haynie, Edward T.	Acting Master's Mate	
Hoge, Francis L.	1st Lt.	VA
Jenkins, H. C.		
King, Joel G.	Asst. Surgeon	NC
Loyall, Benjamin P.	1st Lt. (commanding)	VA
O'Neil, Robert J.	3rd Asst. Engineer	
Palmer, William G.	Acting Master	
Parsons, Edgar O.	Acting Master's Mate	
Petterson, W. M.		
Price, Joseph	1st Lt. (commanding)	NC
Sharp, William	1st Lt. (commanding)	VA
Tucker, John T.	1st Asst. Engineer	VA
Wheless, John P.	Asst. Paymaster	
Worth, Algernon S.	2nd Lt.	VA

CREW
March–October 1864*

Allen, A. A.	Carroll, J. W.	Dillon, Isaiah
Allen, John	Clanahan, A. M.	Downard, John
Arnold, J. H.	Clayton, R. H.	Drew, Washington
Berry, W. R.	Clinton, Michael	Fletcher, James W.
Brown, A. H.	Cooke, John	Forrest, J. T.
Brown, James I.	Crawford, C. D.	Garris, H. B. R.
Brown, Timothy	Crawford, Joham (?)	Hacket, John
Butler, William	Davis, D. M.	Hardy, W. H.

Hass(c)el(l), Dorum
Haynes, G. H.
Heffron, Stephen
Hicks, R.
Hope, Alfred
Jacobs, B. W.
Johnson, N. A.
Knott, A. B.
Lawson, A. W.
Linscut, Isaac
McLaughlin, John D.
Nixon, P. H.
Parsons, William
Peling, Alonzo
Phillips, John
Piercer, Darrin
Pinkney, R. F.
Pittman, F. W.

Plyler, Tobias
Porter, Charles E.
Price, J. B.
Ray, W. H.
Readit, W. H.
Regan, J. R.
Reynolds, John
Rooker, George
Russell, S. E.
Savage, S. P.
Seary, J. H.
Sermonds, D. D.
Shugart, Isaac L.
Smith, George
Smith, John
Smith, Reuben
Stanley, D. R.
Taite, Spencer

Terrell, James E.
Threat, Benjamin
Thrower, O. P.
Tittenton, William R.
Travens, John A.
Turner, J. L.
Tyerlic, Wiley
Wainwright, William
Walker, George W.
Walker, J. T.
Webb, Joseph
White, J. A.
Whitlock, J. D.
Whittey, Josiah
Wilkenson, William
Willerbee, Keder
Wilson, H. J.

APPENDIX 4

OFFICERS AND CREW OF THE CSS NORTH CAROLINA AND/OR THE CSS RALEIGH

April–June 1864

(*Source: Official Records Navy,* ser. II, vol. 1, pp. 295–96)

OFFICERS

NAME	RANK
Muse, William T.	Cmdr.
Maury, William L.	Cmdr.
Jack, E. Alexander	1st Asst. Engineer
McCarrick, Patrick	1st Lt.
Glassell, William T.	1st Lt.
Beck, Charles	Acting Master
Cook, Henry S.	Midshipman
Drury, W. R.	3rd Asst. Engineer
Freeman, Joseph M., Jr.	3rd Asst. Engineer
Garrison, Thomas	Gunner's Mate
Gleason, William	Boatswain
Griggs, William W.	Asst. Surgeon
Ingraham, J. J.	Boatswain
Jenkins, Oliver L.	Acting Master's Mate
Jones, C. Lucian	Asst. Paymaster
Kerr, William A.	1st Lt.
Lamkin, William A.	Acting Master's Mate
Lee, William A.	Midshipman
Lovett, John A.	Gunner
Peck, Charles S.	3rd Asst. Engineer
Porter, Thomas K.	1st Lt.
Roberts, Henry	Lt.
Simpson, Smith L.	Acting Master's Mate
Warren, Henry J.	Midshipman
Wiatt, Americus V.	Lt.

CREW

Adams, William	Aldrich, William	Anderson, J. H.
Aikens, R. H.	Anderson, Thomas J.	Bailey, Thomas

Balance, John
Barco, Caleb
Barwick, Jackson
Bell, John
Best, Joseph
Black, Alexander
Bloom, William
Bolt, John
Boyer, Thomas
Boyer, W. W.
Brantley, William H.
Brasswell, G. W.
Britt, John
Brown, Nelson
Brunner, Joseph
Buchanan, John
Burgess, D. B.
Button, B. L.
Cannon, John B.
Carman, Jacob C.
Carroll, Thomas
Carver, Paul
Certain, Edward
Childs, Charles
Clements, J. N.
Cole, William
Collins, Henry
Condon, Thomas
Connell, Jeremiah
Curtis, William R.
Deans, W. H.
Dougherty, D.
Doyle, George
Dugan, Richard
Edwards, F. M.
Farrady, Andrew
Farrel, M.
Firmer, Valentine
Fork, John W.
Franks, N. D.

Freeise, Frederick
Gee, D.
Gleason, James
Graham, John N.
Griffiths, John
Hamlet, S. W.
Harrington, John W.
Hendricks, Thomas J.
Holmes, C. K.
Horne, T.
Howard, William H.
Jeter, George W.
Jolly, John M.
Jones, H.
Kelly, James
Kirby, William C.
Landford, James M.
Lee, J. H.
Lehne, Samuel
Lillard, J. W.
Little, Christopher C.
Martin, John
May, William
McCall, Edward
McClanney, James
McKay, John A.
McKeller, Archibald
McRae, D. L.
Messick, Nehemiah
Miller, James
Monroe, John H.
Morris, James
Morris, J. H.
Mullins, John
Muse, William T., Jr.
Musgrave, C.
Nelson, Peter
O'Brien, John
O'Donnel, John
O'Neil, John

Oustein, Reuben
Pate, J. W.
Peaden, John
Peaden, Henry
Pence, John H.
Penny, B. F.
Pope, William H.
Porter, Moses
Price, B. F.
Price, F. D.
Pridgen, David
Rafferty, Patrick
Reynolds, Isaac
Reynolds, Murdock
Rhodes, Julius J.
Ryan, James
Saunders, Thomas O.
Saunders, John
Scercey, J. H.
Seeing, J. J.
Shaffer, Benjamin
Showalter, John A.
Shulenbarrier, D.
Shute, Leonard C.
Simmons, M. W.
Simmons, William H.
Skillan, James
Smith, John
Smith, George
Smith, John E.
Smith, Edwin
Solomons, Samuel
Spikes, W. B.
Stoncurch, H.
Strickland, James
Strickland, H.
Temple, Wilson
Thompson, J. B.
Thornton, John
Troxtler, John

Walcott, S. F.
Walker, William A.
Walker, John
Warrick, Alpheus
Welsh, James

West, John
Westcott, John L.
Wheeler, John
White, John
Whittington, Calvin

Williams, R.
Wilson, John
Wood, John K.
Wood, John S.
Wroten, Thomas O.

MARINES

Brady, J.
Haggerty, John
Hickey, John
Joyce, John
McDade, John

McGeehan, Andrew
McLaughlin, Joseph
Mulcahy, John
Murphey, Thomas
Prain, Thomas

Quigley, James
Quinn, T.
Rogers, Thomas
Sullivan, John
Williams, John

APPENDIX 5

CAPTURE OF THE USS UNDERWRITER, IN THE NEUSE, OFF NEWBERN, N. C., FEBRUARY, 1864

Surgeon Daniel B. Conrad, CSN

(From *Southern Historical Society Papers,*
vol. 19 [January 1891]: 93–100)

IN JANUARY, 1864, THE Confederate naval officers on duty in Richmond, Wilmington and Charleston were aroused by a telegram from the Navy Department to detail three boats' crews of picked men and offices, who were to be fully armed, equipped and rationed for six days; they were to start at once by rail for Weldon, North Carolina, reporting on arrival to Commander J. Taylor Wood, who would give further instructions. So perfectly secret and well-guarded was our destination that not until we had all arrived at Kingston, North Carolina, by various railroads, did we have the slightest idea of where we were going or what was the object of the naval raid. We suspected, however, from the name of its commander, that it would be "nervous work," as he had a reputation for boarding, capturing and burning the enemy's gunboats on many previous occasions. Embarking one boat after another on the waters of the Neuse, we found that there were ten of them in all, each manned by ten men and two officers, every one of whom were young, vigorous, fully alive and keen for the prospective work. Now we felt satisfied that it was going to be hand-to-hand fighting; some Federal gunboat was to be boarded and captured by us, or we were to be destroyed by it.

Sunday afternoon, February 1, 1864, about 2 o'clock, we were all quietly floating down the narrow Neuse, and the whole sunny Sabbath evening was thus passed, until at sunset we landed on a small island. After eating our supper, all hands were assembled to receive instructions. Commander Wood, in distinct and terse terms, gave orders to each boat's crew and its officers just what was expected of them, stating that the object of the expedition was to, that night, board some one of the enemy's gunboats, then supposed to be lying off the city of Newbern, now nearly sixty miles distant from where we then were by water. He said that she was to be captured without fail. Five boats were to board her on either side simultaneously, and then when in our possession we were to get up steam and cruise after other gunboats. It was a grand scheme, and was received by the older men with looks of admiration and with rapture by the young midshipmen, all of whom would have broken out into loud cheers but for the fact that the strictest silence was essential to the success of the daring undertaking.

In concluding his talk, Commander Wood solemnly said: "We will now pray;" and thereupon he offered up the most touching appeal to the Almighty that it has ever been my fortune to have heard. I can remember it now, after the long interval that has elapsed since then. It was the last ever heard by many a poor fellow, and deeply felt by every one. Then embarking again, we now had the black night before us, our pilot reporting two very dangerous points where the enemy had out pickets of both cavalry and infantry. We were charged to pass these places in absolute silence, our arms not to be used unless we were fired upon, and then in that emergency we were to get out of the way with all possible speed, and pull down stream in order to surprise and capture one of the gunboats before the enemy's pickets could carry the news of our raid to them.

In one long line, in consequence of the narrowness of the stream, did we pull noiselessly down, but no interrupting pickets were discovered, and at about half past three o'clock we found ourselves upon the broad estuary of Newbern bay. Then closing up in double column we pulled for the lights of the city, even up to and close in and around the wharves themselves, looking (but in vain) for our prey. Not a gunboat could be seen; none were there. As the day broke we hastened for shelter to a small island up stream about three miles away, where we landed upon our arrival, dragged our boats into the high grass, setting out numerous pickets at once. The remainder of us, those who were not on duty, tired and weary, threw ourselves upon the damp ground to sleep during the long hours which must necessarily intervene before we could proceed on our mission. Shortly after sunrise we heard firing by infantry. It was quite sharp for an hour, and then it died away. It turned out to be, as we afterwards learned, a futile attack by our lines under General Pickett on the works around Newbern. We were obliged to eat cold food all that day, as no fires were permissible under any circumstances; so all we could do was to keep a sharp lookout for the enemy, go to sleep again, and wish for the night to come.

About sundown one gunboat appeared on the distant rim of the bay. She came up, anchored off the city some five miles from where we were lying, and we felt that she was our game. We began at once to calculate the number of her guns and quality of her armament, regarding her as our prize for certain.

As darkness came upon us, to our great surprise and joy, a large launch commanded by Lieutenant George W. Gift, landed under the lee of the island. He had been, by some curious circumstance, left behind, but with his customary vigor and daring impressed a pilot, and taking all the chances came down the Neuse boldly in daylight to join us in the prospective fight. His advent was a grand acquisition to our force, as he brought with him fifteen men and one howitzer.

We were now called together again, the orders to each boat's crew repeated, another prayer was offered up, and then, it being about nine o'clock, in double column we started directly for the lights of the gunboat, one of which was distinctly showing at each masthead. Pulling slowly and silently for four hours we neared her, and as her outlines became distinct, to our great surprise we were hailed man-of-war fashion, "Boat, ahoy!" We were discovered, and, as we found out later, were expected and looked for.

This was a trying and testing moment, but Commander Wood was equal to the emergency. Jumping up, he shouted: "Give way hard! Board at once!" The men's backs bent and straightened on the oars, and the enemy at the same moment opened upon us with small arms. The long, black sides of the gunboat, with men's heads and shoulders above them could be distinctly seen by the line of red fire, and we realized immediately that the only place of safety for us was on board of her, for the fire was very destructive.

Standing up in the boat with Commander Wood, and swaying to and for by the rapid motion, were our marines firing from the bows, while the rest of us, with only pistol in belt, and our hands ready to grasp her black sides, were all anxious for the climb. Our coxswain, a burly, gamy Englishman, who by gesture and loud word, was encouraging the crew, steering by the tiller between his knees, his hands occupied in holding his pistols, suddenly fell forward on us dead, a ball having struck him fairly in the forehead.

The rudder now having no guide, the boat swerved aside, and instead of our bows striking at the gangway, we struck the wheelhouse, so that the next boat, commanded by Lieutenant Loyall, had the deadly honor of being first on board. Leading his crew, as became his rank, duty and desire, he jumped and pulled into the gangway—now a blazing sheet of flame, and being nearsighted, having lost his glasses, stumbled and fell prone upon the deck of the gunboat, the four men who were following close up on his heels falling on top of him stone dead, killed by the enemy's bullets; each one of the unfortunate fellows having from four to six of them in his body, as we found out later. Rising, Lieutenant Loyall shook off his load of dead men, and by this time we had climbed up on the wheelhouse, Commander Wood's long legs giving him an advantage over the rest of us; I was the closest to him, but had nothing to do as yet, except to anxiously observe the progress of the hand-to-hand fighting below me. I could hear Wood's stentorian voice giving orders and encouraging the men, and then, in less than five minutes, I could distinguish a strange synchronous roar, but did not understand what it meant at first; but it soon became plain: "She's ours," everybody crying at the top of their voices, in order to stop the shooting, as only our own men were on their feet.

I then jumped down on the deck, and as I struck it, I slipped in the blood, and fell on my back and hands; rising immediately, I caught hold of an officer standing near me, who with an oath collared me, and I threw up his revolver just in time to make myself known. It was Lieutenant Wilkinson, who the moment he recognized me, exclaimed: "I'm looking for you doctor; come here. "Following him a short distance in the darkness, I examined a youth who was sitting in the lap of another, and in feeling his head I felt my hand slip down between his ears, and to my horror, discovered that his head had been cleft in two by a boarding sword in the hands of some giant of the forecastle. It was Passed Midshipman Palmer Sanders, of Norfolk. Directing his body, and those of all the other killed, to be laid out aft on the quarter deck, I went down below, looking for the wounded in the ward-room, where the lights were burning, and found half a dozen with slight shots from revolvers. After having finished my examination, a half an hour and elapsed, and when ascending to the deck again I heard the officers of the various corps reporting to Commander Wood; for immediately after the capture of the vessel, according to the orders, the engineers and firemen had been sent down to the engine-room to get up steam, and Lieutenant Loyall as executive officer, with a number of seamen had attempted to raise the anchor, cast loose the cable which secured the ship to the wharf just under the guns of Fort Stephenson, while the marines in charge of their proper officers were stationed at the gangways guarding the prisoners. The lieutenants, midshipmen and others manned the guns, of which there were six eleven-inch, as it was the intention to convert her at once into a Confederate man-of-war, and under the captured flag to go out to sea, to take and destroy as many of the vessels of the enemy as possible.

But all our well-laid plans were abortive; the engineers reported the fires out, and that it would be futile to attempt to get up steam under an hour, and Lieutenant Loyall, too, after very hard work, reported it useless to spend any more time in trying to unshackle the chains, as the ship had been moored to a buoy, unless he could have hours in which to perform the work. Just at this moment, too, to bring things to a climax, the Fort under which we found that we were moored bow and stern, opened fire upon us with small arms, grape and solid shot; some of those who had escaped having reported the state of affairs on board, and this was the result.

In about fifteen minutes a solid shot or two had disabled the walking-beam, and it then became evident to all that we were in a trap, to escape from which depended on hard work and strategy. How to extricate ourselves in safety from the thus far successful expedition, was the question; but events proved that our commander was equal to the emergency.

Very calmly and clearly he directed me to remove all dead and wounded to the boats, which the several crews were now hauling to the lee side of the vessel, where they would be protected from the shots from the fort. The order was soon carried out by willing hands. They were distributed as equally as possible. Each boat in charge of its own proper officer, and subjected under that heavy fire to that rigid discipline characteristic of the navy, manned by their regular crews, as they laid in double lines, hugging the protected lee of the ship as closely as possible, it was a splendid picture of what a body of trained men can be under circumstances of great danger.

After an extended search through the ship's decks, above and below, we found that we had removed all the dead and wounded, and then, when the search was ended, reported to Captain Wood on the quarter-deck, where, giving his orders where the fire from the fort was very deadly and searching, he called up four lieutenants to him, to whom he gave instructions as follows: two of them were to go below in the forward part of the ship, and the other two below in the after part, where from their respective stations they were to fire the vessel, and not to leave her until her decks were all ablaze, and then at that juncture they were to return to their proper boats and report.

The remainder of us were lying on our oars while orders for firing the ship were being carried out; and soon we saw great columns of red flames shoot upward out of the forward hatch and ward-room, upon which the four officers joined their boats. Immediately, by the glare of the burning ship, we could see the outlines of the fort with its depressed guns, and the heads and shoulders of the men manning them. As the blaze grew larger and fiercer their eyes were so dazzled and blinded that every one of our twelve boats pulled away out into the broad estuary safe and untouched. Then we well realized fully our adroit and successful escape.

Some years after the affair I met one of the Federal officers who was in the fort at the time, and he told me that they were not only completely blinded by the flames, which prevented them from seeing us, but were also stampeded by the knowledge of the fact that there were several tons of powder in the magazine of the vessel, which when exploded would probably blow the fort to pieces; so, naturally, they did not remain very long after they were aware that the ship had been fired. This all occurred as we had expected. We in our boats, at a safe distance of more than half a mile, saw the *Underwriter* blow up, and distinctly heard the report of the explosion, but those at the fort, a very short distance from the ship, sought a safe refuge, luckily for them.

Fortunately there was no casualties at this stage of the expedition. I boarded the boat in my capacity as surgeon, attending to the requirements of those who demanded immediate aid, and I witnessed many amusing scenes; for among the prisoners were some old men-of-war's men, former shipmates of mine in the Federal navy years before, and of the other officers also. Their minds were greatly relieved when I made known to them who their captors were, and that their old surgeon and other officers were present, and as a natural consequence they would be treated well.

Continuing to pull for the remainder of the night, we sought and found by the aid of our pilot, a safe and narrow creek, up which we ascended, and at sunrise hauled our boats up on a beach, there we carefully lifted out our wounded men, placed them under the shade of trees in the grass, and made them as comfortable as possible under the circumstances.

Then we laid out the dead, and after carefully washing and dressing them, as soon as we had partaken of our breakfast, of which we were in so much need, all hands were called, a long pit was dug in the sand, funeral services were held, the men buried and each grave marked. We remained there all that day recuperating, and when night came again embarked on our return trip; all through that night and the four succeeding ones, we cautiously pulled up the rapid Neuse, doing most of our work in the darkness, until when nearing Kingston we could with impunity pull in daylight.

Arriving at Kingston, the boats were dragged up the hill to the long train of gondola cars which had been waiting for us, and then was presented an exhibition of sailors' ingenuity. The boats were placed upright on an even keel lengthwise on the flat cars, and so securely lashed by ropes that the officers, men, even the wounded, seated and laid in them as if on the water, comfortably and safely made the long journey of a day and two nights to Petersburg. Arriving, the boats were unshipped into the Appomattox river, and the entire party floated down it to City Point where it debouches into the James. It was contemplated that when City Point was reached to make a dash at any one Federal gunboat, should there be the slightest prospect of success; but learning from our scouts, on our arrival after dark, that the gunboats and transports at anchor there equaled of the number of our own boats at least, we had to abandon our ideas of trying to make a capture, and were compelled to hug the opposite banks very closely, where the river is nearly four miles wide, and in that manner ship up the James pulling hard against the current. By the next evening we arrived, without any further adventure, at Drury's Bluff, where we disembarked; our boats shown as mementos of the searching fire we had been subjected to—for they all were perforated by many minnie balls, the white wooden plugs inserted into the holes averaging fourteen to each boat engaged; they were all shot into them from stem to stern lengthwise.

Among the many incidents that occurred on the trip there were to which left a lasting impression on my mind, and to this day they are as vivid as if they had happened yesterday. As we were stepping into the boats at the island that night, the lights of the gunboat plainly visible from the spot on which we stood, a bloody, serious action inevitable, several of the midshipmen, youth-like, were gaily chatting about what they intended to do—joyous and confi-dent, and choosing each other for mates to fight together shoulder to shoulder—when one of them who stood near me in the darkness made the re-mark, as a conclusion as we were taking our places in the boats:

"I wonder, boys, how many of us will be up in those stars by to-morrow morning?" This rather jarred on the ears of we older ones, and looking around to see who it was that had spoken, I recognized the bright and handsome Palmer Sanders. Poor fellow, he was the only one who took his flight, though many of the others were severely wounded.

On our route down to Kingston by rail we were obliged to make frequent stops for wood and water, and at every station the young midshipmen swarmed into the depots and houses, full of their fun and deviltry, making friends of the many pretty girls gathered there, who asked all manner of ques-tions as to this strange sight of boats on cars filled with men in a uniform new to them.

The young gentlemen explained very glibly what they were going to do—"to board, capture and destroy as many of the enemy's gunboats as possible." "Well, when you return," replied the girls, "be sure that you bring us some relics—flags, &c." "Yes, yes; we'll do it," answered the boys. "But what will you give us in exchange?" "Why, only thanks, of course." "That won't do. Give us a kiss for each flag—will you?"

With blushes and much confusion, the girls consented, and in a few mo-ments we were off and away on our journey again. On the return trip the young men, never for an instant forgetting the bargain they had made, manufactured several miniature flags. We old ones purposely stopped at all the stations we had made coming down in order to see the fun. The young ladies were called out at each place, and after the dead were lamented, the wounded in the cars cared for, then the midshipmen brought out their flags, recalled the promises made to them, and demanded their redemption. Immediately there commenced a lively outburst of laughter and denials, a skirmish, followed by a slight resistance, and the whole bevy were kissed seriatim by the midshipmen, and but for the whistle of train warning them away, they would have continued indefinitely.

APPENDIX 6

THE CONFEDERATE STATES NAVY YARD AT CHARLOTTE, N. C., 1862-1865

Violet G. Alexander

(From *Southern Historical Society Papers*, vol. 40 [1915]: 183–93)

NOTE: This article appeared in the *Charlotte News*, June 5, 1910—immediately after the unveiling of the Navy Yard Marker. Hon. Josephus Daniels, Secretary of the Navy, visited the site of the Charlotte Navy Yard in May, 1914—and this has aroused a new and wider interest in its history.

THE GREAT DEVELOPMENT OF historic activity in North Carolina during the last few years has been accompanied by the ripening of a taste for historical research and for the collection of matter bearing on county, as well as State and national history; and with this desire to preserve our county and State history has come the patriotic desire to mark historic places within our own borders, so that strangers and guests in each succeeding generation may know the patriotism, courage, bravery and true worth of North Carolina's sons and daughters, from the Colonial, Revolutionary and Confederate periods, even down to the present day.

Much of Mecklenburg's and Charlotte's splendid Colonial and Revolutionary history has been preserved and some of her historic places of those days have been marked, but her part in the Southern Confederacy, when our sons and daughters were one united people in their sacrifice, heroism, bravery and courage, has not received the recognition due her. So the Stonewall Jackson Chapter, U.D.C., through the interest of one of its members, Miss Violet G. Alexander, has returned its attention to the history of the Charlotte Navy Yard, and has marked with an appropriate iron the site of the side of the Confederate Navy Yard, which was established in Charlotte in the spring of 1862 and operated until 1865. The iron marker placed by the Stonewall Jackson Chapter, U.D.C., is a navy shield surrounded by sea anchors with this inscription in gold letters on a black back-ground:

"CONFEDERATE STATES NAVY YARD, CHARLOTTE, N. C., 1862–1865."

This marker is placed on the corner of the brick building of the S. A. L. freight depot, on East Trade street, as this is the site of the former Navy Yard. The tablet was designed by a committee appointed by the U.D.C., composed of Miss Violet Alexander and Mrs. B. D. Heath, and it was cast and placed by the Mecklenburg Iron Works, J. Frank Wilkes, manager. The tablet was unveiled by the Stonewall Jackson U.D.C. on June 3, 1910, which is President Jefferson Davis' birthday—a day of special veneration and observance in the South. Mrs. Stonewall Jackson, life-president of the Chapter, graced the occasion with her presence, and large numbers of veterans of the Mecklenburg Camp of Confederate Veterans, the Stonewall Jackson Chapter, U.D.C., Chapter of Children of Confederacy, as well as many patriotic citizens, were present. A splendid program was provided; Hon. E. R. Preston made an appropriate and patriotic speech; "Dixie," and other loved Southern songs were sung, and prayer and the benediction were said. Miss Violet Alexander, as chairman of the committee appointed by the U.D.C. to mark the site of the Confederate Navy Yard, deemed it advisable to give at this time to the general public a complete account of the Confederate Navy Yard at Charlotte. In compiling the article, she received much valuable aid from many who lived in Charlotte during that period, and some of whom were associated with the Navy Yard during its operations in Charlotte.

Mr. H. Ashton Ramsay, formerly officer in charge of the Navy Yard, with his residence in Charlotte from 1862 to 1865, now (1910) contracting manager of the American Bridge Company of New York, with headquarters in Baltimore, Md., has furnished the following:

"Early in May, 1862, it was determined to evacuate Norfolk, and in order to save some of the tools and machinery and to continue to manufacture ordnance for the navy, a number of the machines, tools, such as lathes, planing machines, and one small steam hammer, were hurriedly shipped to Charlotte, N. C., and Commander John M. Brooke, who was at that time chief of the ordnance bureau in Richmond (afterwards transferred to the army with rank of colonel, and after the war was a professor at the Virginia Military Institute at Lexington, Va., where he died) had assigned to him the United States mint property on West Trade street, and a lot located on and bounded by the railroad tracks of what was then known as the North Carolina Central Railroad, and close to the station used by the S. C. Railroad; this latter lot extended about 3,000 feet on the line of the railroad and faced on a side street parallel with the railroad about 1,000 feet. On this lot there was a small building, which had been occupied as a machine shop, and my recollection is, that the property was purchased from Capt. John Wilkes.

"Capt. R. L. Page, afterward General Page, was placed in command of the works, and had his headquarters, and also his residence, at the U. S. Mint on

West Trade street, where his family lived during his administration of the affairs of the Navy Yard.

"Shortly after the machinery referred to had been forwarded to Charlotte, N. C., the *Merrimac/Virginia,* which had been guarding the approaches to Norfolk, Va., had to be destroyed, together with other Confederate property at Norfolk, and Capt. Catesby Jones and the writer (H. Ashton Ramsay), who was chief engineer of the *Virginia,* were ordered to Charlotte, N. C., in connection with constructing the ordnance works. Subsequently General Page was transferred to the army and ordered to the command of Fort Morgan, near Mobile, Ala., leaving the writer (H. Ashton Ramsay) in command of the naval station at Charlotte, N. C.

"A number of large, frame structures were erected on the property acquired, including a gun-carriage shop, a laboratory and a torpedo shop, and a large forge shop, where the largest steam hammer in the South was built, and where propeller shafting was forged for all the Confederate ironclads; the *Virginia II* at Richmond; the *Albermarle,* which successfully rammed and destroyed several United States gun boats in the Roanoke river; the gun boats built in Charleston and Savannah; the ironclads *Tennessee, Mobile* and other ironclads built at New Orleans; in fact, none of the vessels could have been constructed had it not been for the works at Charlotte. Rifles, solid shot, shell and torpedoes were manufactured at these works in Charlotte and supplied the batteries of all the vessels and shore batteries manned by the Confederate navy.

"In the last six months of the war, when General Stoneman burnt Salisbury, N. C., and was expected to advance on Charlotte, the writer (Ramsay), then in command, was furnished with 300 muskets and directed to form a battalion of three (3) companies from the employees of the naval works and to ship as many of the naval stores and smaller tools as possible on railroad cars to Lincolnton, N. C. and to hold the battalion in readiness to receive from General Beauregard, to whom this battalion had been assigned.

"After the burning of Columbia, S. C., by General Sherman, he advanced toward Charlotte as far as Chester, S. C., but in the meantime the remnant of General Hood's army crossed over the country and came into Charlotte over the railroad bridge across the Catawba river, which we were instructed to plank over so the train could cross. Gen. Johnston then assumed command of all the forces concentrated at Charlotte and immediately transported his troops eastward and confronted General Sherman at Bentonville, where the last battle was fought and the enemy checked for the first time since the capture of Atlanta, Ga. Soon after this, President Jefferson Davis and his cabinet came to Charlotte, N. C., and for a few days Charlotte was the capital of the Confederacy.

"Mr. Davis and his cabinet started from Charlotte soon after the surrender of General Lee, towards Washington, Ga., under the escort of General

Wheeler's cavalry and one company of the navy yard battalion under Capt. Tabb, the other companies remaining to garrison Charlotte, and were surrendered together with the rest of General Johnston's army when the army capitulated at Greensboro, N. C., April, 1865.

"You will note by above that Charlotte, although several times menaced by hostile forces, and at one time the central focus of the Confederacy, was never actually captured by the enemy, their forces not coming into Charlotte until after the surrender at Greensboro."

(Signed) A. Ashton Ramsay,

Late Chief Engineer, C.S.N., and Lieut.-Colonel C.S.A., Baltimore, Md., March 1910.

Miss Alexander was unable to obtain data converging Commander John M. Brooke, referred to by Capt. Ramsay. Mrs. John Wilkes, one of Charlotte's most patriotic and beloved women, at Miss Alexander's request prepared the following sketch of the Charlotte Navy Yard. This article was read by Mrs. Wilkes before the U.D.C., of which she was onetime historian, in April, 1910. A manuscript copy is filled with the U.D.C. Chapter, and it appeared in the Charlotte Observer and the Charlotte News, April 3, 1910.

Mrs. Wilkes' article reads as follows:

"The Confederate Navy Yard In Charlotte, N. C., 1862. 1865.

"As the existence of a navy yard in Charlotte, N. C., has been doubted and derided, it is well to tell its story while there are some persons surviving who know of it and worked in it. I have found a number of workmen and persons, whose memory has aided mine, and here give a true history of the Charlotte Navy Yard.

"Soon after the fight between the *Monitor* and the *Merrimac,* it became apparent to the Confederate government that it would not be possible to hold Norfolk, Va., and the United States Navy would soon take possession of the fort and navy yard. So naval officers were sent to the interior in the spring of 1862 to select a site to which all the valuable movable property in the navy yard would be taken. They came along the only railroad then far enough inland to be safe, and reached Charlotte, N. C., on their mission. Both the officers, Capt. W. D. Murdaugh, and I think Capt. Wm. Parker, were old friends of my husband, Capt. John Wilkes, during his fourteen years' service in the United States navy (1841–1854) and of course he met and welcomed them.

"On talking about their request he showed them a place he had recently purchased, lying about 600 feet along the railroad, with 100 feet frontage on East Trade street. This they thought exactly suited to the purpose, far enough inland to be safe from attack by sea and lying on the only railroad which connected Richmond with the Southern States of the Confederacy. So the Confederate government bought the property on promise to pay for it.

"A large quantity of material and coke ovens, foundry and machine shops were erected. A wooden landing stage was built from the yard to the railroad for convenience in loading and un-loading. This was carried as far as the back of the brick building on East Trade street, near College street, to facilitate the movement of naval stores, and was then and for many years afterward called 'The Navy Yard wharf.' Subsequently it gave the name to all the cotton districts about College street, which has always been known even to this day as 'The Wharf,' an enduring reminder of the navy yard in Charlotte.

"No large guns were cast there, according to the testimony of Capt. Ashton Ramsay, who now lives in Baltimore, and who has given us much information on the subject. He told of a large trip-hammer, which was part of the machinery brought from Norfolk, and which was a great curiosity here. I well remember Capt. Wilkes taking me to see it work. With one blow it flattened a mass of iron, and the next the ponderous mass came down so gently as only to crack an egg placed under it.

"Many workmen came with the machinery from Norfolk, and their families are still with us. Some of the names I recall: B. N. Presson, R. Culpepper, R. W. Grimes, H. W. Tatum and many others. Other men of this vicinity entered the yard—Martin Frazier, Thomas Roberts, John Garibaldi, John Abernathy, John Rigler and many more.

"When the navy became a thing of the past, many of these staunch and good men entered Capt. Wilkes' service in the Mecklenburg Iron Works, where they remained until death, or infirmity terminated their labors forty years afterward. It was a subject of great gratification to Capt. Wilkes that his workmen were so long in his service. Many of the above list, as well as some excellent colored men, were with him until their death, and no strikes or discontent ever disturbed their cordial relations.

"One small gun was brought from Norfolk and passed with other material to the Mecklenburg Iron Works. For many years it was used in the celebrations and parades, but fearing it might burst and injure some one, Capt. Wilkes had it broken up.

"When Richmond was taken by the Federal army, Mrs. Jefferson Davis and her family were in Charlotte, the house on North Brevard street (northeast corner) and East Fifth street, having been rented for her use. When the news reached here the authorities prepared to remove the specie from the treasury and other valuables sent here for safe keeping. Mrs. Davis insisted on accompanying the train with her children and her niece. The men at the navy yard were formed into a company as marines, armed and equipped as well as could be, and ordered out to guard the treasure train. Capt. Wm. Parker was in command. Just before they left he brought his old sword to me, asking me to keep it for him, and it still hangs in my hall.

"The train went by rail to Chester, S. C., and then took up the march for the West. Forty-two (42) wagons with fifty-five (55) men on guard, carried the specie. Mrs. Davis and family and the government officials were in carriages and on horseback. They marched as far as Cokesville, a village beyond Augusta, Ga., and then were ordered back to Newberry, S. C., where the iron-bound boxes of specie were put in a bank. It was a cold, rainy night, and Mr. W. S. Culpepper recalls with pleasure a gracious act of Mrs. Davis. He, a young fellow of 17 or 18 years, was detailed as guard at the door of a little church where her family was spending the night. Mrs. Davis came to the door, bringing him a glass of wine, saying he must be cold and wet, and this was all she could do for him.

"The next day the officials wanted to pay off the 55 men of the guard with pennies, but, remembering the weary tramp back to Charlotte, the men declined the offer and never received any pay for their labor.

"A few days later, in April, 1865, President Davis and his cabinet came to Charlotte and for a few days this was the capital of the Confederate States. One of the last declarations and cabinet meeting was held in the building now occupied by the Charlotte Observer, then the bank, and some of their last acts were sealed and signed there.

"After the news of President Lincoln's assassination was received the government broke up and the officers dispersed. President Davis set out to overtake his family and the sequel is historic.

"The navy yard was abandoned and when the Federal forces marched into Charlotte, it was taken possession of by the United States government as was the mint and all the stores of the Confederacy.

"Later, Captain Wilkes was permitted to repurchase his own property (the Confederacy never having paid him for its use) at a reasonable rate. There he establish the Mecklenburg Iron Works, which occupied the site for 10 years, from April, 1865 to April, 1875. The last casting were made there on the day of our big fire, April 12th, 1875.

(Signed) "JANE RENWICK WILKES.

"March, 1910." (Mrs. John Wilkes.)

Mr. P. P. Zimmerman, of the Mecklenburg Iron Works, a life-time resident of Charlotte, and one of her most honored citizens, gave Miss Alexander invaluable aid in her researches for data and furnished her with the following list of men who came to Charlotte with the removal of the naval works from Norfolk. Mrs. Wilkes has made mention of some of them and paid a fine tribute to their sterling worth and fine loyalty. The list of names given by Mr. Zimmerman is as follows:

Ruben Culpepper.	T. J. Roake, Jr.
W. E. Culpepper.	Robert Culpepper.
Henry W. Tatum.	R. M. Grimes.
Joshua Sykes.	B. M. Presson.
Cornelius Myers.	Thomas Dwyer.
William Myers.	George Dougherty.
Washington Bright.	Jerry Nicholson.
Cope Smith.	Hugh Smith.
Edward Lewis.	Henry Brown.
Isaac Summer.	Henry Tucker.
John Davis.	Henry Goodwin.
James Lloyd.	Elias Guy.
Clay Guy.	Henry Tabb.
Augustus Tabb.	John Thomas.
Andrew Hoffermangle.	John W. Owens.
James Recketts.	Augustus Recketts.
George W. Thompson, Sr.	George W. Thomas, Jr.
Thomas Winfields.	Columbus Walker.
Charles L. Walker.	Joshua Hopkins.
Michael Holey.	George W. Gleason, Sr.
George W. Gleason, Jr.	James Peed.
Thomas Peed.	John Howards.
Willoughby Butt.	Marcellus Thurma.
A. Brewer.	G. J. Rooke, Sr.

Unfortunately, it has been impossible to secure a complete roster of the men who came to Charlotte with the naval works, and who served here from 1862 to 1865, part of that time as members of the three companies of marines. Mr. Zimmerman recalls the names of 51 men, all skilled workmen, who came to Charlotte from Norfolk in 1862. There were many others of whom we have no record, who either died, returned to Norfolk after the war, or moved elsewhere; as we learn from Capt. H. Ashton Ramsey that he was in command of three (3) companies organized from the men of this navy yard.

Capt. Wm. B. Taylor, formerly city tax collector, and one of Charlotte's best known veterans, a member of the Mecklenburg Camp of Confederate Veterans, tells us that Thomas Dwyer, who came to Charlotte from Norfolk with the navy yard men, invented a machine fur turning a perfect sphere, a cannon ball or shell. It was the first successful invention of its kind and was used in the Charlotte navy yard. This valuable invention was confiscated by the United States government and put into use in the United States navy yards, no credit or remuneration ever being given to the Southern inventor.

Capt. H. Aston Ramsey was the officer in charge of the navy yard and Mr. Peters was in charge of the naval store, located at the corner of East Trade street and South College street, convenient to the navy yard. Captain Richard L. Page was the commandant in charge of the entire station, with his official residence at the United States mint, on West Trade street, the latter building having been seized by the Confederate forces and was held by them until the end of the war. Here resided with Captain Page, his niece, Miss Edmonia Neilson, who is still living, at present a resident of Norfolk. Miss Alexander had much correspondence with Miss Neilson, regarding her residence in Charlotte, and she recalled those stormy days most distinctly, and gave many interesting and exciting episodes. She is indebted to Miss Neilson for the following valuable quotation from "The Confederate States Naval History," by Prof. J. Thomas Scharf, A. M., L. L. D., who says: "General Page entered the United States Navy as a midshipman in 1824. He served the United States Navy until 1861, then a Virginian by birth, he cast his lot with the Confederacy and entered the Confederate States Navy, June 10th, 1861, with commission of commander, acting as ordnance officer of the Norfolk Navy Yard until the evacuation of the place by the Confederates. After the evacuation of Norfolk, Commander Page was promoted to the rank of captain, and with the machinery and men removed from the Norfolk shops, established the ordnance and construction depot at Charlotte, N. C., which, under his administration, became of inestimable value to the Confederacy."

APPENDIX 7

THE RAM ALBEMARLE: HER CONSTRUCTION AND SERVICE

Lt. Gilbert Elliott, CSA

(From *North Carolina Regiments, 1861–1865*, 5:315–23)

URING THE SPRING OF 1863, having been previously engaged in unsuccess-ful efforts to construct war vessels, of one sort or another, for the Confederate Government, at different points in Eastern North Carolina and Virginia, I undertook a contract with the Navy Department to build an iron-clad gunboat, intended, if ever completed, to operate on the waters of Albemarle and Pamlico Sounds. Edward's Ferry on the Roanoke river, in Halifax County, North Carolina, about 30 miles below the town of Weldon, was fixed upon as the most suitable for the purpose. The river rises and falls, as is well known, and it was necessary to locate the yard on ground sufficiently free from over-flow to admit of uninterrupted work for at least twelve months. No vessel was ever constructed under more adverse circumstances. The shipyard was established in a corn field, where the ground had already been marked out and planted for the coming crop, but the owner of the land, W. R. Smith, Esq., was in hearty sympathy with the enterprise, and aided me then and afterwards, in a thousand ways, to accomplish the end I had in view. It was next to impossible to obtain machinery suitable for the work in hand. Here and there, scattered about the surrounding country, a portable saw mill, blacksmith's forge, or other apparatus was found, however, and the citizens of the neighborhoods on both sides of the river were not slow to render me assistance, but co-operated, cordially, in the completion of the iron-clad, and at the end of about one year from the laying of the keel, during which innumerable difficulties were overcome by constant application, determined effort, and incessant labor, day and night, success crowned the efforts of those engaged in the undertaking.

Seizing an opportunity offered by comparatively high water, the boat was launched, though not without misgivings as to the result, for the yard being on a bluff she had to take a jump, and as a matter of fact was "hogged" in the attempt, but to our great gratification did not thereby spring a leak.

The plans and specifications were prepared by John L. Porter, Chief Constructor of the Confederate Navy, who availed himself of the advantage gained by his experience in converting the frigate *Merrimac* into the iron-clad *Virginia* at the Gosport navy yard. The *Albemarle* was 152 feet long between perpendiculars; her extreme width was 45 feet; her depth from the gun-deck to the keel was 9 feet, and when launched she drew 6½ feet of water, but after being ironed and completed her draught was about 8 feet. The keel was laid, and construction was commenced by bolting down, across the center, a piece of frame timber, which was of yellow pine, eight by ten inches. Another frame of the same size was then dovetailed into this, extending outwardly at an angle of 45 degrees, forming the side, and at the outer end of this the frame for the shield was also dovetailed, the angle being 35 degrees, and then the top deck was added, and so on around to the other end of the bottom beam. Other beams were then bolted down to the keel, and to the one first fastened, and so on, working fore and aft, the main deck beams being interposed from stem to stern. The shield was 60 feet in length and octagonal in form.

When this part of the work was completed she was a solid boat, built of pine frames, and if caulked would have floated in that condition, but she was afterwards covered with 4-inch planking, laid on longitudinally, as ships are usually planked, and this was properly caulked and pitched, cotton being used for caulking instead of oakum, the latter being very scarce and the former almost the only article to be had in abundance. Much of the timber was hauled long distances. Three portable saw mills were obtained, one of which was located at the yard, the others being moved about from time to time to such growing timber as could be procured.

The iron plating consisted of two courses, 7 inches wide and 2 inches thick, mostly rolled at the Tredegar Iron Works, Richmond. The first course was laid lengthwise, over a wooden backing, 16 inches in thickness, a 2-inch space, filled in with wood, being left between each two layers to afford space for bolting the outer course through the whole shield, and the outer course was laid flush, forming a smooth surface, similar to that of the *Virginia*. The inner part of the shield was covered with a thin course of planking, nicely dressed, mainly with a view to protection from splinters. Oak knees were bolted in, to act as braces and supports for the shield.

The armament consisted of two rifled Brooke guns mounted on pivot-carriages, each gun working through three port-holes, as occasion required, there being one porthole at each end of the shield and two on each side. These were protected by iron covers lowered and raised by a contrivance worked on the gun-deck. She had two propellers driven by two engines of 200-horse power, each, with 20-inch cylinders, steam being supplied by two flue boilers, and the shafting was geared together.

The sides were covered from the knuckle, four feet below the deck, with iron plates two inches thick. The prow was built of oak, running 18 feet back, on center keelson, and solidly bolted, and it was covered on the outside with iron plating, 2 inches thick, and, tapering off to a 4-inch edge, formed the ram.

The work of putting on the armor was prosecuted for some time under the most disheartening circumstances, on account of the difficulty of drilling holes in the iron intended for her armor. But one small engine and drill could be had, and it required, at the best, twenty minutes to drill an inch and a quarter hole through the plates, and it looked as if we would never accomplish the task. But "necessity is the mother of invention," and one of my associates in the enterprise, Peter E. Smith, of Scotland Neck, North Carolina, invented and made a twist drill with which the work of drilling a hole could be done in four minutes, the drill cutting out the iron in shavings instead of fine powder.

For many reasons it was thought judicious to remove the boat to the town of Halifax, about twenty miles up the river, and the work of completion, putting in her machinery, armament, etc., was done at that point, although the actual finishing touches were not given until a few days before going into action at Plymouth.

Forges were erected on her decks, and blacksmiths and carpenters were kept hard at work as she floated down the river to her destination. Captain James W. Cooke, of the Confederate Navy, a native of North Carolina, was detailed by the department to watch the construction of the vessel and to take command when she went into commission. He made every effort to hasten the completion of the boat. He was a bold and gallant officer, and in the battles in which he subsequently engaged he proved himself a hero. Of him it was said that "he would fight a powder magazine with a coal of fire," and if such a necessity could by any possibility have existed he would, doubtless, have been equal to the occasion.

In the Spring of 1864 it had been decided at headquarters that an attempt should be made to recapture the town of Plymouth. General Hoke was placed in command of the land forces, and Captain Cooke received orders to cooperate. Accordingly, Hoke's Division proceeded to the vicinity of Plymouth and surrounded the town from the river above to the river below, and preparation was made to storm the forts and breastworks as soon as the *Albemarle* could clear the river front of the Federal war vessels protecting the place with their guns.

On the morning of 18 April, 1864, the *Albemarle* left the town of Hamilton and proceeded down the river towards Plymouth, going stern foremost, with chains dragging from the bow, the rapidity of the current making it impracticable to steer with her head down stream. She came to anchor about three miles above Plymouth, and a mile or so above the battery on the bluff at Warren's

Neck, near Thoroughfare Gap, where torpedoes, sunken vessels, piles, and other obstructions had been placed. An exploring expedition was sent out, under command of one of the Lieutenants, which returned in about two hours, with the report that it was considered impossible to pass the obstruction. Thereupon the fires were banked, and the officers and crew not on duty retired to rest.

Having accompanied Captain Cooke as a volunteer aide, and feeling intensely dissatisfied with the apparent intention of lying at anchor all that night, and believing that it was "then or never" with the ram if she was to accomplish anything, and that it would be foolhardy to attempt the passage of the obstructions and batteries in the day time, I requested permission to make a personal investigation. Captain Cooke cordially assenting, and Pilot John Luck and two of the few experienced seamen on board volunteering their services, we set forth in a small lifeboat, taking with us a long pole, and arriving at the obstructions proceeded to take soundings. To our great joy it was ascertained that there was ten feet of water over and above the obstructions. This was due to the remarkable freshet then prevailing; the proverbial "oldest inhabitant" said, afterwards, that such high water had never before been seen in Roanoke river. Pushing on down the stream to Plymouth, and taking advantage of the shadow of the trees on the north side of the river, opposite the town, we watched the Federal transports taking on board the women and children who were being sent away for safety, on account of the approaching bombardment. With muffled oars, and almost afraid to breathe, we made our way back up the river, hugging close to the northern bank, and reached the ram about 1 o'clock, reporting to Captain Cooke that it was practicable to pass the obstructions provided the boat was kept in the middle of the stream. The indomitable commander instantly aroused his men, gave the order to get up steam, slipped the cables in his impatience to be off, and started down the river. The obstructions were soon reached and safely passed, under a fire from the fort at Warren's Neck which was not returned.

Protected by the iron-clad shield, to those on board the noise made by the shot and shell as they struck the boat sounded no louder than pebbles thrown against an empty barrel. At Boyle's Mill, lower down, there was another fort upon which was mounted a very heavy gun. This was also safely passed, and we then discovered two steamers coming up the river. They proved to be the *Miami* and the *Southfield*. The *Miami* carried 6 9-inch guns, 1 100-pounder Parrott rifle, and 1 24-pounder S. B. howitzer, and the ferry boat *Southfeld* 5 9-inch, 1 100-pounder Parrott and 1 12-pounder howitzer.

The two ships were lashed together with long spars, and with chains festooned between them. The plan of Captain Flusser, who commanded, was to run his vessels so as to get the *Albemarle* between the two, which would have placed the ram at a great disadvantage, if not altogether at his mercy; but Pilot John Luck, acting under orders from Captain Cooke, ran the ram close to the southern shore; and then suddenly turning toward the middle of the stream, and going with the current, the throttles, in obedience to his bell, being wide open, he dashed the prow of the *Albemarle* into the side of the *Southfield,* making an opening large enough to carry her to the bottom in much less time than it takes to tell the story. Part of her crew went down with her. Of the officers and men of the *Southfield,* seven of the former, including Acting Volunteer Lieutenant C. A. French, her commander, and forty-two of her men were rescued by the *Miami* and the other Union vessels; the remainder were either captured or drowned.

The chain-plates on the forward deck of the *Albemarle* became entangled in the frame of the sinking vessel, and her bow was carried down to such a depth that water poured into her port-holes in great volume, and she would soon have shared the fate of the *Southfield,* had not the latter vessel reached the bottom, and then, turning over on her side, released the ram, thus allowing her to come up on an even keel. The *Miami,* right alongside, had opened fire with her heavy guns, and so close were the vessels together that a shell with a ten-second fuse, fired by Captain Flusser, after striking the *Albemarle* rebounded and exploded, killing the gallant man who pulled the lanyard, tearing him almost to pieces.

Not withstanding the death of Flusser, an attempt was made to board the ram, which was heroically resisted by as many of the crew as could be crowded on the top deck, who were supplied with loaded muskets passed up by their comrades below. The *Miami,* a powerful and very fast side-wheeler, succeeded in eluding the *Albemarle* without receiving a blow from her ram, and retired below Plymouth, into Albemarle Sound.

Captain Cooke having successfully carried out his part of the program, General Hoke attacked the fortifications the next morning and carried them; not, however, without heavy loss, Ransom's Brigade alone leaving 500 dead and wounded on the field, in their most heroic charge upon the breastworks protecting the eastern front of the town.

General Wessells, commanding the Federal forces, made a gallant resistance, and surrendered only when further effort would have been worse than useless. During the attack the *Albemarle* held the river front, according to contract, and all day long poured shot and shell into the resisting forts with her two guns.

On 5 May, 1864, Captain Cooke left the Roanoke River with the *Albemarle* and two tenders, the *Bombshell* and *Cotton Plant,* and entered the Sound with the intention of recovering, if possible, the control of the two Sounds, and ultimately of Hatteras Inlet. He proceeded about sixteen miles on an east-northeasterly course, when the Federal squadron, consisting of seven well-armed gun-boats, the *Mattabesett, Sassacus, Wyalusing, Whitehead, Miami, Commodore Hull,* and *Ceres,* all under the command of Captain Melancthon Smith, hove in sight, and at 2 o'clock that afternoon approached in double line of battle, the *Mattabesett* being in advance. They proceeded to surround the *Albemarle,* and hurled at her their heaviest shot, at distances averaging less than one hundred yards.

The Union fleet, as we now know, had 32 guns and 23 howitzers, a total of 55. The *Albemarle* responded effectively, but her boats were soon shot away, her smokestack was riddled, many iron plates in her shield were injured and broken, and the after-gun was broken off eighteen inches from the muzzle, and rendered useless. This terrible fire continued, without intermission, until about 5 p. m., when the commander of the double- ender *Sassacus* selected his opportunity, and with all steam on struck the *Albemarle* squarely just abaft her starboard beam, causing every timber in the vicinity of the blow to groan, though none gave way. The pressure from the revolving wheel of the *Sassacus* was so great that it forced the after deck of the ram several feet below the surface of the water, and created an impression on board that she was about to sink. Some of the crew became demoralized, but the calm voice of the undismayed captain checked the incipient disorder, with the command, "Stand to your guns, and if we must sink let us go down like brave men."

The *Albemarle* soon recovered, and sent a shot at her assailant which passed through one of the latter's boilers, the hissing steam disabling a number of the crew. Yet the discipline of the *Sassacus* was such that, notwithstanding the natural consternation under these appalling circumstances, two of her guns continued to fire on the *Albemarle* until she drifted out of the arena of battle. Two of the fleet attempted to foul the propellers of the ram with a large fishing seine which they had previously procured for the purpose, but the line parted in paying it out. Then they tried to blow her up with a torpedo, but failed. No better success attended an effort to throw a keg of gunpowder down her smokestack, or what was left of it, for it was riddled with holes from shot and shell. This smokestack had lost its capacity for drawing, and the boat lay a helpless mass on the water. While in this condition every effort was made by her numerous enemies to destroy her. The unequal conflict continued until night. Some of the Federal vessels were more or less disabled, and both sides were doubtless well content to draw off.

Captain Cooke had on board a supply of bacon and lard, and this sort of fuel being available to burn without draught from a smokestack, he was able to make sufficient steam to get the boat back to Plymouth, where she tied up to her wharf covered with wounds and with glory.

The *Albemarle* in her different engagements was struck a great many times by shot and shell, the upper section alone of the smokestack has 114 holes made by shot and shell, and yet but one man lost his life, and that was caused by a pistol-shot from the *Miami,* the imprudent sailor having put his head out of one of the port-holes to see what was going on outside.

Captain Cooke was at once promoted and placed in command of all the Confederate naval forces in Eastern North Carolina. The *Albemarle* remained tied to her wharf at Plymouth until the night of 27 October, 1864, when Lieutenant William B. Cushing, of the United States Navy, performed the daring feat of destroying her with a torpedo. Having procured a torpedo-boat so constructed as to be very fast, for a short distance, and with the exhaust steam so arranged as to be noiseless, he proceeded, with a crew of fourteen men, up the Roanoke river. Guards had been stationed by the Confederate military commander on the wreck of the *Southfield,* whose top deck was then above water, but they failed to see the boat. A boom of logs had been arranged around the *Albemarle,* distant about thirty feet from her side. Captain Cooke had planned and superintended the construction of this arrangement before giving up the command of the vessel to Captain A. F. Warley. Cushing ran his boat up to these logs, and there, under a hot fire, lowered and exploded the torpedo under the *Albemarle's* bottom, causing her to settle down and finally to sink at the wharf. The torpedo boat and crew were captured; but Cushing refusing to surrender, though twice called upon to do so, sprang into the river, dived to the bottom, and swam across to a swamp opposite the town, thus making his escape; and on the next night, after having experienced great suffering, wandering through the swamp, he succeeded in obtaining a small canoe, and made his way back to the fleet.

The river front being no longer protected, and no appliances for raising the sunken vessel being available, on 31 October the Federal forces attacked and captured the town of Plymouth. The *Albemarle* was subsequently raised and towed to the Norfolk Navy Yard, and after being stripped of her armament, machinery, etc., she was sold, 15 October, 1867.

GILBERT ELLIOTT.

St. Louis, Mo.,

20 April, 1888.

NOTE: Gilbert Elliott was born at Elizabeth City, 10 December, 1843, and hence was only 19 years of age when he undertook to build the *Albemarle* After the war he practiced law in Norfolk, Va., St. Louis and New York. He was a brother of Captain Charles G. Elliott, A. A. G., of the Martin Kirkland brigade and of Warren G. Elliott, now President of the W. & W. R. R. Company. He died at Staten Island, N. Y., 9 May, 1895.

APPENDIX 8

THE CONFEDERATE RAM ALBEMARLE

Built to Clear the Roanoke, Neuse and Pamlico Rivers,
She Accomplished Her Mission Brilliantly

Captain James Dinkins

[From the *New Orleans Picayune*, December 28, 1902, January 4, 1903]

ARLY IN 1863 THE Federals had complete possession of all the bays and sounds and rivers along the Virginia and North Carolina coasts.

Pamlico Sound afforded a fine rendezvous for vessels of all kinds, while the towns along the Roanoke, Neuse and Pamlico rivers were garrisoned by Federal troops. From these garrisoned towns foraging parties scoured the country and destroyed or carried away every movable thing, including beast and fowl. The people in that section, being robbed of everything they possessed, appealed to the authorities at Richmond for aid and relief.

On March 14, 1863, Gen. D. H. Hill sent a brigade of infantry and a battery of smoothbore guns, under Gen. J. J. Pettigrew, in response to the call of the people, with instructions to destroy Fort Anderson, on the Neuse river, opposite Newbern, N. C.

General Pettigrew bombarded the place for two hours, but, satisfied he could not capture it by assault, withdrew. Subsequently, Gen. George E. Pickett was ordered from Kinston, with instructions to capture Newbern and destroy the enemy's fleet.

At this juncture the Confederates did not have a vessel of any kind in either of the three rivers named. General Pickett, feeling the need of some diversion on the river, managed to get a lot of skiffs, or new boats, about thirty in all, which he filled with men armed with rifles and cutlasses, under command of Colonel John Taylor Wood, who proceeded down the Neuse, to co-operate with the infantry.

The enemy's fleet at Newbern consisted of five gunboats—the *Lockwood*, *Underwriter*, *Hetzel*, *Commodore Hull*, and the *Hunchback*, while the forts were garrisoned by 4,000 men and fifty cannon. The audacity of the Confederates, therefore, in descending the river with thirty skiffs to attack the Federal fleet of five gunboats and two heavily-armed forts, scarcely has a parallel.

Colonel Wood set out on his desperate mission with as brave a little band as ever went in search of an enemy. There was not a faint heart or a nervous hand in the party. The noble fellows, in fisherman's boats, moved along, hugging the banks as closely as possible, hoping to avoid detection, until they had reached sight of the gunboats. What those men talked about and what hopes they had of surviving an attack against an armored fleet as they glided down the Neuse, would be a pretty story, if it could be told, but we can only surmise what passed between them in their whispered conversations, or what their thoughts reverted to.

About the middle of the night they sighted the *Underwriter,* lying at anchor, and immediately under the big guns of the fort. Nothing daunted, Colonel Wood formed his skiffs in columns of fours, and gave orders to pull for the gunboats. He imparted to the commander of each the part he was expected to perform. He directed the movement with as much deference and ceremony as if he was communicating with captains of modern men-of-war.

On they pulled in the stillness of the night, each crew striving their utmost to be the first to reach the scene. The signal lights hung from the *Underwriter,* but all was darkness without. A sentinel paced the deck to and fro, but otherwise there was no evidence of life on the vessel.

It was well known by the Federals that the Confederates had no vessel of any nature or kind in the river, therefore they felt no anxiety for their safety. Fortunately the tide was in favor of the Confederates, as it ebbed to the sea, and the noise of the waves, as they splashed against the gunboat, drowned the sound of their oars.

Noiselessly the assailants glided into the shadow of the ship, and the four skiffs in front passed by and turned into shore. Instantly, almost, those following were in touch of the gunboat, and when Colonel Wood gave the signal the boys clambered on the sides as nimbly as squirrels. They all knew what was expected of them and went to work. The sentinel was captured before he could arouse his comrades, therefore little difficulty was experienced in making the crew prisoners.

The officers of the vessel tried to rally the crew, and the Commander, Lieutenant Westervelt, and four or five marines, who refused to surrender were killed. The little band of Confederates behaved as if each was a captain, and covered every part of the boat without a moment's delay.

The guns of the fort were not exceeding 100 yards distant, but Colonel Wood's plans were carried out so perfectly and noiselessly the garrison was not aware of what transpired below them. Colonel Wood thought to make the *Underwriter* his flagship, but finding the boilers cold set fire to her, and escaped without the loss of a man or an oar.

The following day General Pickett opened fire on the forts and created the wildest dismay among the enemy, but decided not to assault the works, and on February 3d withdrew his command.

The boldness of Colonel Wood and his little crew excited the wonder of the enemy, and won the warmest commendations from our people, especially those who had felt the ravening hands of the foraging parties.

Soon after the events described above had taken place an ardent and devoted Southerner by the name of Gilbert Elliott, who had some experience in boatbuilding, proposed to the authorities at Richmond that with such aid as the Government could give he would undertake to construct a ram, which he believed would clear the Roanoke river of the meddlesome things which infested its waters. He received all the encouragement the Government could offer, and began the work, under conditions which very few men would have been willing to undertake.

The river was not navigable for the enemy's vessels more than a few miles above Plymouth, therefore Mr. Elliott decided to construct the ram at what was known as Edwards Ferry. To all others it seemed an impossibility. No material or competent workmen at hand, yet he went to work and put so much energy in it, and expressed such confidence in his ability to float a machine worthy a trial, it gave vigor and strength to the undertaking.

It is impossible to say how he obtained the necessary bolts and nuts, besides the iron, to plate her. He prosecuted the work with great caution and secrecy. If the enemy ascertained his purpose an effort would be made to thwart it. Howbeit, he was master of every situation, and by April 10, 1864, the ram was ready for service, and was christened *Albemarle*.

She was built according to the plans of Constructor John L. Porter, Confederate States Navy. She was made of pine timber, 8 x 10 inches thick, dovetailed together and sheathed with four layers of plank. She was 122 feet long, 45 feet beam, and drew 8 feet. Her shield, octagonal in form, was 60 feet long, and was protected by two layers of 2-inch iron plating.

The ram, or the prow, was of solid oak, also plated with 2-inch iron, and tapered like a wedge. She had two engines of 200 horse-power, and when one considers the circumstances and difficulties under which she was constructed, we must confess she was a wonder.

When Elliott reported her ready for service, the Government selected the best men available to man her, under command of Captain J. W. Cooke, and decided to make another effort to capture Plymouth.

On April 18, 1864, the *Albemarle* cut loose from the little town of Hamilton, N. C., and started down the river to co-operate with an infantry force under command of General Hoke. The latter reached the vicinity of Plymouth and surrounded the town, from the river above to the river below, and awaited the advent of the ram.

About a mile and a half above the Federal forts, at Warren's Neck, and near Thoroughfare Gap, the enemy had planted torpedoes and obstructed the channel with wrecks of old boats and other things.

Captain Cooke came to anchor some three miles above Plymouth, and sent out a boat under command of a lieutenant to explore the river. The lieutenant, after a time, returned and reported that it was impossible to pass the obstructions. Captain Cooke thereupon gave orders to bank the fires, and the men were allowed to go to sleep.

Gilbert Elliott, who accompanied Captain Cooke as a volunteer, feeling great dissatisfaction at the conclusion reached, and believing that it was "then or never" with the ram, if she was to accomplish anything, urged Captain Cooke to make the trial. He argued that it would be foolhardy to attempt the passage of the obstructions and the forts in day time, and requested permission to make an investigation also.

Captain Cooke assented, and with the pilot, whose name was John Lusk, and two sailors, who volunteered to accompany them, set out in a small lifeboat. They carried a long pole with them, and, arriving at the obstructed point, began to take soundings. Elliott soon discovered that there was ten feet of water over and above the obstruction (which fact was due to a freshet in the river). The little party, however, pushed along down the stream until they reached Plymouth, and, taking advantage of the darkness, which was increased by the shadow of the trees, pulled to the opposite shore and watched the transport taking on board women and children, whom they were sending away on account of General Hoke's demonstration.

With the greatest caution, almost afraid to take a long breath, for fear of detection, Elliott and his companions made their way back and reached the *Albemarle* after midnight. Elliott stated to Captain Cooke his firm conviction that the ram could pass the obstructions, and urged him to make the attempt.

His earnestness was so great that Captain Cooke at once determined to do so, and had the men aroused, and had orders to get up steam as quickly as possible. The *Albemarle* was soon under way, but the enemy was entirely ignorant of her approach. In fact, they had no knowledge that the Confederates owned a boat in the river. She passed over the obstructions safely, but very soon a gun belched forth from the fort at Warren's Neck, and Captain Cooke realized that he was on a perilous journey.

The Federal battery opened fire vigorously, and the shells rattled against the ram in rapid succession. Elliott had protected her sides with hanging chains, and they proved a very fine shield. The ram was soon beyond the range of the guns, but a little lower down she passed a fort on which was mounted a very heavy gun. The big shells went whizzing over her bow and beyond, crashing through the timber for two miles.

The firing aroused the Federal fleet at Plymouth, and two vessels, the *Miami* and the *Southfield*, started to look for the trouble. The vessels carried each six 9-inch guns, one 100-pounder Parrott rifle, and a 24-pounder howitzer. The two vessels were lashed together, and ascended the river with entire confidence among the officers that nothing in the Roanoke river could check them one minute.

Captain Flusher, the senior Federal officer, stated that his purpose in lashing the vessels together was to get the Confederate craft, whatever it might be, between his vessels, and capture it with little trouble.

Captain Cooke, however, as soon as he sighted the Federal boats, ran the *Albemarle* close to shore, and when in proper position, he suddenly turned her toward the middle of the stream, and, giving her all the steam he could, he dashed the prow into the side of the *Southfield* before a gun was fired. Cutting her almost in twain, she went to the bottom in less than two minutes, taking most of her crew with her.

The chains on the forward deck of the ram became entangled with the *Southfield*, which carried her bow to such a depth that the water began to pour into her portholes. The situation was critical. It looked as if nothing could save the ram, but as the *Southfield* struck bottom she turned over, and the *Albemarle* was released.

The *Miami*, in the meantime, had broken apart from the sunken vessel, and opened fire from her big guns at such close range that the flash passed over and beyond the *Albemarle*.

Here a most remarkable circumstance occurred. A 9-inch shell struck the ram, rebounded, and exploded almost at the lanyard of the gun which it came from, killing Captain Flusher and six men. Notwithstanding the confusion, the Federal crew made an effort to board the ram but were fought off by the Confederates, who used both bayonets and the butts of their rifles, killing a majority of the crew before they could escape.

Seeing how determined the Confederates were, the *Miami*, a very swift vessel, turned tail, and, although pursued by the ram, succeeded in making her escape. She never reversed her engines until she had ploughed into Albemarle Sound.

Captain Cooke successfully carried out his part of the plan by driving every vessel into the ocean. The following day General Hoke attacked the fortifications and carried them, although he lost a good part of his men. General Ransom's Brigade alone left nearly six hundred dead and wounded on the field.

General Ransom distinguished himself by leading his men over the enemy's works, where occurred a hand-to-hand fight.

The Federal Commander, General Wessells, made a gallant defense, but Ransom and Hoke forced him to surrender. The enemy's loss was very heavy. His dead lay in heaps, and his wounded were lying on all sides. During the assault the *Albemarle* played upon the forts also, but the Federal boats were too cautious to return.

After the capture of Plymouth, N. C., April 19, 1864—by Generals Hoke and Ransom—in which action the Confederate ram, *Albemarle,* destroyed one gunboat of the Federal fleet and drove the others into Pamlico Sound; the Confederates were greatly encouraged and the Federals correspondingly discouraged and alarmed. The Yankees spoke of the ram as the "Second *Merrimac,*" and they looked upon her as an unknown quantity, with unlimited capacity for destruction. In fact the Federal Government was laboring under much anxiety because of the changed condition of affairs in the sounds and rivers of North Carolina.

A single boat, the *Albemarle,* had met the entire fleet, destroyed one vessel and defeated the others. Subsequently, she steamed into the open sound, fought seven gunboats and captured one (the *Bombshell*), severely damaged five others and compelled the entire squadron to seek a place of safety. During this engagement the little ram suffered no serious damage.

On May 5, 1864, the *Albemarle* left Plymouth, followed by the *Bombshell,* to meet the Federal fleet, which was reported advancing from the sound, for the purpose of clearing the river of all Confederate boats.

The Federal fleet had been overhauled, reinforced and equipped with all sorts of guns and torpedoes, numerous enough to have alarmed several such crafts as the *Albemarle,* had she been manned by ordinary men and officers.

The Yankee fleet consisted of (what they termed) four double-enders—the *Mattabesett,* Commander John C. Febiger; the *Sassacus,* Lieutenant Commander F. A. Roe; the *Wyalusing,* Lieutenant Commander W. W. Queen; the *Miami,* Lieutenant Charles A. French—and two gunboats, the *Whitehead,* Ensign G. W. Barrett, and the *Ceres,* Commander H. H. Foster. Also, two transports, carrying seven guns each. The double-enders were equipped with four nine-inch Dahlgren guns, two 100-pounder Parrott rifles and one 24-pounder howitzer each. Total, 36 nine-inch Dahlgrens, 8 100-pounder Parrott rifles and 4 24-pounder howitzers.

The gunboats carried eight smoothbore and two rifle guns each, making a grand total of 82 cannon, while the *Albemarle* mounted four 6-inch rifle and two 8-inch smoothbore guns.

The enemy left the sound with full determination to capture or sink the ram.

After leaving the mouth of the Roanoke, the average width of which is about 150 yards, and the depth sufficient to float a vessel drawing sixteen feet of water as high up as Plymouth. Along the shores of Pamlico Sound that beautiful May morning the marsh was gay with little blue flags that nodded to the wind and bowed to the tide as it began to flow.

The birds skimmed lightly over its surface, and looked through the grasses at that splendid array of death-dealing monsters, as they gracefully moved about for positions in line before starting on the hunt for the *Albemarle*.

The sun rose beautifully, and the air was glorious; there was nothing to disturb the sway of the grasses or the chirp of the little marsh birds. Over all that wide expanse of water there was nothing to suggest the desperate encounter and inglorious defeat that awaited the great fleet which floated so grandly over Pamlico Sound. The scene resembled preparations for review.

Everything in readiness, the column headed for the mouth of the river, the *Mattabesett* leading, but the movement was so deliberate, and the order so perfect, no one could have believed that one single vessel would drive them back. It was not reasonable. It could not be possible.

The double-enders were ordered to pass as close to the *Albemarle* as they could, deliver fire, then get out of line as quickly as possible and round to for a second discharge if necessary, while the gunboats and transports were to open from below.

Torpedoes were provided to each boat and instructions given to use them liberally, and, if possible, destroy the propeller of the Confederate ram.

The vessels of the squadron sent to attack the *Albemarle* exceeded in numbers the entire Confederate Navy at that time.

However, the ram had twice before demonstrated its ability to take care of itself even against great odds. As the Federal fleet rounded into the river, they sighted the "Second *Merrimac*," as she steamed toward them. Captain Cooke opened with a shot from one of his rifles, which was quickly followed by another and another.

The aim was skillful. The first shot cut the rail and spars away from the *Mattabesett* and wounded six or seven men. Captain Cooke put on all the steam at his command and made for the Yankee boats. By this time the *Sassacus* came into position and fired a broadside from her 9-inch guns, but such shot as struck the ram skimmed off into the air, and even the 100-pounder rifle shells glanced off as they struck her sloping sides.

By this time five of the Yankee boats were firing on the ram as fast as the guns could be worked, but the smoke settled over all, and became so dense the Federal boats pulled away for fear of being rammed and took new positions.

The *Albemarle* continued to advance, keeping her guns busy.

The Yankee boats, favorably posted in the sound, concentrated their big guns on the ram, hoping to disable it by reaching her port holes. It looked as if the little ram could not survive the combined attack, but she was out for a fight, and floated into the sound as proudly and defiantly as if she was supreme. Quickly she changed her course for the "double-enders," but they set out again and took up new positions, and the ram passed in between them, using her guns with marked effect.

The situation was desperate, and the *Sassacus* was signaled "to ram the *Albemarle*." It was the only hope of success, though it was deemed certain that the *Sassacus* would go under. She moved on the *Albemarle* with a full head of steam, risking everything to save the other vessels. It was a moment of intense anxiety for all as the big ship neared the little *Albemarle*. The latter sent two shots through the Yankee boat just before she struck. A mighty crash, and the boom of cannon. The smoke became intense, and both vessels quivering, rebounded for the second attack. The bow of the *Sassacus* was shattered and she attempted to escape. The ram was still afloat, though, and went in pursuit, sending a shell crashing through the boat and through her boilers. Soon a cloud of steam and boiling water filled every part of the vessel. The shrill screams of the escaping steam almost drowned the sound of the guns, which the ram continued to fire into the unfortunate vessel.

The shouts of the Confederates and the cries of the scalded, blinded and wounded men made a scene which would appall the stoutest heart. The *Sassacus* surged to one side, then to the other, and began to sink. Those of the Yankee crew who survived climbed into the rigging to escape the boiling steam. The tumult always characteristic of battle was doubly intensified by the cries of agony from the scalded and dying men.

No effort was made by the other Federal vessels to give them aid. During all this time the surviving vessels floated at a respectful distance and took no part whatever. When the steam had cleared away the Federal fleet had gone, and the proud little *Albemarle* was master of the field.

One of the Commanders, in reporting the battle, said: "There was no lack of courage on our ships, but the previous loss of the *Southfield,* and the signal from the *Wyalusing* that she was sinking, and the loss of the *Sassacus,* dictated the prudent course they adopted."

The prudent course referred to was to get away as quickly as possible. Captain Cooke picked up the survivors of the *Sassacus* and returned to Plymouth.

From this action may be deduced the following argument: There is nothing in naval affairs which surpasses in brilliancy this battle of the *Albemarle*. The conduct of her crew was glorious; their deeds excited wonder at the time, and should stimulate those unborn when they hear the story. This single boat successfully met and defeated the entire Federal fleet on the North Carolina coast.

This story of the *Albemarle* is not complete. I cannot do her justice, but hope my feeble effort to tell of her matchless deeds will induce some one, better able, to do so.

Let us give a yell for Captain Cooke, his officers and crew.

It may be said, with truth, that the Southern people put more energy into naval affairs than had been done for fifty years before.

Had the Confederacy been able to construct one-third as many boats as the Federals had, there would not have been a blockade of southern ports. This is self-evident when we read the story of the *Merrimac,* the *Albemarle* and the greatest of all, the *Alabama*. When we recall her operations and consider the obstacles in her way, we stand in amazement and congratulate ourselves that Semmes was one of us.

NOTES

Full bibliographical data can be found in the Bibliography

CHAPTER 1: THE COMING STORM

1. U.S. Navy Department, *Official Records of the Union and Confederate Navies in the War of the Rebellion*, ser. 1, vol. 6, 790. (Hereafter referred to as ORN.)
2. Ibid., 21.
3. Tredwell, "North Carolina Navy," 5:299–300.
4. ORN, ser. 1, vol. 6, 22.
5. Ibid., 21.
6. Barrett, *Civil War in North Carolina*, 4–5.
7. Cantwell, "A Capture Before the War," 1:24.
8. U.S. War Department, *The War of the Rebellion*, ser. 1, vol. 1, 476. (Hereafter referred to as OR.)
9. Barrett, *Civil War in North Carolina*, 9.
10. OR, ser. 1, vol. 1, 486.
11. Ibid., 477.
12. Cantwell, "A Capture Before the War," 27.
13. Barrett, *Civil War in North Carolina*, 11.
14. Cantwell, "A Capture Before the War," 27–28.
15. Barrett, *Civil War in North Carolina*, 12.
16. Hill, *North Carolina*, 4:8–9.

CHAPTER 2: PREPARATION

1. Scharf, *History of the Confederate States Navy*, 368–69.
2. Davis, *Boy Colonel*, 76–77.
3. Barrett, *Civil War in North Carolina*, 32–33.
4. Tredwell, "North Carolina Navy," 5:300.
5. ORN, ser. 1, vol. 1, 50.
6. Ibid.
7. Robinson, *Confederate Privateers*, 110.
8. Ibid., 112–13.
9. ORN, ser. 1, vol. 6, 78–80.

10. Ibid., 140–41.
11. Barrett, *Civil War in North Carolina*, 36–37.

CHAPTER 3: DISASTER ON THE OUTER BANKS

1. ORN, ser. 1, vol. 6, 140.
2. Ibid., 141–42.
3. Ibid., 126.
4. Ibid., 139.
5. Scharf, *History of the Confederate States Navy*, 371.
6. ORN, ser. 1, vol. 6, 143.
7. Ibid., 139.
8. Ibid., 144.
9. Barrett, *Civil War in North Carolina*, 45.
10. Scharf, *History of the Confederate States Navy*, 375.
11. Ibid., 45–46.
12. ORN, ser. 1, vol. 6, 223–24.
13. Porter, *Naval History of the Civil War,* 47.

CHAPTER 4: THE CHICAMACOMICO RACES

1. Scharf, *History of the Confederate States Navy*, 377–78.
2. Ibid., 378.
3. Clark, *North Carolina Regiments*, 5:680.
4. Scharf, *History of the Confederate States Navy*, 377.
5. Barrett, *Civil War in North Carolina*, 48–49.
6. Ibid., 50–51.
7. OR, ser. 1, vol. 4, 596–97.
8. Scharf, *History of the Confederate States Navy*, 380.
9. Barrett, *Civil War in North Carolina*, 52.
10. Ibid.
11. Scharf, *History of the Confederate States Navy*, 381.
12. Ibid.
13. Ibid.
14. Barrett, *Civil War in North Carolina*, 54–55.
15. Ibid.
16. OR, ser. 1, vol. 4, 598.
17. Barrett, *Civil War in North Carolina*, 61.
18. ORN, ser. 1, vol. 4, 729.

CHAPTER 5: THE BATTLE FOR ROANOKE ISLAND

1. Ibid., ser. 1, vol. 6, 739.

2. Barrett, *Civil War in North Carolina*, 761.
3. Trotter, *Ironclads and Columbiads*, 70–71.
4. Barrett, *Civil War in North Carolina*, 73–74.
5. ORN, ser. 1, vol. 6, 765.
6. Parker, *Recollections of a Naval Officer*, 246–47.
7. Ibid., 247–48.
8. Ibid., 248.
9. Ibid., 248–49.
10. ORN, ser. 1, vol. 6, 599.
11. Parker, 249–50.
12. Ibid., 250.
13. ORN, ser. 1, vol. 6, 595.
14. Barrett, *Civil War in North Carolina*, 80–82.
15. Ibid., 85.
16. ORN, ser. 1, vol. 6, 595.
17. Ibid., 595–96.
18. Parker, 256–57.
19. Ibid., 257–58.
20. Ibid., 259.

CHAPTER 6: MORE DISASTERS

1. Creecy, *Pasquotank Historical Yearbook*, 1:1954–55.
2. Barrett, *Civil War in North Carolina*, 89.
3. Walcott, *History of the Twenty-first Regiment Massachusetts Volunteers*, 55.
4. Barrett, *Civil War in North Carolina*, 90.
5. Ibid., 92.
6. Ibid., 92–93.
7. OR, ser. 1, vol. 9, 196–96.
8. ORN, ser. 1, vol. 6, 654–55.
9. *Wilmington Journal*, February 27, 1862.
10. Trotter, *Ironclads and Columbiads*, 98.
11. ORN, ser. 1, vol. 7, 117–18.
12. Barrett, *Civil War in North Carolina*, 96.
13. Ibid.
14. Ibid., 104–5.
15. Branch, *Siege of Fort Macon*, 19–22.
16. OR, ser. 1, vol. 1, 747.
17. Ibid., 748.
18. Whittle, "Cruise of the C. S. Steamer *Nashville*," 209.
19. Stern, *Confederate Navy*, 70.

20. Whittle, "Cruise of the C. S. Steamer *Nashville*," 209.
21. Ibid., 210.
22. Barrett, *Civil War in North Carolina,* 117–18.

CHAPTER 7: THE WHITE HALL GUNBOAT

1. C.S. Congress, *Report . . . to Investigate the Affairs of the Navy Department,* 463–64.
2. Bright, Rowland, and Bardon, *CSS Neuse,* 150.
3. Clark, *Histories of the Several Regiments and Battalions from North Carolina,* 5:86.
4. Elliott, "Career of the Confederate Ram *Albemarle.*"
5. ORN, ser. 1, vol. 8, 845.
6. Hill, *North Carolina,* 4:143–44.
7. OR, ser. 1, vol. 18, 61–62.
8. Martin, "History of the Eleventh N. C. Infantry," 42.
9. Howe, *Kinston, Whitehall, and Goldsboro Expedition,* 25.
10. Ibid.
11. ORN, ser. 1, vol. 13, 813–14.
12. Still, "Career of the Confederate Ironclad *Neuse,*" 5.
13. Ibid., 6.
14. Scharf, *History of the Confederate States Navy,* 372.

CHAPTER 8: THE BUILDING OF THE *ALBEMARLE*

1. Barrett, *Civil War in North Carolina,* 172–73.
2. Ibid., 173.
3. Jones, "Construction, Fighting Career and Destruction of the *Albemarle,*" 9.
4. Melton, *Confederate Ironclads,* 184.
5. Elliott, *Ironclad of the Roanoke,* 88–89.
6. Ibid., 90–91.
7. Ibid., 99.
8. Ibid., 115.
9. Scharf, *History of the Confederate States Navy,* 404.
10. Elliott, *Ironclad of the Roanoke,* 139.
11. Ibid., 64–65.
12. Scharf, *History of the Confederate States Navy,* 408.
13. Elliott, "Career of the Confederate Ram *Albemarle,*" 421.
14. Ibid.
15. Scharf, *History of the Confederate States Navy,* 405.
16. Elliott, *Ironclad of the Roanoke,* 142–43.

17. Ibid., 103.
18. Elliott, "Career of the *Albemarle*," 421.
19. Ibid., 422.
20. Elliott, *Ironclad of the Roanoke*, 165.
21. Ibid., 117.

CHAPTER 9: GUN FLASHES ON THE NEUSE

1. Strode, *Jefferson Davis*, 507.
2. Shingleton, *John Taylor Wood*, 90.
3. Ibid., 91.
4. Current, *Encyclopedia of the Confederacy*, 4:1743.
5. Shingleton, *John Taylor Wood*, 91–92.
6. Dowdey, *Wartime Papers of Robert E. Lee*, 657.
7. Conrad, "Capture and Burning of the Federal Gunboat *Underwriter*," 93.
8. Shingleton, *John Taylor Wood*, 92.
9. Donnelly, *Confederate States Marine Corps*, 104.
10. Loyall, "Capture of the *Underwriter*," 137.
11. Ibid.
12. Shingleton, *John Taylor Wood*, 92–94.
13. Ibid., 94.
14. Conrad, "Capture and Burning of the Federal Gunboat *Underwriter*," 93–94.
15. Ibid., 94.
16. Loyall, "Capture of the *Underwriter*," 138.
17. Scharf, *History of the Confederate States Navy*, 396.
18. Conrad, "Capture and Burning of the Federal Gunboat *Underwriter*," 94.
19. Loyall, "Capture of the *Underwriter*," 138.
20. Conrad, "Capture and Burning of the Federal Gunboat *Underwriter*," 94.
21. Ibid.
22. OR, ser. 1, vol. 33, 93–96.
23. Conrad, "Capture and Burning of the Federal Gunboat *Underwriter*," 95.
24. Loyall, "Capture of the *Underwriter*," 139.
25. Shingleton, *John Taylor Wood*, 100.
26. Scharf, *History of the Confederate States Navy*, 397–98.
27. Conrad, "Capture and Burning of the Federal Gunboat *Underwriter*," 95–96.
28. Loyall, "Capture of the *Underwriter*," 140.
29. Ibid.
30. Conrad, "Capture and Burning of the Federal Gunboat *Underwriter*," 96.
31. Scharf, *History of the Confederate States Navy*, 399.

32. Conrad, "Capture and Burning of the Federal Gunboat *Underwriter*," 96.
33. Ibid.
34. Scharf, *History of the Confederate States Navy,* 400.
35. Conrad, "Capture and Burning of the Federal Gunboat *Underwriter*," 97.
36. Loyall, "Capture of the *Underwriter*," 142.
37. Shingleton, *John Taylor Wood,* 105–9.
38. Ibid., 111–12.

CHAPTER 10: THE *ALBEMARLE* ATTACKS

1. Elliott, *Ironclad of the Roanoke,* 166.
2. Ibid.
3. Ibid., 167.
4. Scharf, *History of the Confederate States Navy,* 405.
5. ORN, ser. 1, vol. 9, 656.
6. Barrett, *Civil War in North Carolina,* 216.
7. ORN, ser. 1, vol. 9, 637.
8. Elliott, "Career of the Confederate Ram *Albemarle*," 422.
9. Ibid.
10. Ibid.
11. Elliott, *Ironclad of the Roanoke,* 178.
12. Ibid., 178–79.
13. Jones, "Construction, Fighting Career and Destruction of the *Albemarle*," 43.
14. Elliott, *Ironclad of the Roanoke,* 179–81.
15. ORN, ser. 1, vol. 9, 657.
16. Ibid.
17. Elliott, *Ironclad of the Roanoke,* 185.
18. ORN, ser. 1, vol. 9, 658.

CHAPTER 11: FRUSTRATION AT KINSTON

1. OR, ser. 1, vol. 33, 1061.
2. Ibid., 1101.
3. Ibid., 97.
4. Robert D. Minor to Stephen R. Mallory, February 16, 1864, Minor Family Papers, Virginia Historical Society, Richmond, Virginia.
5. Still, "Career of the Confederate Ironclad *Neuse*," 6.
6. Bright, Rowland, and Bardon, *CSS Neuse,* 10, 153.
7. Benjamin Loyall to Robert D. Minor, March 9, 1864, Minor Family Papers.
8. OR, ser. 1, vol. 33, 1218–19.
9. R. H. Bacot to "Sis," March 19, 1864.

10. Benjamin Loyall to Robert D. Minor, April 7, 1864, Minor Family Papers.
11. Ibid.
12. Ibid.
13. Ibid.
14. R. H. Bacot to "Sis," April 28, 1864.
15. OR, ser. 1, vol. 33, 982.
16. R. H. Bacot to "Sis," May 23, 1864.
17. Bright, Rowland, and Bardon, *CSS Neuse,* 15–16.

CHAPTER 12: STORM OVER ALBEMARLE SOUND

1. Barrett, *Civil War in North Carolina,* 220.
2. ORN, ser. 1, vol. 9, 658.
3. Barrett, *Civil War in North Carolina,* 220–21.
4. Ibid., 221–22.
5. Elliott, *Ironclad of the Roanoke,* 190.
6. Scharf, *History of the Confederate States Navy,* 407.
7. Elliott, *Ironclad of the Roanoke,* 193.
8. OR, ser. 1, vol. 9, 770.
9. Elliott, *Ironclad of the Roanoke,* 196–98.
10. OR, ser. 1, vol. 9, 770.
11. Elliott, *Ironclad of the Roanoke,* 197.
12. Ibid., 197–98.
13. Ibid.
14. OR, ser. 1, vol. 9, 738.
15. Elliott, *Ironclad of the Roanoke,* 200.
16. OR, ser. 1, vol. 9, 744–45.
17. Holden, "The *Albemarle* and the *Sassacus,*" 4:629.
18. OR, ser. 1, vol. 9, 739.
19. Holden, "The *Albemarle* and the *Sassacus,*" 630.
20. Elliott, *Ironclad of the Roanoke,* 209.
21. Ibid., 210.
22. Ibid., 210–11.

CHAPTER 13: WILMINGTON AND THE CAPE FEAR

1. MacBride, *Civil War Ironclads,* 95.
2. Combs, "Confederate Shipbuilding on the Cape Fear River," 2–3.
3. Ibid., 4.
4. Still, *Iron Afloat,* 165.
5. Combs, "Confederate Shipbuilding on the Cape Fear River," 5.
6. Silverstone, *Warships of the Civil War Navies,* 205–6.

7. Combs, "Confederate Shipbuilding on the Cape Fear River," 6.

8. Trotter, *Ironclads and Columbiads*, 298–99.

9. Ibid., 8.

10. C. Lucian Jones Papers, collection 170, folder 21, item 432, Georgia Historical Society.

11. U.S. Navy, *Civil War Naval Chronology*, sec. 6, 277.

12. Donnelly, *Confederate States Marine Corps*, 105–6.

13. ORN, ser. 1, vol. 10, 21–22.

14. Ibid., 23–24.

15. Ibid., 20–21.

16. Doak, *Henry Melville Doak Memoir*, Microfilm # 824, reel, 5, box 12, folder 13.

17. Wise, *Lifeline of the Confederacy*, 238, 247.

18. Scharf, *History of the Confederate States Navy*, 414–15.

CHAPTER 14: THE LOSS OF THE IRONCLADS

1. ORN, ser. 1, vol. 10, 24–25.

2. Flanders, *Memoirs of E. A. Jack*, 31.

3. ORN, ser. 1, vol. 10, 641.

4. Ibid., ser. 1, vol. 9, 734.

5. Ibid., 771.

6. Elliott, *Ironclad of the Roanoke*, 213.

7. ORN, ser. 1, vol. 10, 49–50.

8. Scharf, *History of the Confederate States Navy*, 412–13.

9. Elliott, *Ironclad of the Roanoke*, 228–29.

10. ORN, ser. 1, vol. 10, 718.

11. Warley, "Notes on the Destruction of the *Albemarle*," 4:641.

12. Melton, *Confederate Ironclads*, 197.

13. Cushing, "Destruction of the *Albemarle*," 4:634.

14. Ibid., 634–35.

15. ORN, ser. 1, vol. 10, 571.

16. Warley, "Notes on the Destruction of the *Albemarle*," 642.

17. Ibid., 642.

18. ORN, ser. 1, vol. 11, 372–73.

19. Still, "Career of the Confederate Ironclad *Neuse*," 11.

20. Bright, Rowland, and Bardon, *CSS Neuse*, 16.

21. Ibid., 17.

22. ORN, ser. 1, vol. 12, 191.

23. Bright, Rowland, and Bardon, *CSS Neuse*, 17.

BIBLIOGRAPHY

Amadon, George F. *Rise of the Ironclads*. Missoula, MT: Pictorial Histories Publishing Co., 1988.

Barrett, John G. *The Civil War in North Carolina*. Chapel Hill: University of North Carolina Press, 1963.

Branch, Paul, Jr. *The Siege of Fort Macon*. New Bern: Griffin & Tilghman, 1999.

Bright, Leslie S., William H. Rowland, James C. Bardon. *CSS Neuse: A Question of Iron and Time*. Raleigh: Division of Archives and History, North Carolina Department of Cultural Resources, 1981.

Brooke, George M., Jr., *John M. Brooke: Naval Scientist and Educator*. Charlottesville: University of Virginia Press, 1980.

Burnside, Ambrose E. "The Burnside Expedition." In *Battles and Leaders of the Civil War*, edited by Robert U. Johnson and Clarence C. Buel. 4 vols. New York: Century, 1884–88. 1:660–69.

Campbell, R. Thomas, *Fire and Thunder: Exploits of the Confederate States Navy*. Shippensburg, PA: White Mane, 1997.

———. *Gray Thunder: Exploits of the Confederate States Navy*. Shippensburg, PA: White Mane, 1996.

———. *Iron Courage*. Shippensburg, PA: White Mane, 2002.

———. *Southern Fire: Exploits of the Confederate States Navy*. Shippensburg, PA: White Mane, 1997.

———. *Southern Thunder: Exploits of the Confederate States Navy*. Shippensburg, PA: White Mane, 1996.

Cantwell, John L. "A Capture Before the War." In *Histories of the Several Regiments and Battalions from North Carolina in the Great War, 1861–65*. Edited by Walter Clark. 5 vols. Goldsboro: Nash Brothers, 1901.

Clark, Walter. *Histories of the Several Regiments and Battalions from North Carolina*. 5 vols. Raleigh: State of North Carolina, 1901.

Clark, Walter. *North Carolina Regiments*. Goldsboro: Nash Brothers, 1901.

Combs, Edwin L., III. "Confederate Shipbuilding on the Cape Fear River." *The North Carolina Historical Review* (October 1996): 409–34.

Conrad, Daniel B. "Capture and Burning of the Federal Gunboat *Underwriter*." *Southern Historical Society Papers,* vol. 19 (1892): 93.

C.S. Congress. *Report of Evidence Taken Before a Joint Special Committee of Both Houses of the Confederate Congress, to Investigate the Affairs of the Navy Department.* Richmond: G. Evans & Co., 1863.

Creecy, Richard B. *Pasquotank Historical Yearbook.* Elizabeth City, NC: Museum of the Albemarle, 1954–55.

Current, Richard N. *Encyclopedia of the Confederacy.* 4 vols. New York: Simon & Schuster, 1993.

Cushing, William B. "The Destruction of the *Albemarle*." In *Battles and Leaders of the Civil War,* edited by Robert U. Johnson and Clarence C. Buel, 4 vols. New York: Century, 1884–88. 4:634–40.

Davis, Archie K. *Boy Colonel of the Confederacy: The Life and Times of Henry King Burgwyn, Jr.* Chapel Hill: University of North Carolina Press, 1985.

Doak, Henry M. "Henry Melville Doak Memoir." Tennessee State Library and Archives, Nashville, Tennessee.

Donnelly, Ralph W. *The Confederate States Marine Corps.* Shippensburg, PA: White Mane, 1989.

Dowdey, Clifford. *The Wartime Papers of Robert E. Lee.* New York: Bramhall House, 1961.

Durkin, Joseph T. *Confederate Navy Chief: Stephen R. Mallory.* Chapel Hill: University of North Carolina Press, 1954.

Elliott, Gilbert. "The Career of the Confederate Ram *Albemarle*," *Century Magazine* (July 1888): 427–32.

Elliott, Robert G. *Ironclad of the Roanoke.* Shippensburg, PA: White Mane, 1994.

Evans, Clement A. "North Carolina." *Confederate Military History.* Atlanta: Confederate Publishing Co., 1899.

Flanders, Alan B. *Memoirs of E. A. Jack, Steam Engineer, CSS Virginia.* White Stone, VA: Brandylane Publishers, 1998.

Fonvielle, Chris E. *The Wilmington Campaign: Last Rays of Departing Hope.* Harrisburg, PA: Stackpole Books, 2001.

Gragg, Rod. *Confederate Goliath.* New York: Harper Collins, 1991.

Hawkins, Rush C. "Early Coast Operations in North Carolina." In *Battles and Leaders of the Civil War,* edited by Robert U. Johnson and Clarence C. Buel, 4 vols. New York: Century, 1884–88. 1:632–59.

Hill, Daniel Harvey. *North Carolina.* 4 vols. Atlanta: Confederate Publishing Co., 1899.

Holden, Edgar. "The *Albemarle* and the *Sassacus.*" In *Battles and Leaders of the Civil War.* Edited by Robert U. Johnson and Clarence C. Buel. 4 vols. New York: Century, 1884–88. 4:629.

Howe, W. W. *Kinston, Whitehall, and Goldsboro Expedition, December, 1862.* New York: privately printed, 1890.

Jones, Virgil Carrington. *The Civil War at Sea.* 3 vols. New York: Holt, Rinehart, and Winston, 1960–62.

———. "Construction, Fighting Career and Destruction of the *Albemarle,*" *Civil War Times Illustrated* (June 1962): 9.

Loyall, Benjamin P. "Capture of the *Underwriter.*" *Southern Historical Society Papers,* vol. 27 (1896): 137.

Luraghi, Raimondo. *A History of the Confederate Navy.* Annapolis: Naval Institute Press, 1996.

MacBride, Robert. *Civil War Ironclads.* New York: Chilton Books, 1952.

Martin, W. J. "History of the Eleventh N. C. Infantry, C.S.A." *Southern Historical Society Papers,* vol. 23 (1895): 42.

Melton, Maurice. *The Confederate Ironclads.* New York: A. S. Barnes and Co., 1968.

Moebs, Thomas Truxtun. *Confederate States Navy Research Guide: Confederate Naval Imprints Described and Annotated, Chronology of Naval Operation and Administration, Marine Corps and Naval Officer Biographies, Description and Service of Vessels, Subject Bibliography.* Williamsburg, VA: Moebs Publishing Co., 1991.

Parker, William H. *Recollections of a Naval Officer.* New York: Scribner's, 1883.

Porter, David D. *Naval History of the Civil War.* New York: Sherman Publishing Co., 1886.

Roberts, O. M. *Confederate Military History.* Atlanta: Confederate Publishing Co., 1899.

Robinson, William Morrison. *The Confederate Privateers.* Columbia: University of South Carolina Press, 1990.

Scharf, J. Thomas. *History of the Confederate States Navy.* New York: Rogers & Sherwood, 1887.

Selfridge, Thomas O., Jr. "The Navy at Fort Fisher." In *Battles and Leaders of the Civil War,* edited by Robert U. Johnson and Clarence C. Buel, 4 vols. New York: Century, 1884–88. 4:655–61.

Shingleton, Royce G. *John Taylor Wood: Sea Ghost of the Confederacy.* Athens: University of Georgia Press, 1979.

————. *High Seas Confederate: The Life and Times of John Newland Maffitt.* Columbia: University of South Carolina Press, 1994.

Silverstone, Paul H. *Warships of the Civil War Navies.* Annapolis: Naval Institute Press, 1989.

Stern, Philip Van Doren. *The Confederate Navy: A Pictorial History.* New York: Bonanza Books, 1962.

Still, William N., Jr. "The Career of the Confederate Ironclad *Neuse,*" *North Carolina Historical Review* (January 1966): 137–45.

————, ed. *The Confederate Navy: The Ships, Men, and Organization, 1861–65.* Annapolis: Naval Institute Press, 1997.

————. *Confederate Shipbuilding.* Columbia: University of South Carolina Press, 1987.

————. *Iron Afloat.* Nashville: Vanderbilt University Press, 1971.

Strode, Hudson. *Jefferson Davis, Confederate President.* New York: Harcourt, Brace & World, 1959.

Tredwell, Adam. "North Carolina Navy." In *North Carolina Regiments, 1861–65.* 5 vols. Goldsboro: Nash Brothers, 1901.

Trotter, William R. *Ironclads and Columbiads.* Winston-Salem, NC: John F. Blair, 1989.

U.S. Navy Department. *Civil War Naval Chronology, 1861–1865.* Washington DC: Naval History Division, Navy Department, 1971.

————. *Official Records of the Union and Confederate Navies in the War of the Rebellion,* 30 vols. Washington DC: Government Printing Office, 1894–1927.

U.S. War Department. *The War of the Rebellion: A Compilation of the Official Records of the Union and Confederate Armies.* 130 vols. Washington DC: Government Printing Office, 1880–1901.

Walcott, C. F. *History of the Twenty-first Regiment Massachusetts Volunteers.* Boston: Houghton, Mifflin, 1882.

Warley, Alexander F. "Notes on the Destruction of the *Albemarle.*" In *Battles and Leaders of the Civil War,* edited by Robert U. Johnson and Clarence C. Buel. 4 vols. New York: Century, 1884–88. 4:641.

Wells, Tom Henderson. *The Confederate Navy: A Study in Organization.* Tuscaloosa: University of Alabama Press, 1971.

Whittle, William C. "Cruise of the C. S. Steamer *Nashville.*" *Southern Historical Society Papers,* vol. 29 (1901).

Wise, Stephen R. *Lifeline of the Confederacy.* Columbia: University of South Carolina Press, 1988.

INDEX

284

Campbell, Daniel A., 34
Cantwell, John L., 20–21, 23–24
Cape Fear River, 20, 23, 34, 181,
    183–85, 190, 199, 202, 215, 219,
    228
Carlisle, Hiram, 32
Cassidey Shipyard, 184–85, 187,
    190–91, 220
Cassidey, James, 185
Caswell Street, 111
Chapman, Robert F., 216–17, 219
Chowan River, 9, 28, 84–85, 87–88
Clark, H. J. B., 90
Clark, Henry T., 37, 46, 84
Cobb's Point, 77–79
Confederate Point (Fort Fisher), 183,
    215
Conrad, Daniel B., 129, 131–33,
    137–40
Cooke, Henry M., 121
Cooke, James W., 66, 79, 104–6,
    112–15, 120–22, 124, 143–46,
    148–55, 167–80, 203–4, 206, 211
Cooper, Samuel, 62
Cora, 144
Cotton Plant, 59, 155, 169–70
Cox, Jacob D., 222
Crawford, Allan, 205
Creecy, Richard B., 82
Croatan Sound, 52, 59, 64, 68, 70, 77
Crossan, Thomas M., 16, 30–31, 35
Croton, M. D., 23
CSS Albemarle (side-wheeler), 50
CSS Albemarle (ironclad), 103–4,
    106, 113, 115, 117–25, 127–28,
    143–45, 147–56, 163, 165–69,
    171–81, 183, 187–89, 191, 196,
    202–4, 206–15, 227
CSS Arkansas, 200

CSS (NCS) Beaufort (Caledonia),
    15–19, 31, 66, 69, 72, 74, 78–79
CSS Chattahoochee, 199
CSS Chicora, 207, 228
CSS Curlew, 54, 56–57, 66, 71–72, 121
CSS (NCS) Ellis, 31, 46, 48–49, 66,
    71, 78–79, 121
CSS Equator, 181, 192, 196, 216
CSS Florida, 120, 206
CSS Georgia, 200
CSS Louisiana, 22, 100
CSS Manassas, 207
CSS Nashville, 92–97
CSS Neuse, 90, 101, 103, 105–14,
    117, 120, 126–28, 156–66, 168,
    183, 186–89, 191, 196, 215,
    220–24, 227
CSS North Carolina, 183, 185–92,
    197–200, 202, 215, 228
CSS Palmetto State, 20, 228
CSS Patrick Henry, 129, 220
CSS (NCS) Raleigh, 31, 33, 51,
    54–57, 67, 76
CSS Raleigh (ironclad), 181, 183,
    185–89, 191–200, 202, 215–16, 228
CSS Richmond, 101, 193, 228
CSS Savannah, 192, 228
CSS Squib, 216
CSS Virginia, 89, 100, 126, 157, 184,
    194, 200
CSS Wilmington, 185, 217
CSS (NCS) Winslow, 16, 31, 33, 35,
    40, 44–46, 48–49, 67
CSS Yadkin, 181, 185–86, 192, 196,
    216
Currituck, 18, 83
Cushing, William B., 208–13

Dearing, James, 134
Deep River Basin, 189